Our genuine thanks and appreciation to our publisher,
Matt Brink, for believing in us;
our designer, Anita Jones,
for creating a beautiful book;
and Shannon Reynolds for the adorable
sign language drawings.
And to Jane Van Dusen, our editor, whose patience, skill, and
perseverance guided us through this creative process.

Gratitude and love to David and Opal.
And to the past and present children and families in the Deaf and Hard of Hearing
Preschool Program at Groner Elementary School — for your appreciation of
and enthusiasm for storybook-based teaching. You all inspire me.

~Julie

To all the children I've worked with and learned from;
To Ethan and Eliza for their unyielding, laughter-inducing inspiration;
And especially to Jim for the smile that crinkles his eyes.

~Kate

First and foremost, to Jason — your never-ending love and support is incredible.
To Maria — you are as amazing as they come.
And a sincere thank you to all the children who have ever been
in my classroom — you are invaluable.

~Katy

Contents

Hello Teachers!

As you know, young children love good storybooks. If the books are especially good, children ask to hear them again and again until they've worn out the pages and learned the words by heart. We've created a curriculum for preschool settings that builds on this natural love by structuring activities around 17 favorite storybooks. The storybooks serve as the core of the instruction and provide the themes for all the activities. An added benefit of this curriculum is that it clearly communicates that books have a special value. By modeling the importance and joy of literature for the children, we see that they develop an appreciation for books—an appreciation we hope will follow them for the rest of their lives.

Who is this book for?

The curriculum presented in this book is designed for early childhood educators, speech-language pathologists, daycare workers, and others who teach children ages three to six. It is appropriate for community preschools as well as early childhood special education settings. We've used this storybook-based curriculum to teach children with a wide spectrum of disabilities as well as typically developing children. You will find the activities can easily be adapted to your group of children.

How does it work?

This curriculum includes enough storybooks and activities to fill an entire academic year, from September through May. Each unit focuses on one storybook and provides corresponding activities to last two weeks. We've put the units in an order that will work for most settings, with seasonal and holiday-related units occurring at the appropriate times. Teachers are welcome either to follow the units in order or to pick and choose units or activities as suitable for the needs of your children, your geographic location, the children's interests, and your special skills as a teacher.

For each unit, the teacher reads the storybook each class session over the period of two weeks. Circle time activities enhance the story reading and focus the children's attention on various aspects of the story. Group activities are based on the story's themes, with each of the two weeks having a different focus. And all the songs, poems, art activities, games, room decorations, snacks, and areas in the classroom (dramatic play, sensory, science, art, and books) relate to the story. This immersion allows the children to truly live the story in their classroom for two weeks.

Why is this curriculum effective?

Repetition and immersion are the keys to the success of this curriculum. One time simply isn't enough for a child to hear a story and grasp all the wonders within it. By reading a story each class day over a two-week period, the children don't have to take in everything at once. You, as the teacher, can choose to emphasize different concepts, characters, illustrations, and language each day. The children build on what they learned in the previous days' story readings to eventually, by the end of the unit, thoroughly know and love the story.

Because the classroom environment immerses the children in the language and concepts of the stories, they can put what they are learning at story time into practice. They can create something at the art table to add to the bulletin board, feel something in the sensory table, read a related book in the book corner, explore in the science area, dress up like the characters in the dramatic play area, and eat a funny snack. They can fully live the story!

What is in each unit?

Each unit contains

- A synopsis of the storybook
- A letter to send home to families explaining the storybook unit and activities they can do at home
- Suggestions for setting up your classroom to revolve around the story (dramatic play area, sensory area, art area, science area, book area, and bulletin board)
- Activities separated into two weeks, each week including: a distinctive thematic Focus of the Week; Circle Time activities including songs, poems, fingerplays, and story-reading ideas; and six detailed Group Activities with designated target areas
- Snacks related to the story
- A Pretest and Posttest

Why these storybooks?

We've selected 17 tried-and-true favorites. These are the stories the children in our classes can't hear often enough. They are age-appropriate, high interest stories that contain vivid language, vibrant illustrations, and important concepts for young children. The stories have lovable characters, conflict and resolution, and oftentimes are written using cumulative, repetitive, or rhyming text that encourages children to predict. The storybooks, their authors, and their areas of focus in the curriculum are listed in the "Storybooks and Focus Areas" table on page xiv.

What are the target areas?

The target areas designated for each activity help the teacher pinpoint the areas of development addressed in each activity. The five areas are: cognition, communication, fine motor, gross motor, and social.

- **Cognition** refers to activities involving sensory experiences, predicting, colors, numbers and counting, following directions, memorization, patterning, and sequencing.
- **Communication** encompasses vocabulary development, expressive language, receptive language, and following directions.
- **Fine motor** includes cutting, gluing, writing, tracing, and coloring.
- **Gross motor** comprises running, jumping, dancing, and climbing.
- **Social** incorporates dramatic play, teamwork, and emotions.

The chart at the end of this book cross-references the target areas with the activities in the curriculum.

What are the pretest and posttest?

At the end of each unit in this book you will find a pretest and posttest form. These forms list the concepts that can be taught in each unit. You can either use one form per child or one form for the whole class. Ask the children open-ended questions to see what they can tell you about each concept or word. For example, "What can you tell me about caterpillars?" Note their responses on the forms.

For the pretest, do a quick run-through at the beginning of a unit to see what the children already know about that unit's concepts. This will help you establish which concepts and vocabulary are new, and which you want to expand on using a higher language level. Complete the posttest at the end of the unit to document what the children have learned.

What have we found?

In our classrooms, the children look forward to story time and the new elements that will be incorporated each day. They wonder what their role will be in the story reading and what new twist will surprise them. Story time is an integral part of each class—it's the glue that holds all other aspects of the day together.

During free play time, when surrounded with many options, we've found that the children often choose to interact with the storybook. They gather the props and their friends to reenact scenes. They put on costumes, set the stage, and play without the need of teacher direction. We then see that they generalize the concepts and vocabulary they've learned from the story into other parts of the day.

We see preliteracy skills emerging. The children learn what a title and author are. They can retell the stories by "reading" the pictures and even by recognizing some of the repetitive text. They hear the rhyming or repetitive texts and learn to predict words. They become emergent readers!

Anything else?

Teachers can do several additional related and fun activities with their children either every day, at the beginning of each two-week storybook unit, or three or four times during the year. Consider adding any of the following to the storybook-based activities:

- **Signing In**

  Create a name card for each child. The cards should have the children's names written on them as well as space for the children to write their names themselves. Handwriting lines are helpful. Sentence strips or name cards can be purchased through teacher supply stores or can be homemade. You can make new cards three or four times during the year and use a background on the cards related to the current storybook unit. Laminate the cards. Upon arriving for class, the children find their name cards and sign in on the cards using a dry erase marker. The children then use their name cards to answer the Question of the Day (see next page). The teacher erases the name cards at the end of each day to ready them for use the next day. Once a month, instead of using the name cards, have the children sign in on a regular piece of paper to save as a record of growth throughout the year.

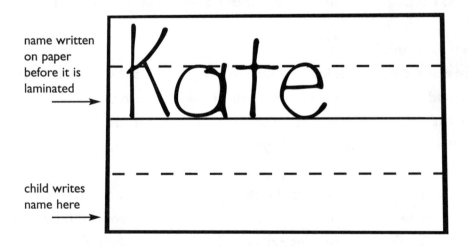

name written on paper before it is laminated →

child writes name here →

• The Question of the Day

The Question of the Day is a simple question related to the current storybook unit. A new question is written on a board each day and read aloud to the children. The children listen to the question and then answer it by placing their name cards in the appropriate places. For example, when reading *There Was a Bold Lady Who Wanted a Star,* the first Question of the Day might be "How did you get to school—in a car or on a bus?" Tape two large envelopes (to hold the name cards) at the bottom of the board. Above one, write *bus,* and above the other, write *car.* The children simply put their name cards in the appropriate envelopes. The results of the Question of the Day can be tallied during Circle Time on a chart or dry erase board. As the year progresses, the children begin to recognize common sight words in the questions and will help to read the questions aloud.

• Morning Meeting

Gather the children together at the beginning of class to discuss the day's agenda. The meeting can begin with a welcoming song or chant and then move into a discussion of the day's activities. Topics to discuss might include: a job chart, the new storybook unit, new areas in the room, hints about what they will have for snack, art activities, games, field trips, and visitors. A closing song or stretching activity brings the meeting to a close and signifies the transition to the next part of the day. The Morning Meeting can last anywhere from two to ten minutes.

• Snack Placemats

Three or four times a year, have the children make laminated snack placemats related to the current storybook. Give each child an 8 1/2-by-11-inch piece of colored construction paper to decorate using pictures of characters in the story, pictures cut out of magazines, stickers, or rubber stamps. The children write their names on their placemats and/or attach photos of themselves to help them find their places at the snack table. Send the old placemats home each time you make new ones.

• Audiotapes and DVDs

Create an audiotape of each story by recording yourself reading the storybook into a tape recorder. Be sure to instruct the listener to "turn the page" at the appropriate time. Set up a listening area in your classroom with a tape player, headphones, and the tape of you reading the story. Consider making a tape for each child to take home, or allowing the children to check out the classroom tape to take home for a night. Some books also have a short video or DVD that is fun to show on the last day of the unit.

Now, how to begin?

The *Happily Ever After* curriculum encourages families to be involved in their children's school experiences. The school year starts not only with an orientation for the children but also with letting families know how they can be involved throughout the year. Copy the letter to the families and the storybooks list (page xiii and xiv) and send them home on the first day of class. Conduct the pretest for your first unit with the children. Then let the stories begin!

Katey   Julie   Kate

Hello Families,

Welcome to what is certain to be a fun and exciting school year. We have a year full of activities planned to spark creativity, playfulness, and a love of learning in your children. Our curriculum is a bit different from most, so we'd like to explain the framework through which we will be teaching this year.

We have selected 17 of our favorite children's storybooks as the basis of our instruction. These are enticing stories with captivating characters, vibrant illustrations, and interesting vocabulary. We'll spend two weeks focusing on each story and all the wonder that lies within it. We will read the story every day of the two-week period, emphasizing different topics during the first and second weeks. We will incorporate puppets, props, music, and other delights to help illustrate key concepts and hold the children's attention. All aspects of our classroom activities and environment will relate to our chosen story—art projects, dramatic play, games, room decorations, even our snacks! Based on our past experience, we predict that by the end of the second week, the children will know the story by heart, they will have learned the concepts and new vocabulary within it, and they will have added it to their personal memory bank—and perhaps home library—of all-time favorite stories.

Every two weeks, we will send home a letter telling you about our new storybook and how we will be spending our time in preschool. We will offer suggestions for activities you can do at home with your child to reinforce what we are doing at school and let you know about other related storybooks to look for at the library. Of course, we offer only suggestions and would love to hear about any activities you create at home that capture your child's interest.

Our goal is to build preliteracy skills and instill in the children a love of books and reading that will last a lifetime. We hope that you will join us in our goal by searching out the storybooks at the library and reading them at home with your child. Indulge your child's request to have the same stories read repeatedly. This repetition is a valuable way to build important prereading skills and an enjoyment of stories. A list of all the storybooks along with their authors and areas of focus is attached.

Thank you for sharing your children with us. We look forward to a wonderful school year.

Storybooks and Focus Areas

Title and Author	Focus Area	
	Week 1	**Week 2**
There Was a Bold Lady Who Wanted a Star (Charise Mericle Harper)	Transportation	Space and stars
Silly Sally (Audrey Wood)	Silly movement	Silly art
My Little Sister Ate One Hare (Bill Grossman)	Counting	Insects and other critters
Go Away, Big Green Monster! (Ed Emberley)	Monsters and emotions	Shapes
Barn Dance! (Bill Martin Jr. and John Archambault)	Farm animals	Dancing, movement, and verbs
I Know an Old Lady Who Swallowed a Pie (Alison Jackson)	Thanksgiving food and turkeys	Harvest and fall season
Gingerbread Baby (Jan Brett)	Gingerbread	Cold weather
Geraldine's Big Snow (Holly Keller)	Winter weather and winter clothing	Waiting and being patient, getting ready for snow
Bear Snores On (Karma Wilson)	Habitats and snow	Cold weather cooking
The Little Mouse, the Red Ripe Strawberry and the Big Hungry Bear (Don and Audrey Wood)	Strawberries, emotions, and *a half*	Prepositions, and problem solving
The Kissing Hand (Audrey Penn)	Love, hearts, and kisses	Hands and forest animals
Pete's a Pizza (William Steig)	Making a pizza	More pizza
The Napping House (Audrey Wood)	Rainbows	Napping
Five Little Monkeys Bake a Birthday Cake (Eileen Christelow)	Sleeping, *noisy* and *quiet*	Birthday parties
The Very Hungry Caterpillar (Eric Carle)	Caterpillars and fruits	Butterflies and metamorphosis
Grow Flower, Grow! (Lisa Bruce)	Growing and seeds	Flowers
Fidgety Fish (Ruth Galloway)	Sea life	Movement

THE
Happily Ever After
CURRICULUM

There Was a Bold Lady Who Wanted A Star

By Charise Mericle Harper

In this clever adaptation of the favorite folk song "There Was an Old Lady Who Swallowed a Fly," we meet a dauntless lady who wants nothing more than to bring a star home to her young child. Her journey takes her through various landscapes requiring different transportation modes. She buys tennis shoes, roller skates, a bicycle, a car, an airplane, and finally a rocket, all in an attempt to get the star. This is a great story about the lengths (and in this case, heights) one might go to in the name of love.

Dear Families,

We've all heard of the old lady who swallowed a fly, but what about the bold lady who wanted a star? Yep, it's a very new twist on a familiar favorite. *There Was a Bold Lady Who Wanted a Star*, by Charise Mericle Harper, is a wacky story about one woman's quest to capture a single star to put in a jar ("it wasn't so far!"). Being as bold as she is, she's up for trying any method she can think of to reach that star: jogging, roller-skating, bike riding, driving, flying, and, naturally, riding on a rocket ship. It's an adventurous story the kids will enjoy listening to as well as singing.

Visit the library or some used bookstores to find this book and the classic storybook *I Know an Old Lady Who Swallowed a Fly*. You may also want to look for *I Know an Old Lady Who Swallowed a Pie* by Alison Jackson and *There Was an Old Lady Who Swallowed a Trout* by Teri Sloat. Both are fun, lively stories, and your child will quickly become familiar with the format. Stories related to transportation also tie in well with this unit. You'll find the library and bookstores have large selections of children's books about cars and rockets. Also look for some children's books about astronomy that explain the constellations and the stories related to each one.

Anybody have any large cardboard boxes lying around? These can be transformed into cars or rockets with a little paint and some creativity. How about a visit to a roller-skating rink (don't forget kneepads)? Practice drawing stars and covering them with gold and silver paint and glitter. Wait for dark and go stargazing. Look for glow-in-the-dark stars and planets to put on the ceiling of your child's bedroom. The possibilities are endless.

Reach for the stars,

Room Setup

Dramatic Play Area

- Set up two rows of chairs and use a puppet theater or small table as the ticket booth. Have paper scraps and writing utensils handy for making tickets and signs. The children can pretend to be riding a bus, plane, or train.

- Create a car wash area with large sponges, towels, squeegees, and buckets for water (real or pretend). Have paper and writing utensils handy as well as play money, and add a table with a toy cash register. Wash any classroom transportation toys.

Sensory Area

- Fill the sensory table with shaving cream or mud and have toy cars available for driving in it. Comment on the variety of tracks the different cars make.

Science Area

- Make exploding mini-rockets: Place an Alka Seltzer tablet into a film canister, add a small amount of water, and place the lid on tightly. Set it on the floor and wait for the blast off. The pressure caused by the tablet mixing with water will cause the top to fly off the canister.

Art Area

- Have old license plates, crayons, and paper available for crayon rubbings.

- Make prints with star-shaped cookie cutters by dipping them into paint and pressing them on a large sheet of paper. Yellow paint on dark blue paper works well. Glitter can be added to the wet paint for more effect.

- Have large car-washing sponges available to dip into paint and make prints on paper. Add two paper circles and a small photo of the child (as the driver) to make a car. These can be used on the bulletin board.

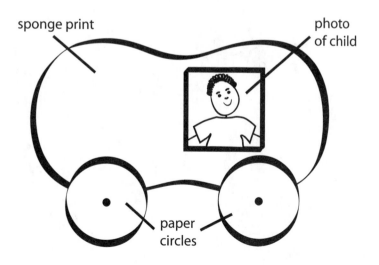

sponge print

photo of child

paper circles

Book Area

- *Astro Bunnies* by Christine Loomis, illustrated by Ora Eitan
- *Draw Me a Star* by Eric Carle
- *I Know an Old Lady Who Swallowed a Pie* by Alison Jackson, illustrated by Judith Byron Schachner
- *I Stink!* and *I'm Mighty!* both by Kate and Jim McMullan
- *Lisa's Airplane Trip* by Anne Gutman and Georg Hallensleben
- *Stargazers* by Gail Gibbons
- *There Was an Old Lady Who Swallowed a Trout* by Teri Sloat
- *This Is The Way We Go To School* by Edith Baer, illustrated by Steve Bjorkman
- *Zoom! Zoom! Zoom! I'm Off to the Moon!* by Dan Yaccarino
- Four books by Donald Crews: *Freight Train, Truck, School Bus, Flying*
- Other books related to transportation and stars

Bulletin Board
- Attach paper rectangles to the board at the children's height to make a road or pathway. Children use the sponge car prints made in the Art Area to "drive" down the road. Ask the children where they would like to travel, print their responses on paper, and attach the papers along with their cars on the board.

Other
- Make license plates using heavy card stock and large letter stickers. Children hang them on the backs of their cardboard box cars (see Week 1, Activity 5).

- Cover a large sheet of black paper with glow-in-the-dark stars and constellation shapes. Tape the paper to the bottom of a table and cover the table with a large blanket. Provide flashlights and books about space along with some pillows to create a cozy spot for reading under the stars.

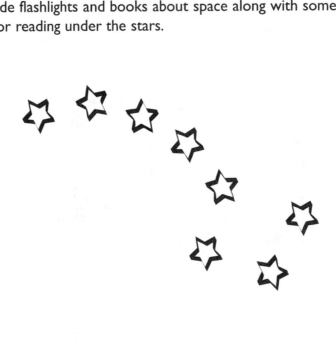

Week 1

Focus of the Week: Transportation

Songs, Poems, and Fingerplays

The Wheels on the Bus
The wheels on the bus go round and round,
Round and round, round and round.
The wheels on the bus go round and round,
All through the town.

Add *doors/open and shut*; *wipers/swish, swish*; *windows/up and down,* and so on

Ten in a Plane
(to the tune of "There Were Ten in the Bed")

Choose one child to be the pilot and give dancing scarves (chutes) to the other children. Begin the song:

There were ten in a plane and the pilot said,
"Jump out, Jump out!"
So they checked their chutes, and one jumped out . . .

One child jumps up and rolls to the floor ("jumping out with the chute"). Continue through the song (*There were nine in a plane . . .*, and so on) with the children, one at a time, jumping out with their chutes. When only the pilot is left, then sing:

There were none in the plane and the pilot said,
"Great job! Well done!"
So they gathered up their chutes and walked on home.

Reading the Story

Introduce the book by discussing the title, author, and dedication. Discuss the book's cover and ask the children to guess what the book will be about.

Read the story every day and, as the children become familiar with it, gradually add in any of the following:

- Make felt cutouts of each mode of transportation, the Bold Lady, a star, and a jar. Use these on a felt board while telling the story.

- The teacher and the children together act out the Bold Lady using each transportation mode as it occurs in the story (run in place, roller-skate, ride a bike, drive a car, fly a plane, zoom up in a rocket).

- Photocopy the Bold Lady and the various modes of transportation. Laminate and tape these pictures onto wooden craft sticks and give one stick puppet to each child. As the story is being read, the children move their puppets (and their bodies) the way their mode of transportation moves. The child with the Bold Lady puppet acts out reaching and grabbing for the star. Encourage the use of dramatic faces, movements, and noises.

- Ask the children to predict which mode of transportation the lady will use next. Have fun substituting the wrong words ("I know a Bold Lady who bought a taxi/motorcycle/train/school bus") and see if the children catch the error.

1. Running Shoes

Target Areas: cognition, fine motor

What you need:
- Heavy-weight paper or foam core cut in the shape of tennis shoes (see next page) (1 pair per child)
- Small pieces of colorful paper (magazine pictures, decorative napkins, tissue paper, junk mail)
- Glue thinned with water
- Paintbrushes

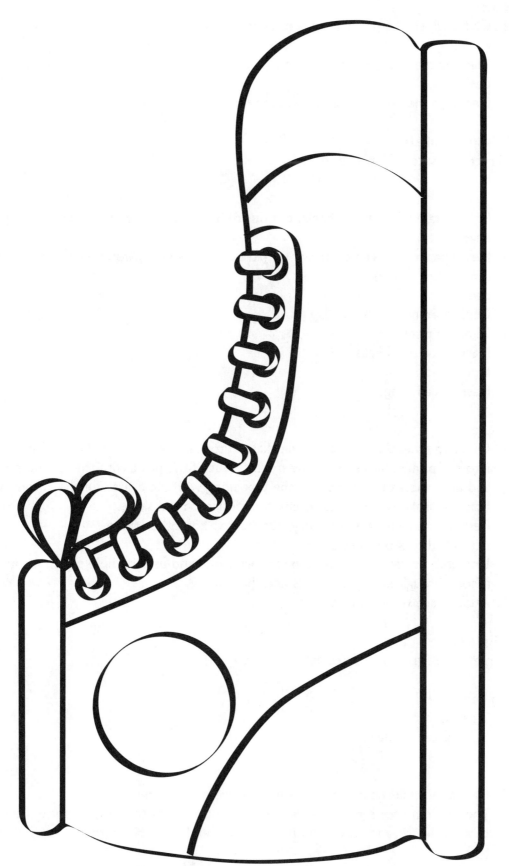

Running Shoe Template

What you do:

1. Give each child a paper (or foam) shoe.
2. Children cover their paper shoes with the thinned glue.
3. They lay the paper scraps on the glue and cover as much of the shoes as desired.
4. Decorate the walls in the classroom with the finished shoes.

2. Rollin' Roller Skates

Target Areas: cognition, fine motor

What you need:

- Roller skate boots (no wheels) cut out of heavy paper (see next page) (2 per child)
- Heavy paper with circles drawn on (to be used as wheels on the skates)
- Brads (4 per child)
- Scissors
- Cardboard box with lid
- Tempera paints
- Marbles or small balls
- Hole punch
- Plastic salad tongs

What you do:

1. One at a time, children place one skate cutout in the box and drop the marbles into the paint. Children pick the marbles out of the paint with the salad tongs and drop the wet marbles into the box along with the skate. Put the lid on the box and shake the marbles to create a design on the skate.
2. Remove the skate and let it dry. Repeat with the other skate.
3. Each child cuts out 4 circles for wheels.
4. Line up 2 wheels on the bottom of each skate and use the hole punch to punch a hole through both the wheels and the skate.
5. Attach each wheel with a brad.

3. Trike Relays

Target Areas: gross motor, social

What you need:

- 2 tricycles
- Large area to ride in

What you do:

1. Divide the children into two teams and give each team a bike.
2. The children race the bike from one end of the room to the other, give the bike to a teammate, and repeat until all the children have had a turn.

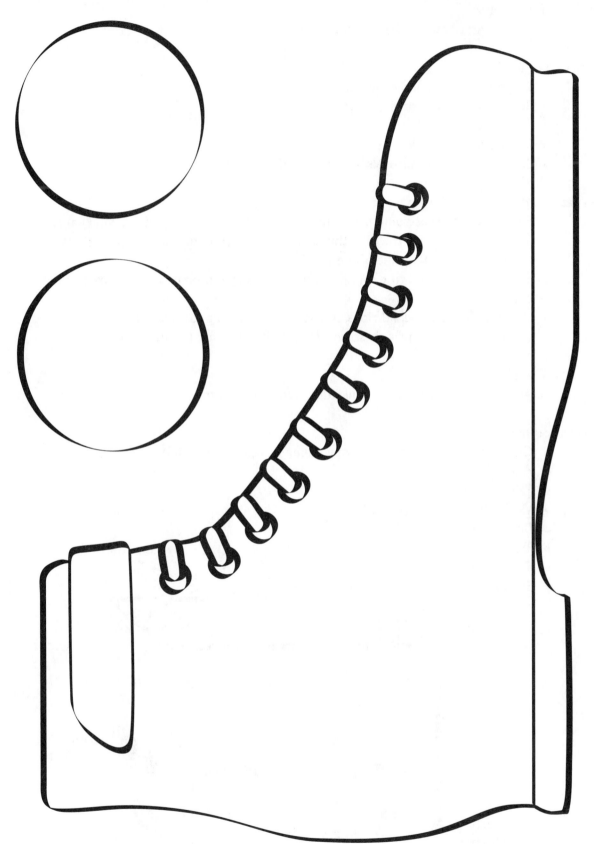

Rollin' Roller Skates Template

4. Bike Paintings
Target Areas: cognition, gross motor, social

What you need:
- Large sheets of butcher paper
- Tempera paints in bright colors
- Tricycles
- Large area to play in
- Tub of soapy water, towels, and a hose (if possible)

What you do:
1. Each child chooses some paint and dribbles it onto the paper in a small area.
2. The child then rides the bike through the paint and continues over the rest of the paper, making a print of the bike's tire.
3. Encourage the child to experiment with turning and reversing to create different patterns.
4. When finished, the child rides to the cleaning area and uses the towel and soapy water to clean the wheels so the tricycle is ready for the next child.

5. Box Cars
Target Areas: cognition, communication, gross motor, social

What you need:
- Cardboard boxes similar to copy paper boxes (1 per child)
- Paints
- Paintbrushes
- Wide ribbon or wide elastic
- Brads (4 per child)
- Transparent tape
- Construction paper
- Scissors

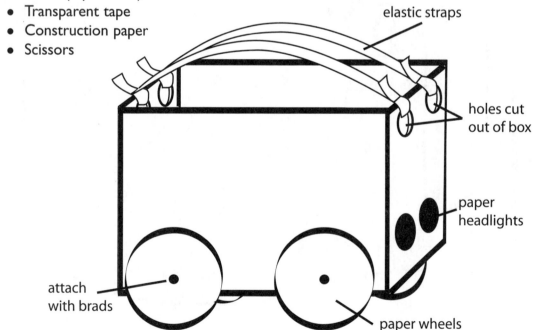

elastic straps

holes cut out of box

paper headlights

attach with brads

paper wheels

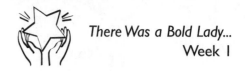

What you do:

1. Open the tops and bottoms of the boxes so they can be slipped over the children's heads and bodies.
2. Children paint the sides of their boxes.
3. When the paint dries, use a pair of scissors and on each box make 2 holes at the tops of 2 opposite sides (4 holes total).
4. Measure out 2 strips of ribbon or elastic to stretch from one side of the box to the other. These will serve as the suspender-like straps that go over the child's shoulders to hold the box up.
5. String one strip of ribbon or elastic through a front hole on one side of the box and a back hole on the other side of the box. Tie each end to secure it. Repeat this with another piece of ribbon or elastic through the remaining two holes.
6. Make construction paper circles for wheels (attach with brads) and headlights (glued to front of box car).
7. The children slip into their boxes and situate the straps on their shoulders.
8. Make a stoplight or stop sign with construction paper or leftover cardboard and take the cars for a drive. Drive to various places in the room, such as the Drive-Thru Restaurant (Snack Area) and the Bookstore (Book Area).

6. Highway to the Stars
Target Areas: communication, fine motor

What you need:

- Several small transportation toys (cars, airplanes, trucks, and the like)
- Paint dishes (1 per child)
- Tempera paint in several colors
- 8 1/2" x 11" pieces of white construction paper (1 per child)
- Small star stickers (1 per child)

What you do:

1. Children attach their star stickers in one upper corner of their papers.
2. Pour paint into the paint dishes and pass out the various transportation toys.
3. Children dip the wheels in the paint, then roll their vehicles from the opposite corner of their papers up to their star stickers.
4. Encourage the children to take various routes to reach their stars: straight lines, curvy lines, loop-de-loops, zigzags.
5. Talk about how many wheels each vehicle has and whether or not the lady in the story bought all the different kinds of vehicles used in this project.

Week 2

Focus of the Week: Space and stars

Circle Time

Songs, Poems, and Fingerplays

Twinkle, Twinkle, Little Star
Twinkle, twinkle, little star, (open and close hands)
How I wonder what you are! (shrug shoulders)
Up above the world so high, (move hands way up high, still twinkling)
Like a diamond in the sky, (make diamond shape with hands)
Twinkle, twinkle, little star, (back to twinkling)
How I wonder what you are! (shrug shoulders)

Star Light, Star Bright
Star light, star bright,
First star I see tonight,
Wish I may, wish I might,
Have the wish I wish tonight.

Reading the Story

Read the story every day and gradually add in any of the following activities:

- Make five index cards with the following words, one word per card: *It was really too far!* Pass out the cards to five of the children, and help each child read the word on his or her card. When the sentence is read out loud during the story, the child with a word, as it is read, jumps up. They line themselves up in the order of the sentence. Redistribute the cards after each page to give everyone a chance to make a "human sentence."
- Before story time, in large print write out on index cards the sentence: *It was really too far!* Make one card for each child and pass out the cards. Children hold their

cards until they hear this repetitive sentence. Model how to use a finger to point to each word as it is read, and have the children point to the words on their cards as they hear them.

- Hang several stars from the ceiling in the story-reading area. Make one larger and more sparkly than the others. Children stand on their tippy toes to try to reach the special star periodically throughout the story. On the last page, lift one child up (as if in the rocket ship) to actually bring the star down and put in a jar or show to the other children.

Group Activities

1. Space Hop
Target Areas: cognition, gross motor

What you need:
- Masking tape (if indoors) or chalk (if outdoors)
- Small pumice rock or piece of sponge cut to resemble a "space rock"

What you do:
1. Lay out a hopscotch board using the tape or chalk.
2. Inside each square, make or draw a shape and a number or letter.
3. Children throw the space rock and identify the shape and number or letter where the space rock landed. Then they hop to the spot to retrieve the space rock.
4. Introduce the term *gravity* and explain that there is no gravity in space. When playing the game, show how to jump from shape to shape with no gravity, using large, slow movements.

2. Star in a Jar
Target Areas: cognition, fine motor, social

What you need:
- Baby food jars with tight-fitting lids (1 per child)
- Light corn syrup
- Water
- Star-shaped sequins
- Glitter
- Food coloring
- Glow-in-the-dark stars that are small enough to fit into the jar (foam stars also work)
- Heavy-duty glue

What you do:
1. Fill three-quarters of each jar with corn syrup.
2. Add water and a few drops of food coloring to bring the liquids nearly to the top of the jar.
3. Add in some star sequins, glitter, and one plastic or foam star.
4. Glue the lid on top.
5. Children shake the jars and watch the star drift through the night sky.

3. Star Finder
Target Areas: cognition, fine motor, social

What you need:
- Toilet paper tubes (1 per child)
- Black tissue or construction paper cut into squares big enough to cover one end of the tubes (1 square per child)
- Tape
- Markers and/or stickers
- Colored construction paper
- Straight pin

What you do:
1. Each child tapes a black paper square to one end of a tube.
2. Carefully use the pin to make small holes in the black paper.
3. Cover the tubes (star finders) with construction paper and tape it in place.
4. Decorate the star finders with markers and stickers.
5. Children look into their star finders and admire the starry patterns they've created.

4. Rocket Ships
Target Areas: cognition, fine motor, social

What you need:
- Empty paper towel rolls
- Aluminum foil
- Construction paper cut into triangles of various sizes
- Glue or tape
- Strips of yellow, orange, and red crepe paper
- Outer space theme stickers

What you do:
1. Cover the paper towel rolls with foil; tape to hold if necessary.
2. Choose 2 triangles and attach them to the bottom sides of the roll to resemble the lower end of a rocket ship.

3. With tape, attach 2 larger triangles to each other at their top points to make the tip of the rocket ship.
4. Slide the rocket's tip down over the top of the roll and attach it with tape to the top of the rocket.
5. Cut the crepe paper into long thin strips and attach several to the bottom of the tube from the inside to resemble flames.
6. Decorate the side of the rocket with the stickers.

5. Constellation Makers

Target Areas: cognition, communication, fine motor

What you need:
- Styrofoam cups
- Straight pin
- Flashlights

What you do:
1. Carefully poke holes in the bottom of a cup using the pin.
2. Make the room as dark as possible an shine a flashlight through the cup onto a wall or the ceiling to create a beautiful starry night sky.
3. Discuss the stars that can be seen at nighttime.

6. Balloon Rockets

Target Areas: cognition, fine motor, social

What you need:
- Balloons
- Drinking straws cut into 1" segments
- Tape
- Smooth string (kite string)
- 4 chairs

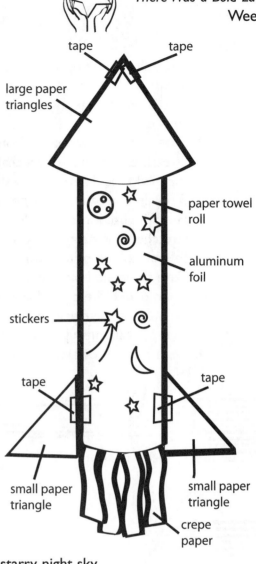

tape tape

large paper triangles

paper towel roll

aluminum foil

stickers

tape tape

small paper triangle

small paper triangle

crepe paper

What you do:

1. Set 2 chairs side by side on one side of the room and the other 2 chairs directly across from them on the other side of the room.
2. Cut 2 long strings and tie the ends to the backs of 2 chairs that are next to each other.
3. Thread one straw segment on each string.
4. Stretch each string to the chair on the other side of the room opposite the chair it is tied to and secure it to that chair (leaving as little slack as possible).
5. Blow up one balloon but don't tie the end.
6. Hold the balloon tightly closed. Orient it so the end points *away* from the stretched-out string and, using a piece of tape, carefully attach the *side* of the balloon to one of the straw segments (do not tape near the end of the balloon).
7. Have someone hold the first balloon closed (but still blown up) and repeat Steps 5 and 6 with the other balloon and the other straw segment, orienting both balloons so their ends point away from the stretched-out strings.
8. Line the balloons up so they are even and, on the count of 3, let them go.
9. Keep track of whose balloon rocket went the farthest!!

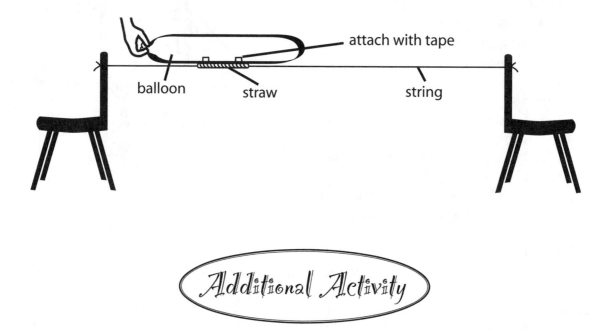

Additional Activity

My Own Transportation

Make a chart with the words *How Did You Get to School Today?* on the top and a variety of transportation modes (walk, bike, car, bus, airplane) on the bottom with lines dividing the modes. Have a name card for each child and have the children put their names on the chart above the mode they used to get to school.

Note: *Be sure that no children are allergic to peanuts before serving snacks with peanut butter. As appropriate, substitute cream cheese, almond butter, or another sandwich spread.*

1. Banana Rockets

What you need:
- Bananas cut in half
- Raisins
- Peanut butter
- A fruit bar or cracker cut into triangles

What you do:
1. Attach 2 raisins with peanut butter to the sides of each half banana to create rocket windows.
2. Put a dollop of peanut butter onto a plate and stand the half banana on end in it.
3. Place a fruit bar or cracker triangle in the peanut butter on each side of the rocket to resemble the lower end of a rocket ship.

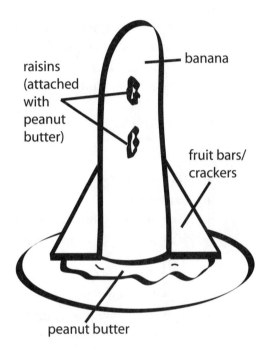

raisins (attached with peanut butter)

banana

fruit bars/ crackers

peanut butter

2. Star Fruits and Sandwiches

What you need:
- Star-shaped cookie cutters of various sizes
- Large fruits that can be cut with the cookie cutters (watermelon, cantaloupe, kiwi, apples, bananas)
- Star fruit
- Peanut butter sandwiches

What you do:
1. Use the cookie cutters to cut star shapes from all the fruits and from the sandwiches.
2 Cut the star fruit and show children the star shape inside.
3. Ask the children to compare the natural star shape to their cookie cutter shapes.
4. Also try cutting the apple in half through the core to show the natural star pattern in the apple.

3. Celery Cars

What you need:

- Celery stalks cut to about 4" lengths (1 per child)
- Carrot disks (4 per child)
- Raisins (at least 4 per child)
- Peanut butter

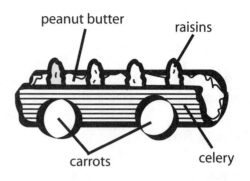

What you do:

1. Spread peanut butter on the celery.
2. Use peanut butter as glue to attach the carrot disks (wheels) onto the sides of the celery (cars).
3. Create drivers and passengers by placing raisins in the peanut butter.

4. Stop Light Snacks

What you need:

- Graham crackers broken in half to make small rectangles
- Peanut butter
- Candy-coated chocolates—red, yellow, and green
- Plastic knives or wooden craft sticks

What you do:

1. Spread peanut butter on the graham cracker.
2. Place the candy pieces on top of the peanut butter to resemble a stoplight: red on top, yellow in the middle, and green on the bottom.
3. Practice this chant:

   Red on top and green below,
   Red means STOP and green means GO,
   Yellow means WAIT, even if you're late!

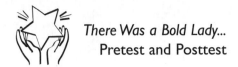

Pretest and Posttest

There Was a Bold Lady Who Wanted A Star

Concepts	Pretest	Posttest
Different types of transportation		
How each type of transportation moves		
Stars		
Outer space		
Wheels and tracks		
Concept of *too far*		
Concept of *gravity*		
Traffic lights		

Notes

Silly Sally

By Audrey Wood

Dancing pigs, leaping dogs, and singing loons are just a few of the silly characters we meet in this story about a wacky girl with an interesting way of taking a stroll to town. All's well until she meets a sheep and the whole traveling gang falls asleep. Now how will they ever get to town? Neddy Buttercup has a plan to wake everyone up and keep the kids entertained until the last page. *Silly Sally* is an amusing tale that introduces the children to a variety of action verbs and prepositions yet includes a silliness that they'll find appealing.

Dear Families,

We don't know about you, but walking all the way to town backwards and upside down sounds pretty impossible to us. Not so for Silly Sally, the main character in our next story, *Silly Sally* by Audrey Wood. Not only does Sally make it to town, she meets several new friends along the way who dance, play, sing, and even take a nap with her. It's a fun, rhyming story that the kids are sure to love.

Naturally, we'll be pretty silly during this unit. Don't be surprised if your child comes home knowing new silly games, faces, and movements. Requests for help walking backwards and upside down may not even be out of the question. Try creating other silly ways to walk together!

Try to locate a copy of this story to read at home with your family. Take special notice of the rhyming words and see if you can come up with some of your own. Create a list of rhyming words together with your child. Feel free to send the list to school for your child to share with the class. We also recommend that you get these related books from the library or bookstore: *The Lady with the Alligator Purse* by Nadine Bernard Westcott, *Sheep in a Jeep* by Nancy E. Shaw, *Miss Mary Mack* by Mary Ann Hoberman, the *Mrs. McNosh* series by Sarah Weeks, and *Shake My Sillies Out (Raffi Songs to Read)* by Raffi.

This is such a simple story that your child will probably be able to tell it to you after just a couple of readings. Your child will enjoy playing "teacher" as you sit and listen (ask a few silly questions along the way just for fun).

See you in town (we'll be the ones walking backwards and upside down),

Dramatic Play Area

- Using masking tape on the floor, tape a "path to town" that extends over a large part of the classroom. Children follow the path as the characters in the book do. Include signs and structures to represent features from the book (mud, doghouse, river).

- Place furniture in the classroom upside down.

- Provide or have kids make costumes for each character in the book. Use the costumes to act out the story.

Sensory Area

- Add sheepskin to the sensory table or add something silly like cooked noodles.

Science Area

- Make silly towers using food instead of blocks. Begin with a few fresh mini-marshmallows, a large bowl of stale mini-marshmallows, and a box of toothpicks. Discuss the differences in the textures of the stale and fresh marshmallows. Poke the toothpicks into the stale marshmallows to make towers, bridges, and houses. Later, add some dried beans that have soaked overnight in water. Again, compare an unsoaked bean to a soaked bean and discuss the differences. Try making structures with the beans and toothpicks.

- Hold a mirror up to an open book. Do the pictures look normal or backward?

Art Area

- Attach paper to the bottom of the tables and encourage drawing with crayons or colored pencils while lying on the floor.

- Set out materials for making silly hats—large sheets of newsprint paper, feathers, markers, tape, paper plates, strips of paper, and so forth.

Book Area

- *The Lady with the Alligator Purse* by Nadine Bernard Westcott
- *Miss Mary Mack* by Mary Ann Hoberman, illustrated by Nadine Bernard Westcott
- *Mrs. McNosh* series by Sarah Weeks
- *Shake My Sillies Out (Raffi Songs to Read)* by Raffi
- *Sheep in a Jeep* by Nancy E. Shaw, illustrated by Margot Apple

- *Take Me Out of the Bathtub and Other Silly Dilly Songs* by Alan Katz, illustrated by David Catrow

- *Today I Feel Silly & Other Moods That Make My Day* by Jamie Lee Curtis, illustrated by Laura Cornell

- Other stories about silliness

Bulletin Board

- Take photographs of the children standing with their legs apart and their arms over their heads. Cut them out so only the children are showing (no background). Turn them upside down and place them on a bulletin board that has been finger-painted green.

Focus of the Week: Silly movement

Songs, Poems, and Fingerplays

<u>*Do Your Ears Hang Low?*</u>
Do your ears hang low?
Do they wobble to and fro?
Can you tie them in a knot?
Can you tie them in a bow?
Can you throw them o'er your shoulder
Like a Continental soldier?
Do your ears hang low?

......

<u>*Happy Birthday (Backwards)*</u>
Yppah yadhtrib ot uoy!
Yppah yadhtrib ot uoy!
Yppah yadhtrib ot (<u>children's backward names</u>)!
Yppah yadhtrib ot uoy!

It might be a good idea to copy this backward rendition to paper; it might be hard to remember!

Reading the Story

Introduce the book by discussing the title, author, and dedication. Discuss the book's cover and ask the children to guess what the book will be about.

Read the story every day and, as the children become familiar with it, gradually add in any of the following activities:

- Using the book as a guide, draw a picture of Silly Sally's journey on a large paper and laminate it if possible. Make and laminate a cutout of each of the characters she meets.

While reading the story, ask the children to predict which
character Sally will meet first, next, and so on. As they
make their predictions, attach the characters to the
picture (using Velcro or sticky tack). Prompt the children
to search for clues to the upcoming characters by looking
at the book's pictures.

- When dismissing the children to other activities, have them
  choose a silly way of moving to the next area. They can
  jump, crawl, walk backwards, skip—the possibilities are
  endless.

- Take moments during the reading of the story to leap like
  Sally and the dog, sing a tune, dance a jig, and pretend to
  nap.

- Children lie on their backs for story time one day. Hold
  the book up over their heads to show the pages. Be very
  silly!

- See if it's possible to read a page while doing a handstand.
  No? Maybe the children want to try!

Group Activities

1. Silly Sally Says

   Target Areas: cognition, communication, gross motor

What you need:
- Large area to move in

What you do:
1. Play a Simon Says game using *Silly Sally* in place of *Simon*.
2. The teacher plays "Sally" and explains his or her role to the children. The children
   do what Sally tells them to do, but only if Sally says "Sally says . . . ." If they do the
   action without "Sally says . . . " being said, they sit down until the game is over.
3. Sally has the children do "silly" actions: make silly faces, flap their arms while
   turning around in a circle, wiggle their fingers under their chins while hopping on
   one foot, and so forth. Continue until all of the children are sitting down.
4. In the next round, make the directions more complex.
5. After the children have practiced with the teacher as Sally, each child gets a turn
   to be Sally.

2. Block Maze

Target Areas: cognition, fine motor, gross motor, social

What you need:

- Wooden blocks
- Ping-Pong ball
- Drinking straws (1 per child)
- Stopwatch
- 1 large sheet of paper
- 1 marker

What you do:

1. The children work as a team to set up a maze using the wooden blocks. The maze should be wide enough for the ball to fit through.
2. Give each child a straw and time the children as they take turns blowing the ball through the maze.
3. Children then sign their names and write their times on the large sheet of paper.

3. Leap Frog

Target Areas: cognition, gross motor, social

What you need:

- Large area to move around in

What you do:

1. The teacher demonstrates the Leap Frog game for the children by squatting down and having another person, standing behind, place his or her hands on the teacher's shoulders and leap over the teacher.
2. The children choose partners and practice playing Leap Frog.
3. When everyone appears to have the hang of it, arrange the children in one long line. The first person squats and the next person in line leaps over the first person and then squats as well. The third person leaps over the first and second person and squats, and so on. Continue until everyone has gone through the line. Then the first squatter leaps over everyone.

4. Dancing Sticks

Target Areas: gross motor, social

What you need:

- Empty paper towel rolls or wooden dowels
- A variety of ribbons and strings
- Markers
- Tape or stapler
- Scissors
- A variety of music to dance to

What you do:

1. Give the children one stick each and let them decorate their sticks using the markers.
2. They then choose ribbons to cut and either tape or staple them to one end of their sticks.
3. When they have finished decorating their sticks, turn on the music and encourage the children to listen to the tempo and move accordingly, using their dancing sticks. Remind them to do some silly dancing!

5. Walk This Way

Target Areas: cognition, communication, gross motor

What you need:

- Large area to move around in

What you do:

1. Play a game of Follow the Leader doing silly things: One child is the leader and instructs the other children to perform an action (bear crawl, crab walk, bird walk, hop on one foot, move backwards).
2. Switch leaders until all the children have had a turn.

6. Silly Cubes

Target Areas: cognition, communication, gross motor

What you need:

- 2 small cube-shaped cardboard boxes (like boxes for coffee mugs)
- Pictures depicting movements (jump, twirl, play air guitar, hula dance)
- Blank index cards cut to fit on the sides of one box
- Markers
- Adhesive-backed Velcro
- Large area to move around in

What you do:

1. Seal the boxes closed and make dice out of them:

   (a) On the first box, stick pieces of one side of Velcro tape (to allow for options) to each of the six surfaces of the box. Then attach a picture of a movement to each side of the box by sticking the other half of the Velcro tape to the backs of the pictures and affixing them to the sides of the box.

   (b) On the sides of the second box, using Velcro as on the first box, attach index cards on which the teacher has written a verbal task (some examples: *Say the ABC's, Count to 10, Name the People in Your Family, Name 5 of Your Classmates, Sing "Old MacDonald," List Colors*).

2. Each child gets a turn to toss the two dice and simultaneously perform the two activities that land face up!

Week 2

Focus of the Week: Silly art

Songs, Poems, and Fingerplays

If You're Silly and You Know It
(to the tune of "If You're Happy and You Know It")

If you're silly and you know it, clap your hands. (clap, clap)
If you're silly and you know it, clap your hands. (clap, clap)
If you're silly and you know it, then your face will surely show it. (silly face)
If you're silly and you know it, clap your hands. (clap, clap)

Add different actions such as *wiggle your fingers*, *stick out your tongue*, *move your eyebrows*.

......

Rhyme Time
Create silly alliterations and rhymes, like the example below, using each child's name and words with the same or similar sounds.

Sally sells seashells down by the seashore.

......

Listen to *Shake My Sillies Out* by Raffi while following the fun directions! (*More Singable Songs by Raffi*: Rounder Records).

Reading the Story

Read the story every day and gradually add in any of the following activities:

- Act out the story with the children using laminated hand-drawn characters. Have the paper characters interact the way they do when they meet in the story.

- Draw a simple stick figure of Neddy Buttercup on a child-size piece of white butcher paper and attach it to a wall in the story-reading area. Keep a couple of shallow containers of yellow paint hidden from view. Give each child one empty thread spool to hold onto until Neddy appears in the story. When he appears, children take turns coming up to dip their spool in the paint and make "buttercup" prints on Neddy's body.

- Give each child a small dry erase board and pen. Model how to draw a picture of Sally, step by step, one new step each time a page is turned. She should be complete and beautiful by the end of the story.

- Children choose their favorite animal in the story and paint small circles on their noses with face paint to represent their characters (pink for pigs, brown for dogs, orange for loons, black for sheep). Children stand up proudly and make appropriate noises when their animals appear in the story.

- Every time the word *silly* is read in the story, all the children make silly faces.

1. These Are the Silly Things I Can Do
Target Areas: cognition, communication

What you need:
- 8 1/2" x 11" pieces of construction paper (3 per child)
- Pencils, markers, or crayons
- Camera and film
- Tape

What you do:
1. Ask each child to think of three silly things he or she can do. If necessary, prompt with questions such as "What's something silly you can do with your feet?"
2. Children draw pictures of themselves doing each action (one action drawing on the top half of each piece of paper).
3. After the children have drawn their pictures, take a photo of each child performing the silly actions.
4. When the photographs are ready, have the children tape them to the bottom halves of their papers with the corresponding drawings.
5. Children compare their drawings to their photos by using words to describe what is the "same" and what is "different." The teacher writes the children's descriptive terms in any empty space surrounding the pictures.
6. The children sign their names on their papers as *Silly (child's name)*.

2. Silly Bag Art

Target Areas: communication, fine motor

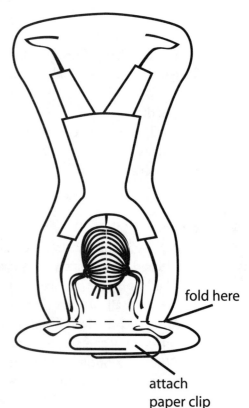

What you need:

- Grocery bags (1 per child)
- Collage materials—including "silly" and surprising items
- Paper plates or large pieces of paper (1 per child)
- Glue
- Tape
- Scissors
- Markers

What you do:

1. Make a bag for each child containing a few collage materials. Each bag's contents should be different from the others.
2. Give each child a plate or piece of paper and a bag of collage materials.
3. The children use the materials in their bags to create a piece of art.
4. After the masterpieces are completed, children stand up and describe their art work to their classmates.

3. Silly Sally Magnet Maze

Target Areas: cognition, communication, fine motor

What you need:

- 11" x 18" pieces of paper (1 per child)
- Small magnets (1 per child)
- Paper clips (1 per child)
- White card stock paper (1 sheet per child)
- Photocopies or drawings of Silly Sally standing upside down and backward (1 per child)
- Glue
- Markers or crayons

fold here

attach paper clip

What you do:

1. Glue the photocopy or drawing of Silly Sally onto the sheet of card stock. Cut out her picture, leaving a 1" margin all the way around her body.

2. Crease and fold the card stock at Silly Sally's wrists and attach a paper clip to the area of her hands so that she stands straight up (albeit upside down) on the paper clip.
3. Children draw a route on their big piece of paper. They can add whatever characters or objects they like to their own route.
4. Place the magnet under the paper and pull Sally along the route.

Optional: Children do this activity using reduced-size copies of their own photos that are on the bulletin board.

4. Silly Wigs

Target Areas: cognition, fine motor, social

What you need:
- Pantyhose (1 pair per child)
- Scissors
- Colorful ribbons

What you do:
1. Children cut the feet off their pairs of pantyhose.
2. Slit each leg into three sections using the scissors.
3. Tie a different-colored ribbon to the bottom of each of the three sections. Children braid the sections using the colored ribbons as a guide (red over blue, yellow over red, blue over yellow). They repeat with the other leg and secure the braids.
4. Place the waistbands on their heads with the braids hanging down on each side.
5. Show the children how to act out the story and have them take turns acting in their silly wigs.

Note: Depending on the abilities of the children, the first two steps may be completed by the teacher.

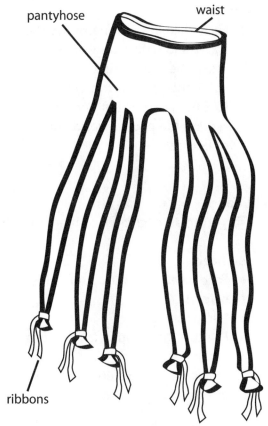

5. Silly Class

Target Areas: communication,
fine motor

What you need:

- Large sheets of white butcher
  paper (1 per child)
- Scissors
- Markers or crayons

What you do:

1. Each child lies on one of the sheets of
   paper and strikes a silly pose.
2. Trace the children and then have them
   color their pictures to resemble themselves.
3. Cut the pictures out and hang them
   around the room—upside down,
   of course!

6. Silly Faces

Target Areas: cognition, communication, fine motor

What you need:

- Face paints in a variety of colors (see recipe for make-your-own face paint
  below)
- Mirrors
- Paintbrushes, Q-tips, facial sponges

Optional: Sample pictures of different items that could be painted on the
children's faces

What you do:

1. Have the children describe what they want painted on their faces. Encourage
   them to use descriptive terms for colors, sizes, and shapes and to use prepositions
   ("a big star below my right eye").
2. While painting the children's faces, ask them to describe how it feels.

Make your own face paint: Mix 2 tbsp. of shortening with 1 tbsp. of cornstarch,
then add 4–5 drops of food coloring. This paint will wash off with soap and water.

Additional Activities

Partner Up, Silly Kids!

Children pair up and the partners face each other. The teacher calls out a body part and the partners touch those parts together. For example, the teacher says "Head!" and the partners touch their heads together. After a few turns the teacher can then say "Snicker Doodles," and everyone finds a new partner.

Silly Dress-up Day

Have the children and teachers wear their clothes backwards for one day!

Snacks

Note: Be sure no children are allergic to strawberries or peanuts before serving snacks with these items. As appropriate, substitute other fruits or jellies and other nuts.

1. Silly Sundaes

What you need:

- Cherries
- Strawberry jelly
- Frozen vanilla yogurt
- Crushed mixed nuts
- Bowls, spoons, forks (1 of each per child)

What you do:

Begin by putting a cherry in the bottom of the bowl.

Sprinkle some nuts onto the cherry. Then drizzle on a little strawberry jelly, and finally add a scoop of frozen yogurt. Give each child a fork to eat it with (have spoons ready for those who don't want to be too silly)!

2. Challenge the children to eat with their nondominant hands. Provide foods such as applesauce and soup to really test their ability. (If they don't know their dominant hands, test them quickly by giving them spoons and seeing which hand they use. Then tell them to switch hands for this activity.) Good fun!

Pretest and Posttest

Silly Sally

Concepts	Pretest	Posttest
Silliness		
Strolling		
Concept of *upside down*		
Concept of *backwards*		
How to use pictures to predict actions		
Getting through a maze		
Body awareness ~ All the silly things a body can do!		

My Little Sister Ate One Hare

By Bill Grossman
Illustrated by Kevin Hawkes

Our next book is an entertaining, and rather stomach-turning, tale of a
little girl who enjoys eating disgusting creatures but is unable to "stomach"
healthy foods. Her sibling, the narrator, was sure the little girl was going
to "throw up then and there, but she didn't." The melodic text and
disgusting subject matter make this a favorite with most children.
Besides the gross-out factor, it is also a counting book full of great pictures.
The last page usually sends children into fits of laughter. When the giggles
subside, it's fun to find each and every creature that had been swallowed.
This is a book that will keep the children in stitches.

Dear Families,

There probably isn't a child out there who hasn't swallowed something unusual at one time or another. But swallowing a hare, snakes, bats, and lizards? Only (we hope) in our very funny next story, *My Little Sister Ate One Hare* by Bill Grossman and Kevin Hawkes. This is a creative counting book with a gross-out factor that the children are sure to love. It's repetitive, yet exciting, with a fantastic ending. We're sure your child will request this one again and again.

Be on the lookout for this and other great counting and silly eating books to read at home. Especially good stories include: *Seven Blind Mice* by Ed Young, *Mouse Count* by Ellen Stoll Walsh, *The Water Hole* by Graeme Base, *Some Smug Slug* by Pamela Duncan Edwards, *The Very Hungry Caterpillar* by Eric Carle, *The Doorbell Rang* by Pat Hutchins, and *There Was an Old Lady Who Swallowed a Fly* by Simms Taback.

We'll be busy counting endless things at school, so the more counting you can do at home to reinforce this, the better! Make a goal to learn a few new numbers over the next two weeks. In addition to counting out loud, you can also practice recognizing written numbers and writing them (try tracing first, then copying a model, then writing them independently).

Insects, worms, and lots of other critters will feature prominently over the next two weeks as we read about all the crazy things our adventurous character swallows. It's sure to be a fun, yet slightly stomach-churning, unit!

Getting ready for giggles,

Room Setup

Dramatic Play Area

- Have props set out so the children can act out the "Little Miss Muffet" nursery rhyme (see Week 2, Songs, Poems section).

- Lay some Hula-Hoops out on the floor and have children act like frogs and jump from hoop to hoop.

Sensory Area

- Fill the sensory table with sand or dirt and add plastic insects and other animals from the story.

- Fill large plastic tubs with "goop" and plastic bugs. To make goop, add cornstarch and water together. When picked up it is a solid, but quickly transforms into a liquid again. Use this to bury the bugs. Add food coloring for added yuckiness.

Science Area

- Set out magnifying glasses and a collection of dead real bugs or plastic insects, depending on what your stomach can handle!

- Make a worm farm. Fill a large clear plastic tub with sand, dirt, shredded newspaper, rocks, and wet leaves. Add about a dozen worms (get them at a bait store or dig them up). Let the children pull them out (carefully) and compare their sizes, have worm races, or just watch them. Teach the children how to handle the worms respectfully. Don't let the worms dry out or get handled too much!

Art Area

- Set out colorful paint, paintbrushes, paper, and rubber snakes, worms, and spiders. Children put paint on the critters and then make prints of the animals on the paper.

- Set out inkpads, paper, and markers for making fingerprint bugs. Make a fingerprint with ink and add legs and antennae to complete the bug.

- Create a Bug: Provide egg cartons (cut apart), pipe cleaners, feathers, wiggly eyes, felt and fabric scraps, sequins, glitter, pom-poms, yarn, and glue. Children use any of the materials to create a bug. See if children can think of silly names for their bugs.

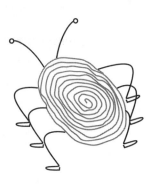

- Ants in Underpants: Cut egg cartons apart so there are three cups in a row on each piece. Children paint the cartons black and stick black pipe cleaners in the sides to form legs. Make small boxer-style underpants cut from white felt with red hearts drawn on to resemble the ants' underpants in the book. Attach the underpants to the backs of the ants with glue.

Book Area

- *The Doorbell Rang* by Pat Hutchins
- *Gregory, the Terrible Eater* by Mitchell Sharmat, illustrated by Jose Aruego and Ariane Dewey
- *I Know an Old Lady Who Swallowed a Fly* (several versions)
- *Mouse Count* by Ellen Stoll Walsh
- *The Picnic* by Kana Riley
- *Seven Blind Mice* by Ed Young
- *Some Smug Slug* by Pamela Duncan Edwards, illustrated by Henry Cole
- *There Was an Old Lady Who Swallowed a Fly* by Simms Taback
- *The Very Hungry Caterpillar* by Eric Carle
- *The Water Hole* by Graeme Base
- Other books related to critters and counting

Bulletin Board

- Begin by covering the bulletin board with white construction paper painted with red vertical and horizontal stripes to look like a plaid tablecloth. Gradually add the following:

  1. The ants in underpants made in the Art Area and any of the other insects and critters children make throughout the unit.

  2. Pictures of the children's faces with their mouths wide open. Have the insects and other animals they make during the unit look as if they are crawling into their mouths.

  3. Numbers cut from construction paper in all colors, sizes, and styles, scattered all over the tablecloth.

Week 1

Focus of the Week: Counting

Songs, Poems, and Fingerplays

Five Little Snakes
Five little snakes (hold up five fingers)
In a frying pan, (make palm flat)
The pan got hot and one went BAM! (one loud clap)

Continue on with *four little snakes, three little snakes,*
two little snakes, one little snake, until:

No little snakes in the frying pan,
Go catch more as fast as you can. (pretend to run and catch snakes)

One Potato, Two Potato
See Week 1, Activity 4 for this counting chant.

Other Counting Songs
"One, Two, Buckle My Shoe"
"Five Little Monkeys Jumping on the Bed"
"Five Little Monkeys Swinging from a Tree"
"Ten in the Bed"

Reading the Story

Introduce the book by discussing the title, author, and dedications (the dedications are at the back of the book). Discuss the book's cover and ask the children to guess what the book will be about.

Read the story every day and, as the children become familiar with it, gradually add in any of the following activities:

- Draw the Sister's "food" items with their corresponding numerals (the numeral 1 with one hare, the numeral 2 with two snakes, and so on) on index cards. Pass the cards out and begin the story. As the items appear in the story, the child with the appropriate card stands up to "read" and count the items on his or her card ("three ants—one, two, three").

43

- Place large numbers 1 through 10 on a flannel board. Attach pieces of Velcro to the backs of the cards with "food" items on them (see previous activity) and hand out a card to each child. At the appropriate time during the story, children stand up and stick their cards on the board under the correct numbers.

- Make small number cards 1 through 10 and pass them out to the children. During the story, the children listen for their number, stand up when they hear it, and sit back down when the page is turned. This continues throughout the entire story reading (#1 will be very busy standing up and sitting down!). By the time #10 is reached, the children may be able to say the numbers and names of the "food" items out loud ("ten peas, nine lizards, eight worms," and so on).

1. Number Hopping

Target Areas: cognition, gross motor

What you need:
- Masking tape
- Large number cards 1 through 10
- A large area to play in

What you do:
1. Using the tape, make a long straight line on the floor.
2. Tape the number cards sequentially along the line.
3. Give the children an action command paired with a number (examples: "Hop to number 5" or "Spin to number 7").
4. When the children have had plenty of practice, they can give the action commands.

2. People Graph

Target Areas: cognition, communication

What you need:
- Name tags for all the children
- Number cards 1 through 10, or higher if needed

What you do:
1. Lay the number cards on the floor in a long line with space between each card.
2. The teacher stands by the number 1 card and says, "If your name has only one letter in it, please stand by the number 1."

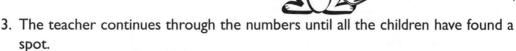

3. The teacher continues through the numbers until all the children have found a spot.
4. Draw a class graph on the white-board demonstrating the results found.
5. The children then can determine which group has the most children, which the least, and which groups have the same number of children.

3. Bugs in a Bucket

Target Areas: cognition, gross motor

What you need:
- Plastic or rubber bugs and other critters
- 6 buckets labeled with numbers 1 through 6 (paper painting buckets work well)
- Number cards 1 through 6

What you do:
1. Each child picks a number card and attempts to toss that number of critters into the bucket with the corresponding number.
2. Children continue picking cards and tossing the correct number of critters into the buckets until all the critters are in buckets.
3. Children close their eyes and grab handfuls of critters from the buckets. They count out how many they have and find the corresponding bucket to throw them into.

4. One Potato, Two Potato

Target Areas: gross motor, social

What you need:
- Large enough area to make a large circle with all the children

What you do:
1. Children stand in a circle with their fists extended out into the middle.
2. The leader begins the chant and gently taps each fist as he or she goes around the circle: "One potato, two potato, three potato, four; five potato, six potato, seven potato, MORE!"
3. When the leader says "seven potato, MORE," the child whose fist is tapped moves it behind his or her back.
4. Continue until only one fist is left; that child becomes the leader.

5. Number Scavenger Hunt
Target Area: cognition

What you need:
- Paper or plastic bags (1 per child)
- Number cards with pictures of common items in the classroom, for example: *1* car, *2* markers, *3* blocks, *4* pencils, *5* buttons (have multiple cards for each number)
- Number cards without pictures

What you do:
1. The children each choose three picture cards and begin searching in the classroom for the needed items. They put the items in their bags.
2. The teacher lays out the plain number cards on the floor.
3. When the children have all their items, they meet in the area where the number cards are laid out. They place their groups of items by the correctly corresponding numbers.

6. Line 'Em Up!
Target Areas: cognition, social

What you need:
- Number cards with numbers on them from 1 up to the number of children in the class

What you do:
1. Show the cards to the children while counting the numbers aloud.
2. Children hide their eyes and the cards are then hidden around the room.
3. All the children search and find one card each, come back, and wait for their classmates.
4. Children form a line in the order of their number cards, beginning with the number 1 card.

Week 2

Focus of the Week: Insects and other critters

Circle Time

Songs, Poems, and Fingerplays

<u>Worms</u>
One worm, two worms, three worms, four,
Five worms, six worms, seven worms, MORE;
Eight worms, nine worms,
Ten worms wiggle.
Put them on your toes and see if you giggle!

<u>Beehive</u>
Here is the beehive, (hold hand in a fist)
But where are the bees?
Hiding inside where nobody sees.
Watch and you'll see them
Come out of their hive,
One, two, three, four, five! (open fingers one at a time)
Buzz, buzz, buzz! (wiggle all fingers)

<u>Little Miss Muffet</u>
Little Miss Muffet sat on a tuffet,
Eating her curds and whey.
Along came a spider
And sat down beside her
And frightened Miss Muffet away!

Reading the Story

Read the story every day and gradually add in any of the following activities:

- Gather together a pea and a collection of small plastic, rubber, or stuffed animals: a small rabbit, a snake, an ant, a mouse, a bat, a shrew, a frog, a worm, and a lizard. Conceal these items in a bag and have the children take turns reaching in and grabbing one item. Children guess what the items are before pulling them out of the bag. After pulling out their critters, they get to hold onto them throughout the reading of the story.

47

- Have a large cutout of a little girl with her mouth open wide. Cut out the opening of her mouth and tape a large baggie to the back side so that items placed into her mouth will fall into the bag. Have laminated cutouts of the critters from the book with their corresponding numbers. During the story reading, the children can help feed the hungry girl. Be true to the story and have all the critters come back up and out of her stomach!

- Make small cards with the animals and peas from the story and pass them out to the children. During the story, the children listen for their item, stand up when they hear it, and sit back down when the page is turned. This continues throughout the entire story reading (the hare will be very busy standing up and sitting down!). By the time the peas are eaten, the children may be able to say the numbers and names of the "food" items out loud ("ten peas, nine lizards, eight worms," and so on).

Group Activities

1. Frog Tongues

Target Areas: cognition, communication, fine motor

What you need:
- Noiseless party blowers (1 per child)
- Self-adhesive Velcro tape
- Small cutouts of critters, colored and laminated

What you do:
1. Roll out the blowers and place a small piece of the soft portion of the Velcro tape on the end.
2. Place the hard part of the Velcro tape on the critter cutouts.
3. The children pretend to be frogs and use their tongues (blowers) to catch the critters.

2. Slinky Snakes

Target Areas: cognition, fine motor

What you need:

- Paper plates (1 per child)
- Scissors
- Markers or paint daubers
- Stapler or tape

What you do:

1. Children cut out the inner circle of the paper plate, leaving the outer ridged edge. Save the inner piece for later.
2. Cut the ridged piece in half, leaving two C-shaped pieces.
3. Position the ends of the two C-shaped pieces together so that they now resemble an S. Staple those ends together.
4. Using the inner piece of the paper plate, children cut out the shape of a snake's head with, if desired, a tongue hanging out.
5. Staple the head onto the end of the S shape to create a snake.
6. Children use the markers or daubers to color the snake in a pattern (for example, an AB pattern: red, blue, red, blue, . . .).
7. Attach the snakes to the bulletin board along with the bugs and other creations.

3. Flyswatter Painting

Target Areas: cognition, fine motor, gross motor

What you need:

- Flyswatters
- Large sheets of paper (1 per child)
- Paint in a variety of colors
- Black markers
- Shallow pans

What you do:

1. On their large papers, children draw little black dots to symbolize flies all over the paper.
2. Dip a flyswatter in some paint and then swat it onto the paper in as many colors as desired.

4. Fishing for Worms

Target Areas: cognition, social

What you need:
- Large amount of rubber fishing worms (no hooks)
- Large clear plastic tub
- Water
- Towels

What you do:
1. Fill the plastic tub with water and add the worms.
2. Children remove their shoes and socks and fish the worms out of the tub with their feet.
3. They race to see how many worms they can get in 30 seconds.

5. Bat Tag

Target Areas: gross motor, social

What you need:
- Sticker sheets, any stickers will do (1 sheet per child)
- Large area to run in

What you do:
1. The children play tag, pretending to be bats, flying around the room all at the same time.
2. When tagged (caught), the child stops and gets a sticker from the tagger. This sticker goes on the child's body (arm, head, face, leg).
3. The first bat to lose all its stickers (all the stickers on the sheet) wins.

6. Ants at the Picnic

Target Areas: cognition, fine motor

What you need:
- White heavy card stock paper
- Red paint
- Black inkpad
- Markers

What you do:

1. Children create a red-and-white plaid design by painting red lines down and across the paper using their fingers.
2. Then make black fingerprints on the red-and-white plaid design. Use the markers to create ants and other bugs out of the fingerprints by adding legs and antennae.

Note: Be sure no children are allergic to peanuts before serving snacks with peanut butter. As appropriate, substitute cream cheese, almond butter, or another sandwich spread.

1. Wash and clean some peas (in the pod), open, and eat. Who can eat ten?

2. Veggie Viper

What you need:

- Carrots
- Celery
- Grape tomatoes
- Cream cheese

What you do:

Cut the carrots and celery into 1" pieces. Spread a small amount of cream cheese on the ends of each piece and then place them side by side in a long row to form a snake, using the cream cheese to stick the pieces together. Use the grape tomato for the snake's head.

3. My Little Students Ate One Hare

What you need:

- Canned pear halves
- Grapes sliced in half
- Slivered almonds
- Raisins
- Cottage cheese

What you do:

Lay a pear half on a plate with the pitted side down. Place a grape half at the small end of the pear for the nose. Add 2 slivered almonds on top for the ears and 2 raisins for the eyes. Place a dollop of cottage cheese at the large end for the tail. Eat and enjoy!

4. Toasty Snakes

What you need:
- Refrigerator breadstick dough
- Raisins
- Aluminum foil (1 square per child)

What you do:

Personalize all the aluminum foil squares with the children's initials and give them to the children. Place one breadstick on each piece of foil. Children shape the dough into a snake shape (like a loose W). Add a raisin for the eye and bake according to the package directions.

5. Nutty Ants

What you need:
- 2 c. powdered milk
- 1 1/2 c. of peanut butter
- 1/2 c. honey
- Chow mein noodles
- Raisins
- Waxed paper squares, personalized (1 per child)

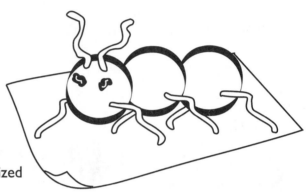

What you do:

Mix powdered milk, peanut butter, and honey in a bowl. Give each child 3 pieces of this dough and have children roll the pieces into 3 balls. Put the balls side by side to make a bug body. Use the chow mein noodles to make legs and antennae and the raisins for eyes. Eat it before it crawls away!

6. Ants on a Log

What you need:
- Celery stalks
- Peanut butter
- Raisins
- Wooden craft sticks

What you do:

Spread the peanut butter on the celery using the wooden craft sticks. Place the raisins on the peanut butter. Eat before the ants get away!

My Little Sister Ate One Hare
Snacks

7. Wormy Ice

What you need:
- Gummy worms
- Ice cube tray
- Water
- Clear plastic cups (1 per child)

What you do:
1. Fill the ice cube tray with water and add a bunch of gummy worms. Make sure they stick out of the top of the tray and over the edges for a better effect.
2. Freeze. Add the wormy ice cubes to water served in the clear cups.

53

Pretest and Posttest

My Little Sister Ate One Hare

Concepts	Pretest	Posttest
Rote counting 1–10		
One-to-one correspondence 1–10		
Numeral recognition 1–10		
Edible vs. nonedible items		
Critters, bugs, insects (comprehension of terms)		

Go Away, Big Green Monster!

By Ed Emberley

Filled with colorful die-cut pages, children find our next book to be empowering and spontaneously interactive. The colors are bright and bold, and the story offers a fun variety of adjectives to describe each of the big green monster's features. With each turn of the page, we are introduced to more and more scary parts of the monster, until finally we see it fully revealed. But, as the book says, "You don't scare me!" and with each turn of the remaining pages the scary features disappear, one by one. The readers are in charge—and that is a very important feature of this book. *Go Away, Big Green Monster!* provides a great avenue for talking about fear and other emotions and ways in which children can recognize, understand, and deal with them.

Dear Families,

What has two big yellow eyes, a long bluish-greenish nose, a big red mouth with sharp white teeth, two little squiggly ears, scraggly purple hair, and a big scary green face? Give up? It's the monster in our next story, *Go Away, Big Green Monster!* by Ed Emberley. This is a short, fun story with wonderful descriptive language. Page by page, the scary monster appears, one feature at a time, and then disappears in just the same way when told, "You don't scare me! So go away . . ." The kids really show the monster who is in charge!

If your child is afraid of the dark or doesn't like to sleep alone, this story is sure to help chase away any nighttime monsters. Are there other things that frighten your child? You could make simple books like *Go Away, Big Green Monster!* to tackle those issues as well. Give your child the power to make the fear disappear. Other home activities you and your child can do during this unit can focus on the descriptive vocabulary used in the story. What else can be big and yellow? Long and bluish-green? Big and red? Sharp and white? Little and squiggly? Scraggly and purple? Green? Go on a giant scavenger hunt!

Since monsters are creatures that fascinate almost all children, the library is filled with plenty of related stories. Some of our favorites are *Where the Wild Things Are* by Maurice Sendak, *There's a Nightmare in My Closet* by Mercer Mayer, *There's a Monster Under My Bed* by James Howe, and *Glad Monster, Sad Monster* by Anne Miranda.

The kids are sure to wear out the pages of this very popular storybook. Let us know what you think of it.

Stay safe!

Room Setup

Dramatic Play Area
- Make a monster den out of a large box. Hang spider webs, fake greenery, and yarn from the ceiling; paint the inside black; cover the walls with little patches of different textures such as fake fur, sand paper, bubble wrap, and contact paper (sticky side out). Add a strobe light and creepy music to enhance the effect.

- Provide costumes, masks, and wigs for the children to dress up like monsters.

Sensory Area
- Put black beans in the sensory table and add blocks of different shapes and colors.

- Spray shaving cream on a table and draw monster faces or shapes in it.

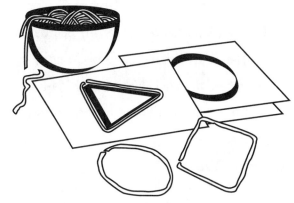

- Put out cooked spaghetti and shape outlines drawn on heavy card stock paper. Children use the shape outlines as templates and form shapes with the spaghetti. Let the shaped spaghetti dry—creating noodle shapes!

- Provide GAK (see Science Area for recipe) for the children to bury and hide Mr. or Mrs. Potato Head parts in, to cut into shapes with cookie cutters, or just to feel and experience the unusual texture.

Science Area
- Green GAK: Mix 1 cup water with 1 cup white glue and 10 drops of green food coloring. Set aside. In a separate bowl, mix 11/3 cups warm water with 4 tsp. borax laundry booster. Stir until the borax is dissolved. Slowly pour the glue mixture into the borax mixture, but don't mix. Tip the bowl and roll the glue mixture around in the borax a few times, then lift the concoction out of the bowl and knead for a few minutes. Store in an airtight container.

- Set out a Mystery Box (see Kissing Hand unit, Week 2, Activity 2) with Mr. Potato Head parts. The children reach into the box and touch an item. They guess what it is without pulling it out.

Art Area

- Use green, yellow, purple, and red paint at the easels.

- Use different shapes cut out of construction paper to create monster faces (some examples: square head, circle eyes, oval nose, rectangle mouth, triangle teeth).

Book Area

- *Glad Monster, Sad Monster* by Anne Miranda, illustrated by Ed Emberley

- *Monster Manners* by Bethany Roberts, illustrated by Andrew Glass

- *My Monster Mama Loves Me So* by Laura Leuck, illustrated by Mark Buehner

- *Skeleton Hiccups* by Margery Cuyler, illustrated by S.D. Schindler

- *There's a Monster Under My Bed* by James Howe, illustrated by David S. Rose

- *There's a Nightmare in My Closet* by Mercer Mayer

- *Where the Wild Things Are* by Maurice Sendak

- Other books related to monsters and things that go bump in the night

Bulletin Board

- Attach the words *Go Away, Big Green Monster!* to the top of the bulletin board. On large, green construction paper circles, make faces that resemble the big green monster. Display the monster faces on the board.

- Add to the board the monster faces the children make in the Art Area.

Week 1

Focus of the Week: Monsters and emotions

Circle Time

Songs, Poems, and Fingerplays

Emotional Monster
(to the tune of "Merrily We Roll Along")

There's a monster in my closet, in my closet, in my closet.
There's a monster in my closet, and it's very sad (BOO HOO!).

Add additional verses: . . . and it's very happy (HOORAY!); . . . and it's very scared
(WHAT'S THAT NOISE?); . . . and it's very tired (YAWN).

Ask the children to suggest ideas for more verses.

Monster Hunt
We're going on a monster hunt.
We're gonna catch a big one!
We're not scared . . .
What a spooooky night.

Is he under the table? We'd better look under it. (Peek, peek.)
Is he out in the hallway? We'd better sneak out there. (Sneak, sneak.)
Is he up in the cobwebs? We'd better look up there. (Brush, brush.)
Is he over by the skeletons? We'd better rush over there. (Rattle, rattle.)
Is he near the black cats? We'd better check it out. (Meow, meow.)
Is he flying with the ghosts? We'd better watch up there. (Whoo, whoo.)
OH NO! I see two yellow eyes, a green nose, and a BIG RED MOUTH!
IT'S THE MONSTER!!!

Gotta go back by the ghosts. (Whoo, whoo.)
Back near the cats. (Meow, meow.)
Back over by the skeletons. (Rattle, rattle.)
Back up by the cobwebs. (Brush, brush.)
Back through the hallway. (Sneak, sneak.)
And back under the table. (Peak, peak.)
And say, "GO AWAY, BIG GREEN MONSTER, AND DON'T COME BACK!"

Play the song "The Monster Mash" by Bobby "Boris" Pickett on *K-tel Presents Halloween Sounds to Haunt Your House*. Dance around the room like monsters.

Reading the Story

Introduce the book by discussing the title and author. Discuss the book's cover and ask the children to guess what the book will be about.

Read the story every day and, as the children become familiar with it, gradually add in any of the following activities:

- Using circles cut out of construction paper, make faces corresponding to each of the stages of the big green monster's developing face. For example, one circle would have two yellow eyes, the next would have two yellow eyes and a long greenish nose, and so on until there is a circle for every stage in the book. Laminate the circles. As the book is read, children place the circles out on the floor in order. They will need to work together. Then they take away the circles in order as they are guided by the book.

- Invite the children to take turns saying "Go Away . . ." along with the story.

- Use silly voices with different volumes, pitches, and durations as you read the story.

- Encourage predicting by asking the children what face part will be on the next page. Give the children picture cards of the face parts and ask them to hold up the one they think will be next.

- Children wait until they hear the word "scare," then make their best scared faces.

1. Monster Masks
Target Areas: cognition, fine motor, social

What you need:
- Green paper plates
- Variety of objects for creating a monster face: cereal, rickrack, buttons, sequins, cotton balls, cotton swabs, pasta, ribbon, pipe cleaners, beans, yarn, colored sprinkles, muffin liners, and so forth
- Glue
- Wooden craft sticks
- Scissors

What you do:

1. Decorate the paper plates using any of the collage items to create a personal monster facemask. Be sure to cut out holes for eyes.
2. Attach the monster mask to a craft stick and use it throughout the week.

2. Monster Toes

Target Areas: cognition, communication, social

What you need:

- Green construction paper
- Scissors

What you do:

1. Make monster footprints cut out of green construction paper in odd shapes—be sure to vary the number of toes. Cut out two of each shape, making sets of left and right feet. Laminate for durability.
2. Before the children arrive, hide one footprint from each set of monster footprints somewhere in the room.
3. Give each child the remaining footprint from one or more of the sets of footprints. The children search for the matching footprints to complete their sets.
4. Encourage the children to work together to find each match. Then they describe what they are looking for using descriptive terms ("I need a triangle-like shape with four toes)."

3. Monster Partners

Target Areas: cognition, fine motor, social

What you need:

- Large sheets of butcher paper
- Markers or paint
- Scissors

What you do:

1. Divide the children into pairs and give each pair one sheet of butcher paper.
2. For each pair, trace one partner as he or she lies on the paper with arms and legs spread out and head turned to one side. Then trace the other partner while lying on top of the first drawing, with arms and legs out and head to the other side. There should be a two-headed, four-armed, four-legged monster on the paper.
3. The partners work together using the markers or paint to decorate their monster.
4. Cut out and hang the monsters around the room.

4. Silly Spaghetti Monsters

Target Areas: cognition, fine motor

What you need:

- Large container of cooked noodles (with a bit of vegetable oil added to decrease stickiness)
- Green tempera paint
- Black paper
- Colored construction paper cut into shapes corresponding to the shapes in the story (eyes, ears, nose, and so on)
- Glue

What you do:

1. Grab a small handful of spaghetti noodles. Dip the noodles into the green paint and drop them onto the black paper. Move them around to make a desired print. Then remove the noodles.
2. Let the paint dry and add construction paper shapes to create a monster face on top of the spaghetti print.

5. Our Many Emotions Book

Target Areas: cognition, communication, fine motor

What you need:

- Camera and film
- Paper
- Tape
- Stapler

What you do:

1. Take a photograph of each child expressing an emotion. Encourage the children to express emotions that are different from each other. Make one copy of each photo for a classroom set.
2. Prepare the book pages for the children to complete (as illustrated): Draw a blank line midway down the page, below that write *is feeling*, and then draw another blank line followed by a period. Give each child one page.

photo goes here

child writes name

child or teacher writes emotion

3. Give each child the copy of his or her emotion photograph. Children tape their photos onto the tops of their book pages.
4. Working individually with each child, have the child write his or her name on the first blank line. Ask the child what emotion he or she is expressing in the photo.

The child (with the teacher's help, if needed) fills in the bottom line of the book page.

5. Staple all of the pages together to make a classroom book to add to the class library.

6. Monster Spray

Target Areas: cognition, communication, social

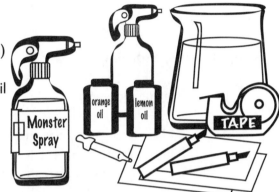

What you need:
- Small empty spray bottles (1 per child)
- Water
- Orange, lemon, or lavender scented oil
- Paper cut to fit around each bottle
- Eyedroppers
- Markers, crayons, or stamps
- Transparent tape

What you do:
1. Discuss fears children may have at bedtime. Explain the concept of monster spray: "When you spray this in the air, only nice friendly monsters or things visit at night."
2. Each child fills a bottle with water and then adds 1 or 2 drops of scented oil (with assistance).
3. Give each child a piece of paper for a label. They color and decorate their labels.
4. Tape the labels onto the bottles and instruct the children to keep the bottles by their beds at night.

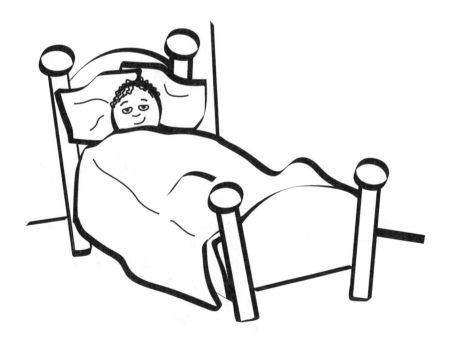

Week 2

Focus of the Week: Shapes

Songs, Poems, and Fingerplays

Shape Hokey Pokey

Make triangle, square, circle, and rectangle shapes cut out of construction paper, enough for 4 different shapes per child. Do the hokey pokey using shape directives instead of body parts:

Put your triangle in, put your triangle out,
You put your triangle in, and you shake it all about.
You do the hokey pokey, and you turn yourself around.
That's what it's all about!

Repeat with other shapes.

......

Look for a Sesame Street Monster album to dance around to during free play time.

Reading the Story

Read the story every day and gradually add in any of the following activities:

- Using a white board, create a face by drawing the parts as they appear in the story. Children take turns using an eraser to make the parts go away.

- Create the monster face as in the previous activity but without using the storybook. Ask the children which parts to draw and which colors to use. Once the monster is drawn, bring out the book to see if the children created the monster correctly.

- Using a white board, create a completely different monster and tell the story based on its characteristics. Children suggest the different shapes and colors to make this unique monster. They take turns using erasers to make the parts go away.

Group Activities

1. Felt Monsters
Target Area: cognition, communication, fine motor

What you need:
- Large piece of green felt
- Large buttons
- Black felt
- Bag or box

What you do:
1. Cut the green felt into a large circle to make a head. Sew the buttons on the head where the eyes, nose, and mouth will be. Cut the black felt into various shapes, each with a slit in the middle big enough to fit the buttons.
2. Show the children the black felt pieces and name the shapes *(triangle, oval, circle)*. Provide words (adjectives), as in the storybook, describing the shapes *(long, skinny, squiggly, sharp)*.
3. Conceal all the black felt shapes in a bag or box.
4. Children take turns reaching in the bag and pulling out a shape. Before they pull it out, they use the descriptive terms to predict which shape it will be ("I think I have a squiggly square." "I think I have a skinny oval.")
5. When a shape is drawn, the child buttons it onto the head.
6. Each child takes a turn, having the option of removing a shape that is already in place. This creates an ever-changing monster face!

2. Shape Treasure Hunt
Target Areas: cognition, communication, social

What you need:
- Shape Treasure Hunt lists (1 per 2 children)
- Pencils (1 per 2 children)
- Clipboards (1 per 2 children)

What you do:
1. Make the Shape Treasure Hunt lists using pictures of different shapes, for example, four pictures of squares, two of triangles, two of stars, and so forth.
2. Children choose partners. Each pair gets a Shape Treasure Hunt list, a clipboard, and a pencil.

3. The pairs look around the room and find the different shapes (*square* chair seat, *circle* pencil holder, and so forth).
4. Each time they find a shape, they check off one of the corresponding shape pictures on their paper.
5. When all the shapes have been checked off, they go to a designated meeting place and wait for the teacher.
6. The children show the teacher where the shapes they found were located.

3. Lost My Shape

Target Areas: cognition, communication, gross motor, social

What you need:

- Various shapes cut out of construction paper and laminated
- Large area to move around in

What you do:

1. Place all the shapes on the floor. Children sit in a circle around the shapes.
2. Choose one child to be the first player. He or she shouts out the name of a shape.
3. The whole group begins singing the following song, using the first player's chosen name of a shape. While they are singing, the first player walks around the circle until the song stops. The first player then retrieves the correct shape from the middle of the circle and dances back to his or her original spot.

(to the tune of "Skip to My Lou")

Lost my (<u>name of a shape</u>), what do I do?
Lost my (<u>name of a shape</u>), what do I do?
Lost my (<u>name of a shape</u>), what do I do?
Skip to my shape, my darling.

4. The child to the first player's right gets the next turn.

4. Shape Twister

Target Areas: cognition, gross motor, social

What you need:

- Large shapes laminated and taped close together on the floor
- Basket of cards showing the same shapes
- Basket of cards with pictures of hands and feet (at least one each for right hand, left hand, right foot, and left foot)

What you do:

1. Two children stand next to the set of shapes on the floor.
2. The teacher draws a card from each basket. Children follow the chosen directions—for example, "Right hand on a circle."
3. The teacher puts the cards back into the baskets and draws another set of cards—for example, "Left foot on a square." Children follow those directions and take the second position without moving out of the first position.
4. Continue until the children become too twisted to move or someone falls over!
5. Select two more children to play. Play until all children have had a turn.

Optional: Set up multiple sets of shapes on the floor around the room. This way, multiple pairs of children can play at the same time.

5. Rip Face!

Target Areas: cognition, communication, fine motor

What you need:

- White board and markers
- Magazines containing photographs of people and animals
- Construction paper, any size or color (1 piece per child)
- Glue

What you do:

1. While drawing a simple picture of a face on a white board, discuss the shapes of the different parts of a face ("These eyes are ovals," "These ears are squares").
2. Each child will be making a picture of a face by ripping out parts of faces from magazines and gluing them onto their papers. Two rules: (1) No two face parts can come from the same photograph! and (2) The parts of the faces should be torn out in identifiable shapes such as triangles, circles, squares, and so forth.
3. Assist the children to identify and rip out the shapes they want.
4. Children make their face pictures using their ripped-out shapes.
5. Display these works of art in the hallway or on the bulletin board.

6. Make a Shape with Your Body

Target Areas: cognition, gross motor

What you need:

- Pictures of the following shapes: circle, triangle, square, star, oval
- Large area to move around in

What you do:

1. Look at and discuss the different shape pictures.
2. Show the children how to make each shape using their bodies: Squat down into a ball for a circle, lie on the floor with arms and legs spread out for a star, lie on the floor with legs spread out and hands at sides for a triangle, and so on.
3. After everyone has practiced, count to 3 and say a shape. The children quickly put their bodies into the position of the shape called. Repeat with different shapes.

Shapely Body Language

Make a set of body parts picture cards (eyes, nose, shoulders, mouth, elbows, hands, legs, neck) and a set of cards with the names of the same body parts. Discuss how different body shapes (positions) convey different meanings. Demonstrate, for example, how smiling eyes convey happiness, a scrunched nose conveys smelling something stinky, and crossed legs convey bathroom time.

Show how the written words on the name cards match the pictures on the other cards. Lay the name cards out on the floor. Place the picture cards into a bag. Children take turns pulling a picture card from the bag and find the matching name card. They take positions using that body part to convey a special meaning. The other children guess the meaning. They put the picture card back into the bag and the next child pulls a card. If the same picture is drawn again, encourage children to take a different position using that body part.

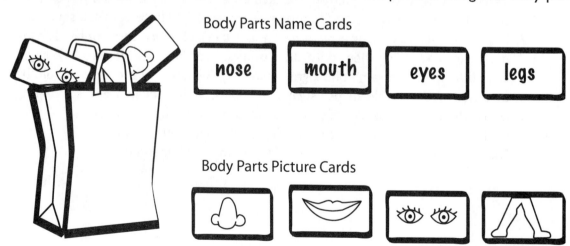

Body Parts Name Cards

| nose | mouth | eyes | legs |

Body Parts Picture Cards

Snacks

1. Serve a variety of crackers with different shapes. The children request the crackers by their shape.

2. Shape Sandwiches

What you need:
- Sandwiches of choice
- Butter or plastic knives

What you do:
    Children choose a shape and cut their sandwiches accordingly.

3. Toasty Monsters

What you need:
- White bread toast
- Food coloring
- Paintbrushes

What you do:
    Use the paintbrushes and food coloring to paint monster faces on the toast.

4. Applesauce Monsters

What you need:
- Unsweetened applesauce colored green with food coloring
- Raisins, orange slices, bananas, grapes, cereals

What you do:
    Put the applesauce into a bowl and use the various foods to create a monster face. Eat and enjoy!

Pretest and Posttest

Go Away, Big Green Monster!

Concepts	Pretest	Posttest
Shapes (circle, square, triangle, rectangle, star, and oval).		
Emotions (name and describe them)		
Descriptive terms (*scraggly, sharp,* etc.)		
Monster information		
Colors		
Body Language		
Right and *left*		

Barn Dance!

By Bill Martin Jr. and John Archambault
Illustrated by Ted Rand

This toe-tappin', lively story tells of a young boy who, by the light of the moon, follows the sounds of music down to the barn. There he finds a fiddle-playing scarecrow leading the farm animals in an old-fashioned hoedown. Shy at first, he eventually joins in the fun, dancing until the sun comes up and the hoot owl signals the end of the party. The boy quietly creeps back up to his bedroom with a memory to last forever. With its rhythmic, rhyming text, the kids will be swinging their partners with this story.

Dear Families,

Are you ready for an old-fashioned, toe-tappin' hoedown? Well, our next story, *Barn Dance!* by Bill Martin Jr. and John Archambault, provides just that. A young boy follows fiddle music out to the barn where the animals and a scarecrow lead him in a night filled with dancing—a night he'll never forget. The fun only stops when the sun comes up. Get ready to grab your partner and do-si-do because this is a story about music, dancing, and fun!

It's easy for you and your child to create some musical instruments right at home. Try making a simple drum (just an overturned pot and wooden spoon will do) and a rattle (a plastic container filled with beans). Books from the library will have more elaborate ideas. Whatever your choice, now is the time to fill your home with music and dance, dance, dance. Dancing is wonderful for your child's physical development and a great way to exercise.

Now is also a perfect time to take a trip to a farm. This story is filled with every kind of farm animal, and it would be fun for your child to see them all up close. Take pictures and send them to school so we can compare the photos of the animals with the pictures in the story. Consider making your own scarecrow to put in your yard or by the front door.

Some related books that you might want to check out from the library along with *Barn Dance!* are *Big Red Barn* by Margaret Wise Brown; *Buzzzzzz Said the Bee* by Wendy Cheyette Lewiston; *Hush, Hush, It's Sleepytime* by Peggy Parish; *Moo, Moo, Peekaboo!* by Jane Dyer; *Rosie's Walk* by Pat Hutchins; and *The Little Red Hen* by Paul Galdone.

See y'all later,

Room Setup

Dramatic Play Area

- Provide any of the following to create a scarecrow: a broom, overalls, a flannel shirt, boots, and a straw hat. Use a brown paper bag for the face and stuff the arms with newspapers.

- Set out masks of all the characters in the book (pig, horse, sheep, scarecrow, and so on).

- Put hay inside a refrigerator box to create a barn for the children to play in.

Sensory Area

- For individual listening, provide a tape recorder or CD player with earphones and some country and western music at the listening center.

- Set up plastic farm animals at the sensory table. Provide bran, oats, or corn flakes as their food.

Science Area

- Put together an ant farm and watch the ants go about their daily chores.

- Lay out a variety of animal puzzles for vocabulary and puzzle practice.

- Place some hay in a box with some plastic child-safe needles and magnifying glasses. Explain how to "find the needle in the haystack."

Art Area

- Set out play dough or paints and a few animal cookie cutters to use with them.

- Encourage children to make turkeys by using brown paper bags for bodies and applying a variety of colorful feathers.

- Provide leaves and crayons or paints for making leaf prints by either (1) placing a leaf under a paper, then rubbing the top with a crayon or (2) painting on the leaf, then pressing the painted side down on paper.

- Make Seed Names: Children write their names (with help, if needed) in big letters on pieces of paper. They outline their names in glue and put on dried pumpkin seeds.

- Children use cornhusks and small rubber bands to create simple cornhusk people (some cornhusks may be available from doing Week 2, Activity 5).

73

Book Area

- *Big Pumpkin* by Erica Silverman, illustrated by S.D. Schindler

- *Big Red Barn* by Margaret Wise Brown, illustrated by Felicia Bond

- *Buzzzzzz Said the Bee* by Wendy Cheyette Lewiston, illustrated by Hans Wilhelm

- *Farmer Duck* by Martin Waddell and Helen Oxenbury

- *Hush, Hush, It's Sleepytime* by Peggy Parish

- *The Little Red Hen* by Paul Galdone

- *Moo, Moo, Peekaboo!* by Jane Dyer

- *Pigs in the Corner: Fun with Math and Dance* by Amy Axelrod, illustrated by Sharon McGinley-Nally

- *Rosie's Walk* by Pat Hutchins

- *Too Many Pumpkins* by Linda White, illustrated by Megan Lloyd

- Other books related to farm animals, dancing, and fall

Bulletin Board

- Attach a simple farm scene with a house, gate, and barn. Add the children's art projects as the unit progresses.

- Glue a picture of each child on a Popsicle stick. These can be used as props for acting out scenes with the bulletin board. The children can use their pictures to visit the house, climb under the gate, and dance in the barn.

- Create a fence using Popsicle sticks.

Other

- Set a large pumpkin in the middle of the floor and let children take turns trying to throw a Hula-Hoop over it.

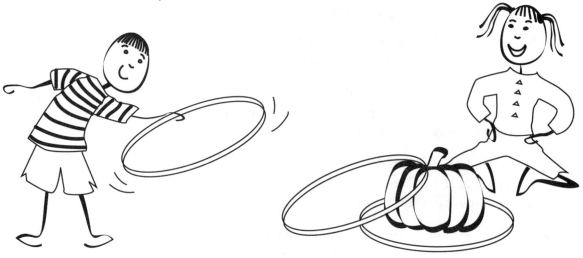

Week 1

Focus of the Week: Farm animals

Songs, Poems, and Fingerplays

Old MacDonald Had a Farm
Old MacDonald had a farm, E-I-E-I-O.
And on this farm he had a cow, E-I-E-I-O.
With a moo-moo here and a moo-moo there,
Here a moo, there a moo, everywhere a moo-moo,
Old MacDonald had a farm, E-I-E-I-O.

Continue singing the song, changing the animals and sounds they make.
Some ideas are: *chicken, horse, pig, dog, rooster,* and *duck.*

The Farmer in the Dell
The farmer in the dell,
The farmer in the dell,
Hi-ho the Derry-o,
The farmer in the dell.

On succeeding verses, substitute the following for "the farmer in the dell":
The farmer takes a wife; the wife takes a child; the child takes a nurse; the nurse
takes a cow; the cow takes a dog; the dog takes the cat; the cat takes the rat; the
rat takes the cheese; the cheese stands alone.

As they sing "The Farmer in the Dell," the children are in a circle holding
hands. One child starts in the middle as the farmer. As they sing the song, the
farmer chooses another child to be the wife. The wife joins the farmer in the
middle of the circle. Then the wife "takes a child," and so on, until the end of
the song. If more than one child is left as the cheese, the teacher can pick
one of them to be the next farmer. If you sing all the verses, the song works
best with 9 or 10 children.

Five Little Ducks
Five little ducks went out to play,
Over the hills and far away.
Mama Duck said, "Quack, quack, come back!"
But only <u>four</u> little ducks came waddling back.

Repeat the song, reducing the number in the last line until <u>no</u> little ducks come waddling back. Then, on the last verse, sing:
All five ducks come waddling back. Yeah!

Reading the Story

Introduce the book by discussing the title, authors, and dedication. Discuss the book's cover and ask the children to guess what the book will be about.

Read the story every day and, as the children become familiar with it, gradually add in any of the following activities:

- Each child chooses an animal he or she would like to be. When the animals in the story run into the barn, the children make the appropriate animal sounds, creating a noisy parade into the barn. They can also make their animal noises when the animals in the story dance.

- Read the story while sitting in a large box made to look like a barn (see Dramatic Play Area). Paint animal noses on the children or have them wear animal headbands. Invite them to sit on real hay or brown paper, which they pretend is hay, while listening to the story.

- Using any variety of puppets (Popsicle stick puppets, finger puppets, whole-hand puppets), the children bow to each other and dance when the animals in the story have their hoedown. They quietly lay their animals down for a rest at the end of the story.

1. Marble Paint Hay
Target Areas: cognition, fine motor

What you need:
- Brown paint
- White paper 8 1/2" x 11" (1 sheet per child)
- Colored pencils or markers
- Marbles
- Shallow paint containers (several)
- Medium-sized box lids (several)
- Optional: Plastic salad tongs

What you do:

1. Each child has a piece of paper. The children take turns putting their pieces of paper inside one of the box lids and doing steps 2 through 4.
2. Put one marble in a small container of paint and roll it around until it is completely covered.
3. Using the salad tongs, pick up the marble and place it in the box lid on top of the white paper.
4. Wiggle the box lid all around until the marble runs out of paint.
5. The finished product will look like some hay from the barn. Children can draw characters from the story on the paper after it is dry. These hay paintings can be displayed in the room or laminated and used as placemats.

2. Paper Bag Puppets

Target Areas: fine motor, social

What you need:

- Brown paper lunch sacks (1 per child)
- Faces of animals in the book, enlarged and photocopied onto white paper
- Colored pencils
- Glue
- Scissors

What you do:

1. Each child chooses which animal puppet to make and takes the chosen animal face.
2. Color and then cut out the animal face and glue it to the flat part on the bottom of a lunch bag (with the bottom folded up).
3. On the inside of the fold, draw the tongue of the animal.
4. These puppets can live in the barn area and be used during free play.

3. The Guessing Game

Target Areas: cognition, communication

What you need:

- Paper or plastic animals that live on a farm (at least 10 different animals)

What you do:

1. The teacher tells the children the names of 10 animals while lining them up on a table.
2. The children then close their eyes, and the teacher removes one animal.
3. When the children open their eyes, the teacher says: "There were ten animals, now there are nine. Guess which one is not in line."

4. The children try to guess which animal is missing.

5. After they have played this a couple of times with the teacher, let the children take turns hiding one animal.

6. To make this more challenging, remove 2 animals and see if they can remember which 2 are gone.

4. Swingin' Characters

Target Area: fine motor

What you need:

- Enlarged photocopies of the characters in the book (several per child)
- Various collage materials (straw, buttons, paint daubers, felt, sandpaper, feathers, string)
- Wire coat hangers (1 per child)
- String in a variety of colors and lengths
- Glue
- Transparent tape

What you do:

1. Children decorate the characters from the book using the collage materials. Encourage creativity in the decorating (buttons for the cow's spots, straw for the boy's hair, and so forth).

2. Cut out the characters and tape each one to a string.

3. When all of the characters are complete, tie the strings of each child's characters to a coat hanger and, voilà, everyone has a mobile!

4. See if the children can make their characters swing and dance with each other.

5. Bat Feet

Target Areas: cognition, fine motor

What you need:

- Black paint
- Heavy white paper
- Tub of soapy water and towels
- Wiggly eyes (1 pair per child)
- Glue
- Scrap construction paper (white and black)
- Scissors

What you do:

1. For each child, paint the bottom of one foot black.

2. Press the child's painted foot onto a piece of heavy white paper to create a footprint.

3. Wash the paint off the first foot and paint the bottom of the other foot black. The child places the heel of the second foot so it overlaps the heel of the first footprint, with the toes pointing in directly opposite directions (the heels make the bat's body and the rest of the feet make the bat's wings). Wash the second foot!

4. When the print dries, add eyes, a mouth, and pointy ears.

5. Cut out the bat prints and hang them up in the classroom or barn.

6. Boingy Nose Pig Hat

Target Areas: cognition, fine motor

What you need:

- Thick paper strips, long enough to fit around a child's head (1 per child)
- Strips of paper 1" wide x 5" long (1 per child)
- Large pig face and a separate pig nose drawn on an 8 1/2" x 11" piece of white paper (use the drawing on page 80 or make one) (1 copy per child)
- Scissors
- Stapler
- Pink crayons, pens, colored pencils, watercolors, paint

What you do:

1. Each child creates a pink pig face and extra nose by cutting out and coloring a pig face and nose drawing.

2. Fold the 5" strip of paper accordion-style and attach one end to the extra nose with a stapler or tape.

3. Attach the other end to the nose on the pig face.

4. After the nose is attached, staple or tape the pig face to the headband.

5. Decorate the rest of the headband with rubber stamps of animals or the letters P-I-G, or draw some grass on it.

6. The children will love the boinginess of their noses!

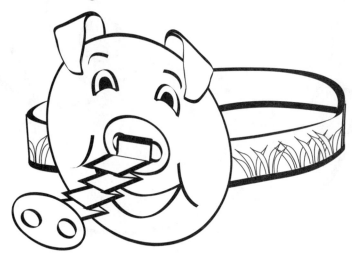

Boingy Nose Pig Hat Template

Week 2

Focus of the Week: Dancing, movement, and verbs

Songs, Poems, and Fingerplays

B-I-N-G-O
There was a farmer had a dog and Bingo was his name-o.
B-I-N-G-O, B-I-N-G-O, B-I-N-G-O, and Bingo was his name-o.
There was a farmer had a dog and Bingo was his name-o.
(Clap)-I-N-G-O, (clap)-I-N-G-O, (clap)-I-N-G-O, and Bingo was his name-o.

Continue substituting letters with claps, until there are no more letters, only claps.

If You're Happy and You Know It!
If you're happy and you know it, clap your hands. (clap, clap)
If you're happy and you know it, clap your hands. (clap, clap)
If you're happy and you know it, then your face will surely show it.
If you're happy and you know it, clap your hands. (clap, clap)

Continue the song with these verses:
If you're happy and you know it, stomp your feet. (stomp, stomp)
If you're happy and you know it, shout "Hooray!" (Hooray!)
If you're happy and you know it, do all three. (clap, clap, stomp, stomp, Hooray!)

Head, Shoulders, Knees, and Toes
Touch body parts as they are named in this poem:

Head, shoulders, knees and toes, knees and toes,
Head, shoulders, knees and toes, knees and toes,
Eyes and ears and mouth and nose,
Head, shoulders, knees and toes, knees and toes.

Reading the Story

Read the story every day and gradually add in any of the following activities:

- Create an obstacle course for children to follow while the story is read. The children take turns working their way through each step as it occurs in the story: *tiptoe* down the stairs past the sleeping dog (stuffed animal, or child pretending to be the dog); *creep* through the fence posts (crawl under chair); *run* into the barn (cardboard box or structure like a barn); *dance* around with animals in barn (other children acting out animals); *watch* the sun come up (through a fake window frame); *tiptoe* past the sleeping dog back up the stairs; *climb* into bed and then *chomp* an apple. Emphasize the verbs used in each of these activities. Periodically ask the children what they are doing, to check comprehension of the terms.

- Using musical instruments, play a song while the boy and animals are dancing. Musical instruments could include coffee-can drums or two paper cups taped together with beans inside. Maybe it will turn into a conga line . . . who knows?

- Children tiptoe, run in place, and dance when these actions occur in the story.

1. Dance Time!
Target Areas: gross motor, social

What you need:
- Open floor space
- Book or video from the library on square dancing

What you do:
1. Teach this sequence of "dance steps," having children "bow to their partners" before beginning:

    (arms) up, down; (hands) shake, shake, shake;
    (hips) wiggle, wiggle, wiggle; (feet) jump, jump, jump.
2. Or, get a book on square dancing for young children and teach a real square dance!
3. Teach other dances. Don't forget the Hokey Pokey!! What about the Chicken Dance? Know any line dances? Everybody Hand Jive!

2. Walk Like the Animals

Target Areas: cognition, communication, gross motor

What you need:

- Open floor space

What you do:

1. Demonstrate to the children how a few animals move. Some examples: strut like a chicken, saunter like a cow, run like a dog, waddle like a duck, and hop like a bunny.
2. Name one animal at a time, and ask the children to act out its movement.
3. When the children have practiced moving like all of the animals, increase the speed at which the animals are named until the children are going so fast that they can't tell which animals they are anymore!

3. Drawing to the Music

Target Areas: fine motor, social

What you need:

- Large rectangular piece of paper
- Pencils, pens, or crayons
- Country and western music

What you do:

1. Lay the paper down on the floor with room to walk around it.
2. Children choose a crayon, pen, or pencil and then pick a place somewhere on the side of the paper as their starting point.
3. Children start drawing in their area. They can draw whatever comes to mind.
4. The country and western music starts, and the children stand up, hold on to their pencils, and dance around the paper clockwise until the music stops.
5. They sit down wherever they are and continue drawing on that area.
6. Repeat steps 4 and 5 until the paper is filled.
7. The end product will be a beautiful picture made by all of the children.

4. Corny Relay

Target Areas: gross motor, social

What you need:

- 1 ear of corn (in or out of husk)

What you do:

1. Divide the class into two groups. The groups go to opposite sides of the room and line up.
2. The first child in one line has to get the ear of corn over to the other line and give it to the first child in that line. The child in that line has to carry it back across the room to the next child on the other side.
3. The relay continues this way, but there are two hitches: They cannot use their hands to carry the corn, and no child can carry it the same way another child has already carried it!
4. Add some lively fiddlin' music to really get this relay going! Hee-Haw!

5. Corn on the Cob Painting

Target Areas: cognition, fine motor

What you need:

- Unshucked raw ears of corn (1 per child)
- Paint in a variety of fall colors
- Shallow and wide containers for paint
- Paper in a variety of fall colors (1 piece per child)
- Country and western music and music player

What you do:

1. Children shuck their pieces of corn. (Save the husks for the Art Area.)
2. Children roll their ears of corn in the paint and then roll them along their papers. Play music while painting with the corn. Who can roll slowly? Who can roll quickly? Can anyone use the ear of corn like a paintbrush?
3. Talk about how and where corn grows, which farm animals eat corn, whether the children like corn, and different ways humans eat corn (on the cob, from a can, popcorn). Has anyone ever been in a corn maze?

6. Make Your Own Band

Target Areas: cognition, communication, fine motor

What you need:

- Empty shoeboxes
- Rubber bands, a variety of types and sizes
- Empty milk cartons (pint-sized and clean!)
- Beans
- Empty toilet paper or paper towel tubes
- Waxed paper
- Contact paper for decorations
- Markers of various colors
- Transparent tape
- Stapler

What you do for **guitars**:
1. Stretch rubber bands around empty shoeboxes, using different-sized rubber bands to get a variety of pitches and tones.
2. Pluck away!

What you do for **shakers**:
1. Put beans or other noisy objects into each milk carton.
2. Close the tops of the cartons and staple shut.
3. Decorate the cartons with contact paper.
4. Shake, shake, shake!

What you do for **kazoos**:
1. Decorate toilet paper or paper towel tubes with markers.
2. Secure a piece of waxed paper over one end of the tube with a rubber band.
3. Put a piece of tape over the rubber band to keep it in place.
4. Blow and hum into the kazoo!

Old MacDonald Had Some Shapes
Write the names of the animals in "Old MacDonald" on sentence strips and attach associated pictures. Teach the song during a structured circle, then leave the sentence strips out for children to play with as they sing the song during free play time. Once they know this song well, sing "Old MacDonald had some *shapes*, E-I-E-I-O. With a *triangle* here, and a *triangle* there," and so forth. Put the various shapes on the floor, and the children can jump from shape to shape.

1. Make homemade applesauce or apple cider in a blender or juicer.

2. Use oriental noodles as pretend hay for animal crackers or animal fruit chews to eat. Crunch, crunch.

3. **Homemade Butter**

What you need:
- Pint of whipping cream
- Crackers or bread
- Baby food jar
- Optional: salt

What you do:

Allow a pint of whipping cream to reach room temperature. Pour a small amount of the cream into a baby food jar. Place the lid on the jar and shake. The butter will form a ball. There will be a residue of watery milk. Remove the ball of butter and serve on crackers or bread. Salt to taste.

4. Cook up some Tater Tots and serve them as "bales of hay"!

Pretest and Posttest

Barn Dance!

Concepts	Pretest	Posttest
Farm animals		
Scarecrow		
Farm		
Corn		
Dancing		
Different styles of music		
Musical instruments		
Verbs (action words—*strut, waddle, tiptoe, crawl,* etc.)		

Notes

I Know an Old Lady Who Swallowed a Pie

By Alison Jackson
Illustrated by Judith Byron Schachner

This silly tale, a takeoff on a popular folktale, is a perfect treat for the Thanksgiving holiday. A little old lady comes to Thanksgiving dinner offering a delicious pie. No one even gets a tiny bite, however, before she eats the whole thing. Each page reveals something else the insatiable, funny lady consumes. Finally full, and with a very large tummy, she becomes a hilarious contribution to the Thanksgiving Day Parade!

Dear Families,

Our next story, *I Know an Old Lady Who Swallowed a Pie*, written by Alison Jackson and illustrated by Judith Byron Schachner, is just the story to read right about the time your taste buds are gearing up for Thanksgiving dinner. The old lady devours all our old favorites, including rolls, squash, salad, and of course turkey. But she manages to digest a few unusual things as well. The familiar rhyme continues until the funny old lady is stuffed; but, unlike the unfortunate old lady who swallowed the fly, our friend finds herself in quite a different predicament at the end (you'll have to check the book out to see what happens!).

This is a perfect story to start the holiday season. Now is the time to talk about any upcoming family gatherings. Think about making place cards or centerpieces to contribute to the events. Explore the fall season with your child, looking for colorful leaves and other pieces of nature to add to your decorations. Make shopping lists and venture to the grocery store together. Of course, cooking together provides endless fun and opportunities to learn about different measurements (half and whole, teaspoon and tablespoon, cup) and cooking terms (*stir, beat, whip, spread, bake, broil,* and so on).

See if you can find this and other Thanksgiving stories at the library. Among our favorites are *Feast for Ten* by Cathryn Falwell, *It's Thanksgiving* by Jack Prelutsky, and *Pumpkin Pumpkin* by Jeanne Titherington. Some of these stories will help you explain the traditions and history behind the holiday and encourage conversations about things to be thankful for.

Who's hungry?

Special Note: The Thanksgiving holiday season is a good time of year to invite grandparents to a Grandparents' Day at school. They could come for a snack and visit the classroom. Try to fit in a Grandparents' Day during the two weeks of this unit.

Dramatic Play Area

- Set up a grocery store with bags, cash register, price tags, and bins (containers or boxes) to display assorted foods (fruits, vegetables, meats, dairy). Have a table nearby equipped with paper, pencils, and word cards with food words and a matching picture card of each of the foods. The children use these cards to help write a grocery list before they go shopping at the store.

- Supply placemats, dishes, and silverware. Set out cards or paper and pencils, crayons, or markers. Provide word cards with words needed to create invitations to a dinner party. Children make invitations and set a table for a Thanksgiving dinner party.

Sensory Area

- Fill the sensory table with one of the following foods: oatmeal, beans, split peas, cornmeal, or popcorn. Then hide various items inside, such as small foods, small pumpkins, or small Indian corn. Children use utensils (forks, spoons) and cups and saucers to dig out, search for, and bury the food.

Science Area

- Classroom Pumpkin Patch: Gather together several orange pumpkins in a variety of sizes and, if possible, some unusual pumpkins too (for instance, white or striped). Have a large scale available to weigh the pumpkins and paper and pencils for recording the weights. Children guess which pumpkin will weigh the most. Chart the results.
Discuss the differences in the pumpkins. Ask questions such as: Do all these pumpkins have the same number of lines? What's inside the pumpkins? Make comparisons by cutting open a carving pumpkin, a pie pumpkin, and an ornamental gourd shaped like a pumpkin.

- Glue two lines of popcorn kernels to strips of poster board. Make sure each line has the same number of kernels, but spread one line out longer than the other. Ask the children to look at each line and guess which line has more kernels. The children count the kernels to get their answers. Provide pencils and paper for recording results.

Art Area

- Set out orange, yellow, red, and brown paints at the art easel.

- Color dried pumpkin seeds with mixtures made from food coloring or liquid watercolors (1 tsp. vinegar, 1 c. water, several drops color) and set the colored seeds out for gluing onto paper. Let the children know that the seeds are for art only, not for eating (nevertheless, paint should be nontoxic).

- Provide glue, papers shaped like cake layers, and materials for decorating the cakes: sequins, glitter, buttons, cotton balls, colored paper clips, cupcake sprinkles, and so on. Stack the layers to create a ten-layer cake as mentioned in the book.

- Potato Heads: Set out large baking potatoes, face materials (buttons, yarn, ribbons, sequins, paint, feathers, fabric scraps), glue, and toothpicks. Children use the materials to make faces on the potatoes. The toothpicks can be used to carefully anchor buttons or sequins. Children take home their potato friends for Thanksgiving centerpieces.

Book Area

- *Alligator Arrived with Apples: A Potluck Alphabet Feast* by Crescent Dragonwagon, illustrated by Jose Aruego and Ariane Dewey

- *Feast for Ten* by Cathryn Falwell

- *Grateful: A Song of Giving Thanks* by John Bucchino, illustrated by Anna-Liisa Hakkarainen

- *It's Thanksgiving* by Jack Prelutsky, illustrated by Marilyn Hafner

- *The Night Before Thanksgiving* by Natasha Wing, illustrated by Tammie Lyon

- *Pumpkin Pumpkin* by Jeanne Titherington

- *Too Many Pumpkins* by Linda White, illustrated by Megan Lloyd

- *'Twas the Night Before Thanksgiving* by Dav Pilkey

- Other books related to feasting and family traditions

Bulletin Board

- Send home several paper feathers with each child. They can decorate these with their families however they want and then bring them back to school. Children help attach their feathers to one large class turkey body. Then display the beautiful bird on the bulletin board. Attach a heading that reads *Teamwork Turkey*.

- Cover the board with the school Pumpkin Patch (see Week 1, Activity 5).

Week 1

Focus of the Week: Thanksgiving food and turkeys

Songs, Poems, and Fingerplays

Listen and Add To Game
With everyone sitting in a large circle, begin by chanting, "I know a preschooler who swallowed a (name a food) <u>cookie</u>." The next child recites the same line and adds another food, for example, " . . . an apple and a cookie." Continue around the circle for as long as possible.

Turkey Dance
Play the music to the "Chicken Dance" song and teach the children how to do the motions: First open and close hands (like beaks), then flap, then wiggle, then clap. At the chorus, each child locks elbows with a classmate and spins one way, then changes elbows and spins the other way.

Reading the Story

Introduce the book by discussing the title, author, and dedication. Discuss the book's cover and ask the children to guess what the book will be about.

Read or sing the story every day and, as the children become familiar with it, gradually add in any of the following activities:

- Give the children felt or laminated paper cutouts of each of the food items from the story to hold up as they are mentioned during the story reading.

- On the floor, place a large paper cutout of an old lady dressed like the old lady in the book. The children can then place the food cutouts (see previous activity) in the old lady's tummy.

- At the end of the story, blow up a balloon and hold it closed without tying it. Draw a picture of an old lady on it. On the count of 3, let the balloon go and watch it fly around the room.

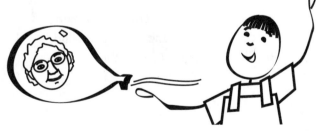

Group Activities

I. Thanksgiving Pie

Target Areas: cognition, fine motor

What you need:

- Paper bowls (1 per child + several extra)
- Orange construction paper (1 piece per child)
- Orange tissue paper
- Spray bottle with cinnamon-scented water (boil cinnamon sticks in water for 5 minutes and let the mixture sit overnight for scented water)
- Pumpkin pie spice or cloves, nutmeg, allspice, and cinnamon
- Sharp pencil or pen
- Glue

What you do:

1. The children fill their bowls with pieces of torn orange tissue paper.
2. Spray the tissue paper with the cinnamon-scented water and, while the paper is wet, sprinkle on the pumpkin pie spice.
3. Using an empty paper bowl turned upside down, each child traces a circle onto a piece of orange construction paper and then cuts it out. This circle will be the top crust of their pie.
4. Poke 5–6 holes in the center of each child's orange circle, using the pen or pencil.
5. Glue the circles to the tops of the paper bowls.
6. Children shake their paper pumpkin pies to smell the fragrant aromas!

2. Thankful Turkeys

Target Areas: communication, fine motor, social

What you need:

- Turkey body shapes cut out of brown construction paper (1 per child)
- Feathers of different colors made out of paper (about 13 per child)
- Plastic baggies (1 per child)

What you do:

1. Ask the children to think of things that they are thankful for in their lives. Give an example: "I am thankful for having a great dog."
2. When the children have thought of a couple of things they are thankful for, they write one thing on each feather (or the teacher can do the writing).
3. They glue their written-on feathers on their turkeys.
4. When the child takes the turkey home, also send a baggie with 10 more feathers in it and a note to the family. It could say something like this:
   I am thankful for these things on my turkey. Next year, let's get this turkey out and glue on some more feathers. I am sure that I will have more things to be thankful for next year, and the year after that, and the year after that.

(Signed by the child) _____

3. Colors of the Season

Target Areas: cognition, communication, fine motor

What you need:

- Red or pink, yellow, and blue gelatin, each color mixed separately and set
- Clear plastic baggies (1–2 per child)
- Spoons

What you do:

1. Each child chooses two different colors of gelatin to scoop into one baggie.
2. Ask the children to predict what color they will have after they've mixed the two colors.
3. Children squeeze the gelatin until it makes a new color.

4. Feathered Friends

Target Areas: communication, fine motor, social

What you need:

- Wooden ice cream spoons (1 per child)
- Small brown paper circles (1 per child)
- Feathers cut out of different colored construction paper
- Paper scraps in yellow and red
- Pipe cleaners
- Wiggly eyes
- Glue
- Clear tape

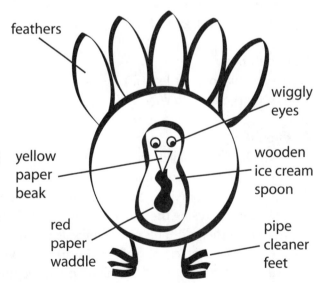

feathers

wiggly eyes

yellow paper beak

wooden ice cream spoon

red paper waddle

pipe cleaner feet

What you do:

1. Children glue the wooden ice cream spoon to the middle of the brown circle to serve as the turkey's head and neck.
2. Glue the colorful feathers around the edge of the back of the brown circle.
3. Add wiggly eyes and cut a beak and waddle from the paper scraps and attach them to the spoon with glue.
4. Finish the turkeys by cutting the pipe cleaners, bending them into the shapes of turkey feet, and attaching them to the back of the circle with clear tape.

5. Pumpkin Patch

Target Areas: cognition, fine motor

What you need:

- Large sheet of yellow or white butcher paper
- Orange and green paint
- Paintbrushes
- Cotton swabs

What you do:

1. On the top or in the middle of the butcher paper, write the name of your school and the words *Pumpkin Patch* (for example, *Rainbow Preschool's Pumpkin Patch*).
2. Each child makes a fist and paints the top (the four finger knuckles and fingers out to the first joints) with orange paint.
3. Press their fists onto the paper to make "pumpkin" prints. Make as many as possible over the large sheet of paper.
4. After they've washed off the orange paint, dip the children's fingertips into the green paint and make green "stems" with their fingertips on the tops of their pumpkin prints.
5. Use cotton swabs dipped in green paint to draw green vines.

6. Corn on the Run

Target Areas: gross motor, social

What you need:

- Corncobs (at least 2)
- Large area to run in

What you do:

1. Divide the children into two teams. Designate the playing field, making sure to explain the boundaries.
2. One member of each team runs from one end of the field to the other end and back carrying the corncob. The runners hand the cobs to the next players in line, who then do the same. (*Optional:* Children could crawl, skip, gallop, pretend skate, tiptoe, bear crawl, walk backwards, or walk sideways.)
3. The first team to have all its players complete the relay wins.

Week 2

Focus of the Week: Harvest and fall season

 Circle Time

Songs, Poems, and Fingerplays

<u>*Oats, Peas, Beans, and Barley Grow*</u> (traditional)

Chorus:
Oats, peas, beans, and barley grow,
Oats, peas, beans, and barley grown,
Can you or I or anyone know
How oats, peas, beans, and barley grow?

Verse 1:
First the farmer sows his seed, (plant seeds)
Stands erect and takes his ease, (stand
straight)
He stamps his foot and claps his hands, (stamp, clap)
And turns around to view his lands. (turn and shade eyes)

Repeat Chorus

Verse 2:
Next the farmer waters the seed, (water seeds)
Stands erect and takes his ease, (stand straight)
He stamps his foot and claps his hands, (stamp, clap)
And turns around to view his lands. (turn and shade eyes)

Repeat Chorus

Continue with two more verses, changing only the first lines as follows.

Verse 3: *Next the farmer hoes the weeds* (hoe weeds)
Verse 4: *Last the farmer harvests his seed* (collects food)

Read and learn together the leaf poem from Week 2, Activity 3.

Reading the Story

Read the story every day and gradually add in any of the following activities:

- Each child chooses an item from the story to represent. Children then wear something to indicate what they are pretending to be (beak for turkey, cooking pot on head, and so forth). Select one child to be the Old Lady. The Old Lady pretends to eat the children as the items they represent appear in the story.

- Write the words *I know an old lady who swallowed a* _____ on a long piece of paper. Write on separate index cards the names of the items the Old Lady comes across in the story. Hand the cards out to the children. As each page is turned, point out the word(s) on the page that match an index card. Ask the children, "Who has this item on a card?" The child with the right card brings it to the sentence strip and holds it over the blank line until that page has been read.

- Substitute foods and other items related to different holidays ("I know an old lady who swallowed some firecrackers," "I know an old lady who swallowed a jack-o-lantern") to see if the children notice the errors and can identify the holiday referred to.

Group Activities

1. Veggie Head Fred
   Target Areas: communication, fine motor, social

What you need:
- 1 large pumpkin
- Variety of vegetables (the more exotic, the better): green onions, bean sprouts, radishes, mushrooms, peppers, turnips (great noses), green beans, lettuce
- Toothpicks
- Heavy gloves for pushing toothpicks into pumpkin (rubber-tipped garden gloves work well)

What you do:
1. Gather the children around the large pumpkin and explain that they are going to make a face using some or all of the vegetables displayed on the table.
2. Tell the children the names of all the vegetables.
3. The children choose which vegetables will be used for the eyes, ears, nose, mouth, hair, mustache, beard, and eyebrows.
4. Carefully secure the chosen vegetable in place, using the toothpicks. Toothpicks may need to be broken in half to hide them better.
5. When all the parts have been secured, have the children decide on an appropriate name for their pumpkin head.

2. Maple Leaf Turkeys

Target Areas: cognition, fine motor

What you need:

- Large leaves (maple leaves work well) in a variety of fall colors
- Paper plates (1 per child)
- Brown paint or markers
- Orange, red, and yellow construction paper
- Glue
- Wiggly eyes (1 pair per child)

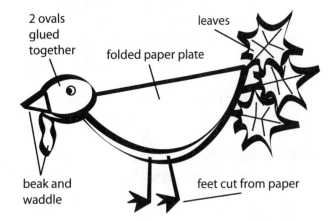

2 ovals glued together

leaves

folded paper plate

beak and waddle

feet cut from paper

What you do:

1. Children paint or color their paper plate brown and fold it in half when dry, painted side out.
2. Holding the plate with the fold on top, the children attach 3 to 4 leaves to one end with glue.
3. On the other end, glue 2 ovals cut from orange paper, lined up with each other, one on each side of the plate fold. Together these ovals make the head.
4. Cut a triangle out of orange paper and attach it for a beak.
5. Add the wiggly eyes and a waddle cut from red paper.
6. Make the turkey's feet by cutting them out of the yellow construction paper. Glue them onto the plate.

3. Leaf Rubbing Book

Target Areas: cognition, communication, fine motor

What you need:

- 2 or 3 leaves of each of 4 different types of leaves (8–12 leaves total) collected as a group on a nature walk
- White copier paper (5 pieces per child)
- Copies of the following poem on the same size of white paper (1 per child)
- Red, yellow, green, and brown crayons
- Stapler
- Transparent tape

What you do:

1. Tape the edges of the leaves onto a table in a couple of different spots, making sure to separate the leaves into 4 sections by type (should have 4 areas with 2-3 leaves each).
2. Designate each area with a color and set out the appropriate crayons.

3. Give each child a piece of paper to place over a leaf and begin rubbing with the side of a crayon.

4. When finished, give each child another paper to do a different leaf with a different color. In the end, each child should have 4 different leaf rubbings, one of each different type of leaf, each in a different color.

5. Give each child another blank paper. They copy the words *My Leaf Book* on it.

6. Give each child a poem page and read the poem aloud.

> *The leaves are falling down,*
> *The leaves are falling down,*
> *Red, yellow, green, and brown,*
> *The leaves are falling down.*

7. For each child, staple together the title page, the 4 leaf-rubbing pages, and the poem page to make a book.

4. Cranberry-Red Napkins

Target Areas: cognition, communication, fine motor

What you need:

- Fresh or frozen cranberries
- 4 squares of 12" x 12" white muslin fabric per child (cut squares with pinking shears to reduce fraying)
- Rubber bands or string

What you do:

1. Boil cranberries in water and set aside to cool.
2. Tie the fabric squares into knots or use rubber bands or strings to tie them.
3. Dip the fabric squares into the cranberries and water for a few minutes and then set them aside to dry.
4. When dry, untie the knots or ties. Iron the tie-dyed napkins.
5. Use the napkins at snack time, or wrap and send them home for Thanksgiving gifts. Be sure to include directions so that families can make some at home, too. (The dye should be permanent after being ironed, but families are also welcome to heat-set the napkins' dye in a clothes dryer prior to use.)

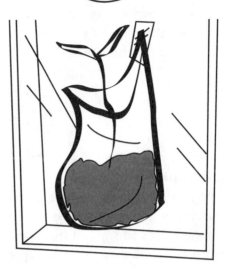

5. Growing Popcorn

Target Areas: cognition, communication, fine motor

What you need:
- Clear baggies
- Potting soil
- Popcorn kernels
- Water
- Transparent tape
- Marker for writing on baggies
- Graph paper and marker

What you do:
1. The children put dirt into a baggie, then add a small amount of water and a few popcorn kernels.
2. Write their names on the baggies and use the tape to hang the baggies in a window that gets a good amount of sun.
3. Ask children to guess what they think will happen to their popcorn kernels. Write their responses on graph paper and check back throughout the growing process.
4. In a few days, the kernels will begin to sprout. Discuss how the children's predictions compare with the results.
5. Talk with the children about how corn is harvested. Perhaps there is a cornfield nearby that the class could visit.

6. Handy Turkey

Target Areas: communication, fine motor

What you need:
- Clear plastic gloves (1 glove per child)
- Tissue paper pieces in brown, red, yellow, purple, and orange
- Popped popcorn
- Twist ties
- Wiggly eyes (1 pair per child)
- Small triangles cut out of red construction paper (1 per child)

What you do:
1. Each child fills each finger of a glove with a different color of crumpled tissue paper, using the brown tissue paper for the thumb.
2. Fill the rest (palm) of the glove with either brown tissue paper or popcorn and tie the bottom with a twist tie.

3. Glue eyes to the thumb and tape a red triangle (beak) under the eyes.
4. Use the turkeys as a centerpiece at snack time, and then children take them home for their families.

Additional Activity

Magic Pumpkin Seeds

Put some pumpkin seeds in a special bag and show them to the children. Tell them the seeds are magic and lead them out to the playground. Encourage the children to think of some magic words to say and then have them throw the seeds onto the ground. The next day, before the children arrive, pick up the seeds and replace them with mini-pumpkins. Show the children the "magic" pumpkins and let each of them choose one to take home.

Snacks

1. Apple Tart Pies

What you need:
- Refrigerator biscuits (1 biscuit per child)
- Chunky Applesauce
- Powdered Cinnamon
- Muffin or cupcake liners
- Muffin pan

What you do:
1. Each child puts one biscuit into a liner, pushing down and out to line the bottom and sides.
2. Then add a spoonful of applesauce and sprinkle with cinnamon. Bake at 350° for 12–15 minutes.

2. Turkey Roll-ups

What you need:
- Small flour tortillas
- Sliced deli turkey
- Cream cheese
- Wooden craft sticks or plastic knives

What you do:

> Spread the cream cheese on the tortilla using a craft stick. Put a slice of turkey on top of the cheese. Roll the tortilla and eat!

3. Decorated Mini-Muffins
Note: Be sure no children are allergic to peanuts before using peanut butter in this snack. As appropriate, use a different topping.

What you need:

- Healthy muffin mix and required ingredients
- Mini-muffin pan
- Cream cheese, peanut butter or other nut spread, or sugarless jam or jelly (for topping)
- Decorative edible sprinkles
- Wooden craft sticks

What you do:

> Mix the muffins according to the directions on the box and pour into the mini-muffin pan. Bake as directed on the box. When the muffins have cooked and cooled, divide them evenly among the children. Children decorate the muffins using the craft sticks, topping, and sprinkles. Encourage them to stack them to make a layered cake like in the book. Eat and enjoy!

> *Note:* It's a good idea to have a batch of the mini-muffins already made before class.

4. No-Bake Pumpkin Pie

What you need:

- Large can of pumpkin fruit
- Large container of prepared whipped topping
- Graham cracker pie shell (cooked as directed)

What you do:

> Mix the pumpkin with the whipped topping and put into the pie shell. Refrigerate until ready to eat, then enjoy.

5. 2x2 Drop Biscuits ("She swallowed it whole, the entire roll!")

What you need:

- 2 c. flour
- 2 tbsp. baking powder
- 1 tsp. salt
- 2 tbsp. granulated sugar
- 2 tbsp. grated cheese (optional)
- 2 c. milk

What you do:

Preheat oven to 400°. Mix all dry ingredients together in a bowl. Stir in milk until just blended. Using a small scoop, drop dough onto a baking sheet and bake for 12-15 minutes.

6. Warm Apple Cider

What you need:

- 1/2 gallon apple juice
- 4 tbsp. of orange juice concentrate
- 5 cinnamon sticks
- Large pot or crock pot

What you do:

Put all ingredients into the pot and bring to a boil. Reduce heat and simmer for 5 minutes. Let cool, pour into cups, and enjoy.

7. Fresh Salad

What you need:

- Lettuce and fresh vegetables
- Cutting boards
- Butter knives or plastic knives for chopping
- Dressings
- Large salad bowl and salad utensils
- Small salad bowls (1 per child)

What you do:

Children help wash the vegetables. Carefully, and with ample supervision, children help cut the vegetables and place them in the salad bowl. Talk about how to be safe when using knives. Use the salad utensils to mix the salad, and then serve.

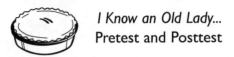

Pretest and Posttest

I Know an Old Lady Who Swallowed a Pie

Concepts	Pretest	Posttest
Concept of *Thanksgiving*		
Thanksgiving foods		
Turkeys		
The fall season		
Leaves		
Corn		
Pumpkins		

Notes

Gingerbread Baby

By Jan Brett

In this adorable adaptation of the classic tale, a little boy opens the oven too soon and out jumps the Gingerbread Baby! A great chase follows with everyone but the little boy trying to get the Gingerbread Baby. In the delightful border illustrations, we see the little boy carefully creating a gingerbread house for the Gingerbread Baby to hide in. In the end, the pursuers are left empty-handed and the Gingerbread Baby finds a safe, warm place to live.

Dear Families,

The smell of gingerbread cookies baking in the oven is hard to beat. Your child will certainly become familiar with this smell as we read our next story, *Gingerbread Baby* by Jan Brett. It's the popular tale you know, complete with a cookie that escapes and people who chase it, but the ending is sure to surprise you. Jan Brett provides beautiful illustrations with pictorial previews of upcoming story events in the borders of each page—a wonderful way to encourage predicting skills.

You will want to check out some of Jan Brett's other great stories when you head out to find *Gingerbread Baby*. It would also be fun to find versions of the traditional tale to compare and contrast with this new spin on the story. As you read through the traditional versions, ask your child how these stories are the same or different from the one we are reading at school. We also recommend *The Cajun Gingerbread Boy* by Berthe Amoss, *The Gingerbread Boy* by Paul Galdone, and *The Gingerbread Man* by Eric A. Kimmel.

Here's a good gingerbread cookie recipe to try at home:

Gingerbread Cookies

Ingredients

2 1/4 c. all-purpose flour	3/4 c. margarine, softened
2 tsp. ground ginger	1 c. white sugar
1 tsp. baking soda	1 egg
3/4 tsp. ground cinnamon	1 tbsp. water
1/2 tsp. ground cloves	1/4 c. molasses
1/4 tsp. salt	2 tbsp. white sugar

Directions

1. Preheat oven to 350°. Sift together the flour, ginger, baking soda, cinnamon, cloves, and salt. Set aside.
2. In a large bowl, cream together the margarine and 1 c. sugar until light and fluffy. Beat in the egg, then stir in the water and molasses. Gradually stir the sifted ingredients into the molasses mixture. Shape dough into walnut-sized balls and roll them in the remaining 2 tbsp. sugar. Place the cookies 2" apart on an ungreased cookie sheet and flatten slightly.
3. Bake for 8 to 10 minutes. Allow cookies to cool on baking sheet for 5 minutes before removing to a wire rack to cool completely. Store in an airtight container.

Gotta run!

$$\mathscr{Room\ Setup}$$

Dramatic Play Area

- Cut a large appliance box to look like a house (doors, windows, and roof). Cut 6"-wide strips of brown butcher paper the lengths of the walls of the house. Children decorate these strips using a variety of candy-shaped construction paper cutouts: First they place candy cutouts in a pattern (mint-gumdrop-mint-gumdrop- . . .). When the children have a pattern they like, they glue the cutouts to the brown strips. Then they attach the strips to the house.

- Set up a kitchen with cookie trays, oven mitts, cookie cutters, spice jars, aprons, and spatulas.

Sensory Area

- Fill the sensory table with flour (a large bag's worth) and gingerbread spices (cinnamon, cloves, allspice, and nutmeg). If you wish, add some salt for texture. Add measuring cups, sifters, funnels, and spoons. Enjoy the sweet smell of gingerbread throughout the classroom.

Science Area

- Copy color photographs from books or the Internet or draw pictures of the characters in the story and glue them on one 8 1/2" x 11" piece of paper. Cut a 2" square out of a piece of construction paper (anywhere on the paper) but leave one of the four sides of the square uncut to make an opening like a little door. Place the construction paper over the pictures. Children look through the "door" and guess what character they are looking at. Make several different pieces of construction paper with various sizes of doors in different locations on the papers so children can see different aspects of the same pictures or photographs.

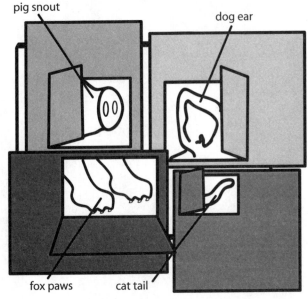

pig snout

dog ear

fox paws   cat tail

Art Area

- Set out a variety of collage materials including various cutouts of gingerbread friends.

- Provide brown construction paper houses along with puffy paints and sequins, both in a variety of colors. The children decorate the papers to resemble gingerbread houses.

Book Area

- *The Cajun Gingerbread Boy* by Berthe Amoss
- *Cookie Count: A Tasty Pop-Up* by Robert Sabuda
- *The Gingerbread Boy* by Paul Galdone
- *The Gingerbread Man* by Eric A. Kimmel, illustrated by Megan Lloyd
- *The Musubi Man: Hawaii's Gingerbread Man* by Sandi Takayama, illustrated by Pat Hall
- Cookie cookbooks with color pictures and other books related to baking, cookies, and winter

Bulletin Board

- Cover the bulletin board with blue paper and white snowflakes. Use artwork from Activities 1 and 3 in Week 1 (Gingerbread Baby Snow Globes and Class of Gingerbread Babies) and from other activities to decorate the board throughout the unit.

Week I

Focus of the Week: Gingerbread

Songs, Poems, and Fingerplays

Gingerbread Man
(to the tune of "Do You Know the Muffin Man?")

Do you know the Gingerbread Man?
The Gingerbread Man? The Gingerbread Man?
Do you know the Gingerbread Man?
Who ran and ran and ran.

Other verses:
Yes, I know . . . ; Can you catch . . . ; I ate up . . . yum yum yum!

Eat Your Gingerbread
(to the tune of "Row, Row, Row Your Boat")

Eat, eat your Gingerbread Baby
Before (he/she) runs away,
Faster, faster, faster, please,
Catch up with (him/her) today!

Reading the Story

Introduce the book by discussing the title, author, and dedication. Discuss the book's cover and ask the children to guess what the book will be about.

Read the story every day and, as the children become familiar with it, gradually add in any of the following activities:

• Use mask patterns from Jan Brett's Web site (www.janbrett.com) to act out the story as it is read.

• Gingerbread Match: Make a set of cards with pictures of the Gingerbread Baby doing the actions in the book. Each card should have a different picture on it. Pass them out to the children. As each page is read, see who has the matching Gingerbread Baby. Children can stand up and act out whatever action the Gingerbread Baby is doing.

111

- Wear oven mitts while telling the story. Of course, the children will have to help turn the pages! Give the children an oven-mitt high five to indicate when it is their turn to flip a page.

1. Applesauce Ornaments

Target Areas: cognition, fine motor

What you need:

- Applesauce
- Cinnamon
- Drinking straw
- Ribbon
- Small bowls (1 per child)
- Cookie cutters in gingerbread people shapes

What you do:

1. Spoon about 1/2 cup of applesauce into each child's bowl. Add enough cinnamon to make it pasty.
2. Spread out the paste and cut out the gingerbread people using the cookie cutters.
3. Use the straw to make a hole at the top of each gingerbread person.
4. Allow to air dry about 2 days.
5. Hang with the ribbon.

2. Life-Size Gingerbread Friends

Target Areas: fine motor, social

What you need:

- Large sheets of brown butcher paper
- Pencils
- Fabric scraps, pom-poms, rickrack, ribbons, buttons
- Glue
- Scissors and stapler

What you do:

1. Lay each child down on a sheet of paper and trace his or her whole body.
2. Cut out each child's shape.
3. Using the collage materials, children decorate their gingerbread friends.
4. Staple the gingerbread friends flat on the ceiling or have them hang down from the ceiling into the classroom.

3. Class of Gingerbread Babies
Target Areas: fine motor, social

What you need:
- Gingerbread Babies cut out of brown construction paper
- Picture of each child in class (head shots cut to fit the Gingerbread Babies)
- Glue
- Collage materials for decorating the Gingerbread Babies

What you do:
1. Each child finds his or her picture and glues it to a Gingerbread Baby.
2. Decorate the Gingerbread Baby with the collage materials.
3. Display the class of Gingerbread Babies on the bulletin board.

4. Gingerbread Lace-Up
Target Area: fine motor

What you need:
- Gingerbread people cut out of 8 1/2" x 11" brown construction paper (2 per child)
- Markers or crayons
- Yarn
- Hole punch
- White hole-reinforcement stickers
- Newspaper strips

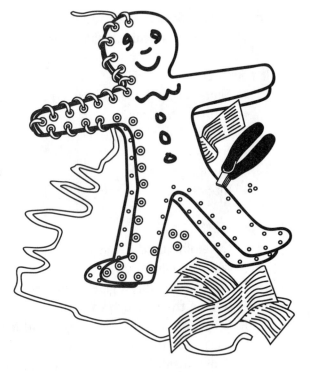

What you do:
1. Children use the markers or crayons to decorate their pairs of gingerbread people (one for a front and one for a back).
2. Hold the decorated pairs of gingerbread people together and punch holes around the edges.
3. Cover each hole on the front gingerbread person with the hole-reinforcement stickers.
4. Lace the yarn through both sets of holes, leaving a small opening.
5. Stuff some crumpled strips of newspaper in through the opening.
6. Finish lacing and secure the ends of the yarn.

5. Gingerbread Play Dough

Target Areas: cognition, fine motor

What you need:

- 2 c. flour (more as needed)
- 2 c. boiling water
- 1 c. salt
- 4 tsp. cream of tartar
- 2 tsp. oil
- 1 tbsp. any or all gingerbread spices: allspice, cinnamon, ginger
- Play dough toys

What you do:

1. Combine all ingredients but the last in a large bowl and mix thoroughly.
2. Use the toys to manipulate this wonderfully scented play dough.

6. Gingerbread Sandpaper Ornaments

Target Areas: cognition, fine motor

What you need:

- Gingerbread Babies cut from sandpaper
- Cinnamon sticks
- Colored glue
- Felt scraps
- Small buttons
- Ribbon

What you do:

1. Carefully rub the Gingerbread Babies with the cinnamon sticks.
2. Using the colored glue as the frosting, outline the Gingerbread Baby.
3. Glue on the buttons for eyes and felt scraps for the nose and mouth.
4. Punch a small hole in the top and thread a piece of ribbon through to hang.

Focus of the Week: Cold weather

Circle Time

Songs, Poems, and Fingerplays

<u>*Gingerbread Is Yummy!*</u>
(to the tune of "Jingle Bells")
Children sing the song and perform the pretend actions.

Gingerbread, gingerbread
It is so yummy, (rub tummy)
Mix it (stir), *bake it* (put in oven), *decorate* (decorate),
Then put it in your tummy! (eat it)

<u>*I Say "Brrrrrr"*</u>

I say "Brrrrrr"
It's cold out here.
There must be some clouds in the atmosphere.

I say "Brrrrrr"
It's cold out here.
There must be some water in the atmosphere.

I say "Brrrrrr"
It's cold out here.
There must be some SNOW in the atmosphere!

This chant is best performed outside. With each verse, children speak
louder and shiver harder.

Reading the Story

Read the story every day and gradually add in any of the following activities:

- Children sit in a circle with the teacher in the center reading the story. One child is
  the Gingerbread Baby. While reading the story, the teacher moves around in a circle.

The child the teacher's toes point to when the teacher stops moving becomes the character from the page of the story just read. Both that character and the Gingerbread Baby stand up and run around the circle once. The Gingerbread Baby tries to sit in the character's spot before being touched by the character. While running around the circle, the Gingerbread Baby calls out, "I'm the Gingerbread Baby. Catch me if you can!"

- Attach a photocopy of each character, including the Gingerbread Baby, to a Popsicle stick. Pass these stick puppets out to the children. With each page, children predict which character will be on the next page. When the character is revealed, the child with that puppet uses the puppet to chase the Gingerbread Baby puppet around.

- Everyone gets all bundled up and, if possible, goes outside for the story reading one day. If it's too cold to go outside, everyone pretends to be cold and shivers through the story reading. To warm up cold hands and toes, children get up and run in place along with the Gingerbread Baby (either a puppet or a designated child).

Group Activities

1. Indoor Ice Skating
Target Areas: cognition, gross motor, social

What you need:
- Waxed paper squares or plastic bags large enough to cover each child's feet and ankles
- Large rubber bands
- Music
- Large area to move around in

What you do:
1. Cover each child's feet with waxed paper or plastic bags, making sure to cover the shoes and up to the ankles. Secure the waxed paper or plastic bags with rubber bands around the ankles.
2. Turn on the music and invite the children to skate around the room.

2. Ice Cube Relay

Target Areas: cognition, fine motor, gross motor

What you need:
- Ice cubes
- Spoons
- Large area to move around in

What you do:
1. Divide the children into two teams and give each child a spoon.
2. The children race from one spot to another carrying an ice cube on the spoon.
3. When they get back to the line, they pass the ice cube to the next child in line.
4. The team that finishes first wins.

3. Gingerbread Baby Snow Globe

Target Areas: cognition, fine motor

What you need:
- Circle (the size of a CD) cut out of blue construction paper (1 per child)
- Gingerbread Baby cut out of brown construction paper, small enough to fit in the circle (1 per child)
- Triangle cut out of black construction paper (all points should fit just inside the circle) (1 per child)
- Markers
- Hole punches and white paper scraps
- Iridescent glitter
- Clear contact paper
- Glue

What you do:
1. Give each child a blue circle, a Gingerbread Baby cutout, and a black triangle.
2. Use the markers to decorate the Gingerbread Baby. Then glue the Gingerbread Baby to the blue circle.
3. Use the hole punch to make small white circles from the white paper scraps (for snow) and sprinkle them all over the blue circle. Add some glitter, and then carefully cover the circle with clear contact paper and press it down. Trim the contact paper around the circle.

4. Glue the triangle onto the back of the circle so that two points of the triangle show at the bottom. The triangle is now the base of the snow globe.
5. Display on the bulletin board or in the window.

4. Freeze Tag

Target Areas: gross motor, social

What you need:
- 1 set of mittens
- Large area to move around in

What you do:
1. Ask the children, "What can you do to warm up when you're feeling cold?" If necessary, prompt for someone to suggest running around.
2. Give the set of mittens to one child. This child is "it." The other children run around to try to get away from "it." When "it" touches another child, that child "freezes" right in place.
3. The only way children can melt and run around again is if a classmate touches them; then they "melt." (Show how to melt before taking off running again.) The child who is "it" tries to freeze the whole class.

Optional: This can be played with two children wearing mittens and being "it."

5. Ice Sculptures

Target Areas: cognition, communication, social

What you need:
- Sandcastle molds or large plastic cups filled with water and then frozen
- 3 small containers of saltwater
- Red, yellow, and blue food coloring
- 3 eyedroppers
- Large plastic container (such as a sweater storage box)

What you do:
1. Add one color of food coloring to each of the containers of saltwater.
2. Place the frozen molds or cups in the large container. Children use the droppers to drop the colored saltwater onto the ice castles.
3. Discuss the effects the saltwater has on the ice.

6. Winter Trees

Target Areas: cognition, fine motor

What you need:
- Dark blue paper (1 sheet per child)
- Green construction paper triangles for treetops (2–3 per child)
- Brown construction paper rectangles for tree trunks (2–3 per child)

- Variety of empty thread spools
- White tempera paint

What you do:
  1. Children glue brown trunks onto the blue paper and add the green triangles to create trees.
  2. Dip one end of a spool into the white paint and press it onto the paper to create snowflakes.

It's Showtime!

Act out the story using character masks attached to Popsicle sticks (see Week 1, Reading the Story section, for a source for mask patterns). Practice each day and then put on a play for families. Make sure to serve gingerbread cookies!

A Classroom Gingerbread Tree

Set up a real or artificial tree in the room. Decorate it with the Applesauce Ornaments (Week 1, Activity 1), the Gingerbread Lace-ups (Week 1, Activity 4), and the Gingerbread Sandpaper Ornaments (Week 1, Activity 6).

1. **Decorate Gingerbread Cookies:** Children use sprinkles, icing in tubes, and small candies to decorate either homemade (see our recommended recipe in the letter to families at the beginning of this unit) or store-bought gingerbread cookies in gingerbread people shapes.

2. **Gingerbread Toast**

What you need:
  - Bread
  - House-shaped cookie cutter (optional)
  - Toaster
  - Butter
  - Teddy-bear shaped mini-cookies or miniature gingerbread man cookies
  - Cinnamon-sugar mixture
  - Butter knife

What you do:

> Toast the bread and cut it into the shape of a house. Children decorate the toast with butter and then with the cinnamon-sugar mixture. Add the small teddy bear or gingerbread man cookie as the house's inhabitant.

3. Gingerbread Graham Crackers

Note: Be sure that no children are allergic to peanuts before making this snack. As appropriate, substitute almond butter, cream cheese, or another sandwich spread for the peanut butter.

What you need:

- Graham cracker squares
- Peanut butter
- Yogurt-covered raisins
- Granola
- Popcorn
- Small pieces of dried fruits and nuts

What you do:

> Spread peanut butter on one graham cracker square (as the house). Break another square in half and use the two pieces to make a roof. Attach the roof to the house with peanut butter. Decorate using the other foods.

4. Warm and Fuzzy Milk

What you need:

- Milk
- Vanilla flavoring
- Cinnamon
- Nutmeg
- Honey
- Microwave
- Cups (1 per child)
- Spoons (1 per child)

What you do:

> Warm up the milk in the microwave. Add spices and honey to the milk, and stir. Children sit around and drink their hot drinks, pretending to be warming up in front of a fire after running in the snow.

> *Optional:* Use the frothing mechanism on an espresso maker to make the milk fluffy!

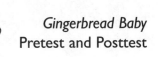

Pretest and Posttest

Gingerbread Baby

Concepts	Pretest	Posttest
How to make cookies		
Gingerbread		
Concept of *real* vs. *pretend*		
How does ice melt?		
Ways to get warm		
Concept of *next*		

Notes

Geraldine's Big Snow

By Holly Keller

In this sweet story, a little pig, Geraldine, waits patiently for a predicted snowstorm. As she walks outside, wishing for the flakes to start falling, she encounters several animal friends preparing for the snow in different ways. Later, as a still hopeful Geraldine sleeps, softly and quietly the snowflakes gather on houses and trees. Geraldine awakens with glee, excited to finally put on her snow boots and take her sled to the top of the hill.

Dear Families,

Ahhhh! White, fluffy, beautiful snow! It's many children's winter dream and what they wait for all season long. Geraldine, the main character in our next storybook unit, is no exception. *Geraldine's Big Snow*, by Holly Keller, tells the story of an anxious little pig who simply cannot wait for the flakes to start falling so she can go sledding. We learn about patience, winter weather, and how different friends prepare for the impending snowstorm. Happily for Geraldine, the snow finally comes and she is able to put her sled to use. Will we be so lucky? Let's hope so!

For the next two weeks we'll be waiting right alongside Geraldine and getting ready for the big snow. We'll be watching weather reports, getting our winter clothes ready, making trips to the library for plenty of reading material, making sure the birds have enough to eat, and baking apple pies to share with friends. It would be wonderful if your home activities could coincide with what is happening at school. Call your child's attention to the winter weather. Pack away summer and spring clothes and, if you have them, bring out boots, mittens, hats, and coats. Watch the newspaper and magazines for pictures of snowy places to use in making a collage. If possible, take a trip to the snow to go sledding!

Look in the library for *Geraldine's Big Snow,* as well as for other children's books related to snow. Some of our favorites are *The Snowy Day* by Ezra Jack Keats, *The Snowman* by Raymond Briggs, *Froggy Gets Dressed* by Jonathan London, *The Mitten* by Jan Brett, and *Here Comes Winter* by Janet Craig.

Let it snow!

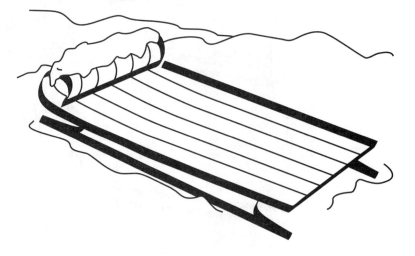

Special Note: This unit may require a little extra creativity for classrooms in areas where it does not snow. Consider looking for snowy pictures in magazines or showing the class a quick video containing snow scenes before reading the story. Talk about how winter in snowy areas differs from winter in your area. Use it as an opportunity to learn about different places. Note that the families' letter may need a bit of adjusting to better suit your location.

Room Setup

Dramatic Play Area

- Fill the area with winter clothes (hats, mittens, coats, and scarves). Point out that there are no boots available yet; the children will have to be patient and wait. Later, add boots to the area, explaining to the children that they can pretend it has finally snowed and they need their warm boots.

- Using a crate and soft pad, create a place for the children to pretend to climb up the hill (step onto the crate) and slide down (jump onto the soft pad).

- Set up a pond for ice fishing: Bring in a small plastic wading pool and cover it with white butcher paper or an old white sheet. Cut a hole in the center and place a large bucket under it. Fill the bucket with magnetic fish. Children use magnetic fishing rods to catch the fish.

Sensory Area

- Fill the sensory table with birdseed and scoops. Children will learn during the unit about how people can feed the birds when their food is scarce.

Science Area

- Supply snowflake cutouts, pictures of snowflakes, and magnifying glasses with which to examine the snowflakes. Encourage the children to observe that no two snowflakes are alike.

- Add scratch or tracing paper and pencils for children to draw their own snowflakes or to trace ones that are on the table.

- Set out a variety of birds' nests and magnifying glasses for examining the nests. Talk about why nests are empty in the winter.

Art Area

- Supply pictures of winter scenes and winter clothes for the children to paint or color and cut out (draw simple sketches for the children or search online for coloring pages related to clothing and seasons).

- Teach the children to make simple cutout snowflakes using folded tissue paper or coffee filters.

- Supply cotton swabs, white tempera paint, and dark blue construction paper for the children to paint white snowflakes.

- Glue cotton swabs together onto paper in the shapes of snowflakes. To add different aspects to the designs, cut some of the cotton swabs in half.

Book Area

Make the Book Area cozy like a cabin in winter with lamps, pillows, blankets, and a rocking chair.

- *Froggy Gets Dressed* by Jonathan London, illustrated by Frank Remkiewicz
- *Geraldine's Blanket* by Holly Keller
- *Here Comes Winter* by Janet Craig, illustrated by G. Brian Karas
- *The Jacket I Wear in the Snow* by Shirley Neitzel, illustrated by Nancy Winslow Parker
- *Katy and the Big Snow* by Virginia Lee Burton
- *Lily and Trooper's Winter* by Jung-Hee Spetter
- *The Mitten* by Jan Brett
- *The Snowman* by Raymond Briggs
- *The Snowy Day* by Ezra Jack Keats
- Other stories related to snow, winter, pigs, and patience

Bulletin Board

- Create a dark blue background and add the heading *Here Comes Winter*. As children complete pictures from the Art Area and the Group Activities, attach them to this bulletin board.

- Using cotton swabs and white paint from the Art Area, children add snowflakes to the blue background paper on the bulliten board.

- Take a close-up photo of each child wearing a winter hat (one with ear flaps would be funny!). Cut out and glue their pictures on snowflakes that they made in the Science or Art Areas.

Week 1

Focus of the Week: Winter weather and winter clothing

Songs, Poems, and Fingerplays

<u>S is for Snow</u>
S *is for* <u>s</u>now.
N *is for* <u>n</u>ow.
O *is for* <u>o</u>utside.
W *is for* <u>w</u>ow!
S-N-O-W, *snow!!!*

<u>The Snow in the Air</u>
(to the tune of "The Wheels on the Bus")

The snow in the air comes falling down, falling down, falling down.
(children fall down)
The snow in the air comes falling down, all through the town.

The people on the ice go slip, slip, slip; slip, slip, slip; slip, slip, slip.
(pretend to slip around)
The people on the ice go slip, slip, slip, all through the town.

The children at school say, "Brr, brr, brr; Brr, brr, brr; Brr, brr, brr."
(hug shoulders and shiver)
The children at school say, "Brr, brr, brr," all through the town.

The snowmen on the lawn they stand up proud, stand up proud, stand up proud.
(puff out chest)
The snowmen on the lawn they stand up proud, all through the town.

Reading the Story

Introduce the book by discussing the title, author, and dedication. Discuss the book's cover and ask the children to guess what the book will be about.

Read the story every day and, as the children become familiar with it, gradually add in any of the following activities:

- While the story is read, children put on winter clothing items as Geraldine heads outside to wait for the snow. They put boots on only after the snow has fallen.

- Make a picture checklist of winter clothing and attach it to the wall at story time. The children take turns coming up to the front to check off the items as Geraldine puts them on.

- Introduce a pig puppet and manipulate it to interact with the children during the story reading.

Group Activities

1. Winter Clothes Relay

Target Areas: fine motor, gross motor, social

What you need:
- Paper bag containing about 5 winter clothing items (hat, mittens, boots, scarf, and coat)

What you do:
1. Children take off their shoes.
2. Divide the children into two groups lined up at opposite ends of the room.
3. The first child in one of the lines opens the bag and, as quickly as possible, puts on all the items of clothing. Lead the rest of the children in cheering and chanting the name of the clothing article as their classmate puts each item on.
4. Once all the items are on, the child runs to the other end of the room and, with the help of the first child in that line, removes the items. The child who has just run sits on the floor and helps with the cheering.
5. The first child in the new line then puts on the items to cheering and chanting and runs to the other line.
6. Children go back and forth until they have all had a turn.

2. What's Missing?

Target Areas: cognition, communication

What you need:
- 5–10 winter clothing items

What you do:
1. The teacher lays all of the items in a line on the floor in front of the children and says the name of each item while laying it down. Give the children a few minutes to look at the items, telling them that the goal is to remember where each item is placed.
2. Children cover their eyes. Then the teacher removes one item from the line.
3. Tell the children to uncover their eyes. If they think they know which item is missing, they raise their hands.
4. Call on the children one at a time until the right answer is revealed. Reward right answers with a high five (making sure all children end up with a high five by the end of the game).

Optional: If using ten items, recite this poem before the children begin guessing:
> *There were ten items, now there are nine,*
> *Guess which one is not in line.*

If using five items, try this poem:
> *There were five items, now there are four,*
> *Guess which one is not on the floor.*

3. Describe It!

Target Areas: cognition, communication

What you need:
- Any or all of the same winter clothing items used in Week 1, Activities 1 and 2

What you do:
1. Hide the items behind a barrier.
2. The children take turns listening to a description of one of the items (color, size, texture, which part of the body it covers).
3. Lift the barrier to see if the child can remember the description and select the correct item.
4. Switch roles with the children so that they describe the items to the teacher and to each other.

4. Winter Class Collage

Target Areas: communication, fine motor

What you need:

- Printed materials (magazines, brochures, catalogs) that contain winter-themed pictures
- Table-sized piece of blue paper
- Scissors (1 pair per child)
- Glue bottles to share

What you do:

1. Either at the table or on the floor, the children go through the materials looking for pictures of winter things (clothes, snow, winter activities) and cut them out.
2. The children then glue their pictures to the large paper to create one giant class collage.
3. As they are gluing, ask them what is shown in their pictures. Write their words next to their pictures.
4. Hang the completed collage in the room or in the hallway for all to admire.

5. What Will the Weather Be?

Target Areas: communication, social

What you need:

- 1 or 2 video-recorded weather reports from the local TV news
- Television set with a VCR
- Video camera
- Wall-sized map

What you do:

1. Show the class the videos of TV weather reports.
2. Standing or sitting in front of the large map, model for the class the things they might say in a weather report related to Geraldine's story. (Example: "A big snowstorm is coming soon. We will have one foot of snow! Be sure to have your winter clothes and sled all ready to go.") The children practice what they will say when it is their turn to be on the news.
3. One at a time, videotape the children giving their weather reports.
4. When everyone is done, turn off the lights and watch the class's recorded news reports (maybe even with popcorn). Pause so each child can take a bow after his or her segment.

Note: If a video camera is not available, try audio tape recording the children giving their reports. Then listen to the tape(s) and see if the children can recognize their own voices.

6. Summer in Winter

Target Areas: gross motor, social

What you need:

- A selection of winter clothes
- Optional: Summer equipment (see step 2)

What you do:

1. Invite the children to wear summer clothes (a visor or sun hat, T-shirt, shorts, sandals) to school during one day of the unit.
2. Consider making the whole day a little silly by bringing in lawn chairs, umbrellas, and a small swimming pool with a small amount of water for wading.
3. During activity time, invite one child at a time to come stand in front of the group. The other children take turns selecting a winter clothing item to help dress the child for the winter season (just put the winter clothes on over the summer clothes).
4. As children help dress their classmate for winter, they explain why he or she should put on the item they chose. The teacher models language the children can use (Examples: "Your feet will be too cold in sandals. You need boots"; "It's too cold outside for shorts. You need snow pants.")
5. Allow each child a chance to get dressed for winter.

Week 2

Focus of the Week: Waiting and being patient; getting ready for the snow

Songs, Poems, and Fingerplays

Snow, Snow
(to the tune of "Rain, Rain, Go Away")

Snow, snow, come today.
Little (name of child) wants to play.

The teacher goes around the circle, taking turns inserting each child's name and fluttering fingers over that child's head as if it were snowing.

Ten Little Snowflakes
(to the tune of "Ten Little Indians")

One little, two little, three little snowflakes,
Four little, five little, six little snowflakes,
Seven little, eight little, nine little snowflakes,
Ten snowflakes on Geraldine.

Reading the Story

Read the story every day and gradually add in any of the following activities:

- Provide props such as a pig nose, simple masks, or hats for the characters of Mom (pig), Mrs. Wilson (sheep), Mr. Peters (porcupine), Mr. Harper (fox), the birds, and Uncle (pig). The children can use these to act out the story.

- Set out books, apples, and birdseed to use as props when the characters in the story use these items.

- On the last day, suspend a sheet filled with packing peanuts or cotton balls from the ceiling above the story area. Children pretend to sleep while Geraldine is sleeping. When the time is right, loosen the sheet to send the "snow" fluttering down. Then, of course, take time to play in the snow.

Group Activities

1. Snowball Bowling

Target Areas: cognition, gross motor

What you need:

- 2-liter plastic bottles (1 per child; ask families to send one if possible)
- Pictures of characters and/or items from the story (pig, apple, book, birds, and so forth) (1 per child)
- Checklist with corresponding pictures (1 copy per child)
- Pencils
- Rubber tee balls or rubber softballs

What you do:

1. Tape one of the pictures onto each bottle.
2. Line up the bottles in a horizontal line.
3. The first child rolls the "snowball" and tries to hit the bottles. The other children practice being patient like Geraldine and waiting for their turn.
4. When a bottle is knocked down, children mark that character or item off on their lists.
5. Children continue taking turns "bowling" until they have knocked down all the items on the checklists.

2. Biscuit Birdfeeders

Target Areas: cognition, fine motor

What you need:

- Package of refrigerator biscuits
- Birdseed
- Scoops
- Small paper plates
- Yarn

What you do:

1. Discuss how birds have a hard time finding food in the snow and how it can help them to be fed by people.
2. Each child gets an uncooked biscuit, makes a hole in the middle with a finger, then ties a piece of yarn through the hole.
3. Children scoop some birdseed onto a paper plate and press the biscuit into the seeds. Then they flip the biscuit over and cover the other side with seeds the same way.
4. Bake the seed-covered biscuits according to the package directions.
5. When cool, hang the birdfeeders in the trees to feed the birds.

3. Book Search

Target Areas: cognition, communication, social

What you need:

- A place with an assortment of books (either the school library or another accessible area in the classroom or school where there is, or where you have set up, a supply of books)
- Several blankets and pillows

What you do:

1. Refer to the part in the story where Mr. Peters is going to the library to get books to read during the snowstorm. Explain to the children that now it is their turn to find a special book to bring to the classroom to read during the "storm."
2. Go to the library (or other place with a supply of books). Allow each child to select a book.
3. Once settled back in the classroom, the children explain why they chose their particular books.
4. Tell the children the storm is coming and it's time to get wrapped up in blankets and rest on comfortable pillows with their books. Turn the lights low and flutter your hands (like snow) over the children as they read their books. They can trade books as they finish reading them.

4. Hungry Birds

Target Areas: fine motor, gross motor

What you need:

- Birdseed from the sensory table
- Scoops
- Ziplock bags (1 per child)

What you do:

1. Children put a scoop or two of birdseed into their ziplock bags and seal them.

2. After providing some suggestions, decide as a class on a special place on the ground outside to spread the birdseed for hungry birds to come and eat.

3. Get bundled up, bags in hand, and take a walk outside to the special place. Spread the seed all over the ground.

4. Over the next few days, check the status of the seed on the ground to see if any birds have visited. Make a chart of how much seed is still on the ground each day. One child can draw "a lot," "a little," or "no" seeds on the chart.

5. Be Patient!

Target Area: cognition, communication

What you need:
- Ice cubes (2 per child)
- Dish with hot water (1 per child)
- Watch with a second hand

What you do:
1. Explain that the children will watch ice cubes melt and see how long it takes. Emphasize that they will need to practice patience—just as Geraldine did—as they wait for the ice cubes to melt.

2. For the first round, provide each child with an ice cube. Note the time in minutes and encourage the children to rub their ice cubes between their hands, to lick them (no chewing), and to breathe on them to try to get them to melt. Record the time in minutes when all of the ice cubes have finally melted.

3. For the second round, give each child a dish of hot water to put his or her ice cube in. Note the time, give each child an ice cube, and record the melting time again.

4. What did they notice? Did they need to be as patient the second time around? Talk about which time was faster and which was slower. Ask the children for ideas on why the ice melted faster when it did.

6. Here Comes the Snowplow

Target Areas: gross motor, social

What you need:
- Large supply of packing peanuts or cotton balls
- Large piece of cardboard
- Stop sign

What you do:
1. Children sit at one end of the room while the teacher scatters the packing peanuts or cotton balls on the floor at the other end, as if a snowstorm just hit the room.

2. Explain that the children are now drivers in their pretend cars. They drive slowly toward the snow.

3. When they reach the snow, the teacher holds up the stop sign and explains that the cars can't come through due to the snow. They must wait patiently while the teacher "plows" the snow out of the way with the "snowplow" (cardboard).

4. Once the road is clear, they can drive through and around the rest of the room.

5. Give each child an opportunity to be the snowplow operator. The other children can be creative about how they are traveling (walking, skateboarding, rollerskating . . .).

Note: For all snack ideas using peanut butter, be sure that no children are allergic to peanuts. As appropriate, substitute cream cheese, almond butter, or another sandwich spread.

1. Provide the children with slices of several different kinds of apples. Talk about how fall and early winter are the seasons when apples are ripe, ready to fall from the trees, and ready to eat. Have an apple taste test and record which kind was the most popular. Which would make the best apple pie?

2. Sliced apples or celery sticks with peanut butter are always kid favorites. Serve some, and point out that liking peanut butter isn't just for the birds!

3. Shiver while eating icy treats such as ice pops, flavored shaved ice, or snow cones.

4. Play (or pretend to play) outside in the cold weather, then come into the cozy room to warm up with hot cider and cinnamon sticks.

5. **Ready-to-Play Sandwiches**

What you need:

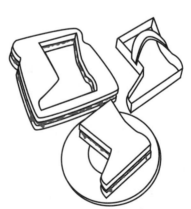

- Boot-shaped cookie cutters
- Sandwich bread
- Peanut butter and jelly in single-portion cups (1 each per child)
- Plastic knives

What you do:

1. Demonstrate how to spread peanut butter and jelly on a piece of bread and then place another piece of bread on top. Then give the children a chance to try.

2. Take turns placing the cookie cutter in the center of the sandwich and pressing all the way through to create a boot shape. The children may need help to press hard enough to go through the entire sandwich.

3. Before eating, the teacher pretends to walk a sandwich up to the top of the hill, then slides it down into a waiting mouth. Children imitate the teacher and enjoy their sandwiches.

6. Apple Crumble

What you need:
- 4 c. peeled, sliced apples
- 1/4 c. water
- 4 tsp. firmly packed brown sugar
- 2 tsp. lemon juice
- 1 tsp. cinnamon
- 1/2 c. oats (quick or old-fashioned)
- 1 tbsp. firmly packed brown sugar
- 1 tbsp. soft margarine
- Stirring spoon
- Mixing bowl
- 8" x 8" baking dish sprayed with nonstick coating
- Access to an oven (or take it home to bake and bring it back the next day)

What you do:
1. With the children helping every step of the way, combine the first five ingredients and mix well.
2. Arrange the mixture in the baking dish.
3. Combine remaining three ingredients and sprinkle over the top.
4. Bake for 40 minutes at 375° or until the apples are tender and the topping is lightly browned.

Pretest and Posttest

Geraldine's Big Snow

Concepts	Pretest	Posttest
Snowflakes		
Snow		
Winter clothes (description/ function)		
Summer clothes (description/ function)		
Activities to do while it is snowing		
Names of the four seasons		
How to predict the weather (look outside, news, what season is it?)		
Concept of *patience*		

Bear Snores On

By Karma Wilson
Illustrated by Jane Chapman

This is a wonderful wintertime story about a hibernating bear.
When several animal friends come into the cave to escape the winter cold,
the bear misses all the fun. The other animals feast, dance, and have a merry
time, all while the bear slumbers on. The bear has fun in the end, though,
when the friends offer to have the party all over again after he awakes.
But they're so worn out by the end that now it's the friends' turn to snooze.
Too bad the bear is now wide awake! The rhythmic, rhyming text
will engage the children on the very first reading.

Dear Families,

Our next book, *Bear Snores On*, was written by Karma Wilson and illustrated by Jane Chapman. This beautifully told wintertime story has a lively, rhyming text and a variety of interesting animals the children will soon know and love. It's the story of a hibernating bear who misses all the fun of a spontaneous party when his animal friends come into his cozy cave to escape the winter cold. Bear has his fun in the end, though, when his friends offer to have the party all over again after he wakes up. They're so worn out by the end that it's *their* turn to take a long nap. It's a story about life's basic pleasures—food, friends, and fun.

We'll focus our attention on animal habitats (snow, caves, and wilderness) and all the yummy foods the animals in the story feast on. Now is a perfect time to pop some popcorn, brew some tea, make a hearty stew, and have your own little party at home. Watch for a letter coming home soon about our Teddy Bear's Picnic. You, your child, and your child's favorite teddy bear will be invited to a potluck (be thinking about what bears might find delectable) on the last day of this unit.

We encourage you to find a copy of *Bear Snores On* to read as a sweet bedtime story. You can find it at the library or in a bookstore. We also recommend you look for two other books by Karma Wilson, *Bear Stays Up for Christmas* and *Bear Wants More*, as well as *How Do Bears Sleep?* by E.J. Bird, and *Castles, Caves, and Honeycombs* by Linda Ashman.

The rhyming text in *Bear Snores On* is one your child will begin to know and predict before too long. Pause before reading the last word in each sentence so that your child can read the word for you. Or, say a word that doesn't rhyme and see if your child catches the mistake. These techniques help keep a familiar story fun and interesting while encouraging prereading and thinking skills.

Stay warm and rested,

Dramatic Play Area

- Make a cave for children to play in by using a large cardboard box or setting up a tent that doesn't require stakes. Decorate the cave with flashlights, stuffed animals, and artificial plants.

- Provide empty shoeboxes (caves) with small characters. Children decorate the boxes throughout the week with moss, dirt, and sticks.

Sensory Area

- Fill the sensory table with popcorn (first week unpopped, second week popped).

- Smelling center: Use empty jars with facial tissue secured on the top with a rubber band. Fill jars halfway with a fragrant item: pepper, garlic, tea bags, lavender, onion powder, cloves, baby powder, peanut butter, orange rind, cinnamon, and so forth. Label each jar with a permanent marking pen.

- Provide a tub of ice-cold water. Children stick their hands in and count how many seconds they can keep them in. Then, provide shortening (Crisco or other brand) in a ziplock bag. Children put a hand in the bag and cover it with shortening. Then they stick that hand back in the freezing water and see how long they can keep it in. Graph their times on a large sheet of paper. Explain that the shortening mimics the layer of fat that polar bears have as insulation to help them stay warm.

Science Area

- Make some ice cubes from water mixed with various food colorings. Each day, put out some of these ice cubes. Provide magnifying glasses, squirt bottles filled with water, and forks for exploring and experimenting with the ice.

- Provide shaved ice and squirt bottles with colored water. Squirt the colored water on the ice. Watch the "snow" melt.

- Make up some water bottles, some with just water and some with water and salt. Set them out along with some ice. Make predictions about which kind of water will make ice melt more quickly. Experiment to see the result, using forks to move melting ice "sculptures" around.

- Freeze plastic bears in water in plastic bags or ice cube trays. When frozen, put them in the sensory table and discuss how long it will take before the bears get out.

Art Area

- Have the following materials available to make character masks: paper plates, string, yarn, tongue depressors, fake fur, feathers, colored cotton balls, pipe cleaners, tape, glue, scissors, paint, and colored pencils. Keep the storybook close by to remind the children of the characters.

- Make play dough balls in a variety of sizes. Children create bear shapes out of the balls.

Book Area

- *Bear All Year: A Guessing Game Story* by Harriet Ziefert
- *Bear Stays Up for Christmas* by Karma Wilson, illustrated by Jane Chapman
- *Bear Wants More* by Karma Wilson, illustrated by Jane Chapman
- *Castles, Caves, and Honeycombs* by Linda Ashman, illustrated by Lauren Stringer
- *Happy Baby: Who Lives in the Wild?* by Roger Priddy
- *How Do Bears Sleep?* by E.J. Bird
- *Ragged Bear* by Alan Marks and Brigitte Weninger
- Other books related to bears, hibernation, and the wilderness

Bulletin Board

- Snowstorm! (see Week 1, Activity 2)

- Hang plastic snowflakes from ribbons of different lengths over the winter snowstorm scene to enhance the three-dimensional effect.

Week 1

Focus of the Week: Habitats and snow

Songs, Poems, and Fingerplays

The Bear Went Over the Mountain
(to the tune of "For He's a Jolly Good Fellow")

The bear went over the mountain,
The bear went over the mountain,
The bear went over the mountain
To see what he could see.

And all that he could see,
And all that he could see,
Was the other side of the mountain,
The other side of the mountain,
The other side of the mountain
Was all that he could see.

Reading the Story

Introduce the book by discussing the title, author, and dedication. Discuss the book's cover and ask the children to guess what the book will be about.

Read the story every day and, as the children become familiar with it, gradually add in any of the following activities:

- Discuss how the bear snores. See if the children can snore too. When the bear snores, have the children join in. Who is the loudest? The quietest? The funniest?

- Each child holds a Popsicle stick with a picture of a bear attached to it. The challenge is to hold the puppet as quietly as possible until the bear in the story sneezes. The children then raise their puppets up and sneeze loudly along with the bear.

- On each page, stop reading *before* the line "But the bear snores on." Let the children fill in the blank and practice their snoring until the next page!

1. Create a Cave!

Target Areas: fine motor, social

What you need:
- Large cardboard furniture box (furniture or refrigerator stores are good sources)
- White or blue bed sheet
- Black, brown, and gray paint
- Floor fan
- Newspapers

What you do:
1. Lay out newspapers on the floor. Set the box on top of the papers.
2. Provide the children with black, brown, and gray paint.
3. Several children paint the inside of the box as a cave, with the box resting on its side. The other children paint the outside of the cave. Let it dry overnight.
4. Attach a sheet to the opening of the cave. Tell children that this is the snow.
5. Have the fan blow on the sheet to create a snowstorm!

2. Snowstorm!

Target Areas: communication, fine motor

What you need:
- Large black sheet of butcher paper
- White paint
- Paintbrushes and other painting tools (scrapers, flyswatters, forks, and so on)
- Packing peanuts
- Glitter
- Paper bears and other book characters (made with a die cutter or printed from online clip art)
- Glue

What you do:
1. Tape the sheet of butcher paper to a large table.
2. Explain to the children that they will be making a snowstorm.
3. Demonstrate different ways to use the materials provided to make a winter scene (glue on peanuts and glitter, paint on "wild" snow with various painting tools).
4. Draw or paint a half circle. This represents the entrance to a cave.
5. Children make the collage of the cave in a snowstorm.

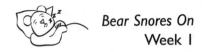

6. When the collage is dry, add paper bears and other characters from the book.

7. Use the collage as a bulletin board for use throughout the unit or display it elsewhere for all to enjoy.

3. Shaving Cream Snow
Target Areas: cognition, fine motor

What you need:
- Several cans of non-menthol shaving cream
- Large table
- Paint smocks

What you do:
1. Discuss how snow can cover up and hide things on the ground.
2. Children put on paint smocks.
3. Allow children time to experiment with spraying the shaving cream and with the shaving cream sensations.
4. Place some small plastic animals in the middle of the table.
5. Children spray shaving cream on the animals until the animals are covered up.
6. Demonstrate how to use your fingers and write the word *snow* in the shaving cream.
7. Children use their fingers and take turns writing the letter *S* or the word *snow* in the shaving cream.

Note: Be aware that this project may provide too much sensory input for some children. Allow children to come and go freely from this activity.

4. Wilderness of Arms
Target Areas: communication, fine motor

What you need:
- Long sheet of butcher paper
- Marking pens, paint, or colored pencils
- Scissors
- Paints, crayons, glitter, glue, ribbons, leaves, twigs, and other tree-decorating materials

What you do:
1. Each child places an arm on the butcher paper. Trace each child's arm, from armpit to fingertips and back to armpit, onto the butcher paper. Children spread their fingers as wide as possible. Explain that their arms are the trunks and their hands are the tops of the trees.
2. Children decorate their trees in their own individual styles.
3. Cut out each tree after it is decorated.
4. When all of the trees have been cut out, hang them on a clothesline in a row. This will create a wilderness in your classroom.

5. Sparkling Snow Dough

Target Areas: cognition, social

What you need:
- 2 c. water
- 2 c. flour
- I c. salt
- 4 tsp. cream of tarter
- 4 tsp. oil
- Iridescent glitter
- Bowl

What you do:
1. Discuss how snow sparkles at night in the moonlight and during the day in the sunlight.
2. Combine all of the ingredients except the glitter in a large bowl. Allow each child to add one ingredient. Discuss what units you are using to measure (for example, "I put in 2 *cups* of water").
3. Cook on medium heat until lumpy, stirring with a wooden spoon.
4. Let the concoction cool. Then add the glitter.
5. When playing with the dough, challenge the children to create snow people, snow caves, snowdrifts, igloos, and other snowy things.
6. Store the dough in a ziplock bag.

6. Footprints in the Snow

Target Areas: cognition, communication

What you need:
- White construction paper (I sheet per child)
- Blue paint
- Pipe cleaners
- Animal fact books or encyclopedias

What you do:
1. Discuss and research what the feet of each animal in the story look like. Go online, or look in an encyclopedia or other books.
2. Bend and twist the pipe cleaners to make them look like the various animal feet. Each child will make his or her own pair of feet for one of the animals.
3. Making sure that the pipe cleaners are flat on the bottom, dip them into the blue paint, and then transfer them to the paper. This should create a nice little footprint.
4. When the children have made several footprints in the snow (the white paper), have them copy the names of the animals corresponding to the footprints.

Week 2

Focus of the Week: Cold weather cooking

Circle Time

Songs, Poems, and Fingerplays

<u>Oh Mr. Sun</u>
Oh Mr. Sun, Sun, Mr. Golden Sun,
Please shine down on me.
Oh Mr. Sun, Sun, Mr. Golden Sun,
Hiding behind a tree.
These little children are asking you,
Please come out
So we can play with you.
Oh Mr. Sun, Sun, Mr. Golden Sun,
Please shine down on,
Please shine down on,
Please shine down on me.

<u>The Popcorn Song</u>
Play the "Popcorn Song" by Greg & Steve on the CD *We All Live Together,*
Volume 2 (Portland: Newsound, 1987). Listen and move to the popcorn-y
sounds!

Reading the Story

Read the story every day and gradually add in any of the following activities:

- Act out the story. Each child chooses a character and wears a simple corresponding
  mask (paper plates masks are easy to make). Pass out the appropriate props for each
  character (popcorn, a tea pot, mugs for drinking, a pot for stew, a bag of nuts). Of
  course the bear "sleeps" through the first half of the story, but joins in the fun for
  the second half.

- Children smell and taste black pepper like the pepper used in the story. See if anyone
  sneezes!

- Glue red and orange tissue paper (crumpled up) onto a piece of cardboard. Read the
  story while everyone sits around the warm fire.

1. Pepper Letters

Target Areas: cognition, fine motor

What you need:

- Glue (1 per child)
- Construction paper: 8 ¹/₂" x 11" in assorted light colors
- Large container of black pepper

What you do:

1. Children use the glue to write each letter in their names. They either write one letter per paper or their whole name on one sheet.
2. Sprinkle pepper over all of the exposed glue.
3. Leave papers lying flat overnight to dry.
4. When dry, shake off excess pepper.
5. Voilà! You have pepper letters. Did anyone sneeze during this activity?

2. Stew

Target Areas: communication, social

What you need:

- Electric crock pot
- Large can of vegetable soup
- Chopped potatoes, carrots, and celery
- Bread
- Ladle
- Bowls (1 per child)
- Spoons (1 per child)

What you do:

1. Set up the crock pot, and assemble the vegetables, soup, and kitchen utensils.
2. Each child adds a handful or cup of ingredients to the crock pot.
3. Explain that the crock pot will get very hot, and the children are not to touch it. Ask, "How did the animals in the book heat their stew when they didn't have electricity?"
4. Show the picture in the book that shows the animals making stew.
5. When all ingredients are warm and tender, unplug the crock pot, ladle up some stew, and enjoy a nice hearty snack.
6. Offer the children bread to dip into their stew.
7. Discuss how the animals worked together to make the stew.

4. Show the picture in the book that shows the animals making stew.
5. When all ingredients are warm and tender, unplug the crock pot, ladle up some stew, and enjoy a nice hearty snack.
6. Offer the children bread to dip into their stew.
7. Discuss how the animals worked together to make the stew.

3. Parachute Popcorn

Target Area: gross motor

What you need:

- Large bed sheet or parachute
- White scrap paper
- Large floor space

What you do:

1. Have children crumple up the paper and place it on the parachute (sheet).
2. Everyone takes a handle around the edge of the parachute.
3. When you say, "Make some popcorn!" the children start shaking the parachute up and down. The papers flying through the air are popcorn kernels being popped!
4. Throw back the pieces of popcorn that fall off to keep the game going.
5. Play until small arms get tired.

4. Beary Good Quesadillas

Target Areas: communication, fine motor

What you need:

- Flour tortillas (2 per child)
- Block of cheddar cheese
- Can of olives
- Jar of salsa
- Microwave
- Paper plates
- Plastic knives
- Plastic spoons
- Cheese grater
- Bear-shaped cookie cutters

What you do:

1. Each child uses a cookie cutter to cut 2 bears (cut with the same cutter) out of the tortillas.
2. Children help in the preparation by shredding the cheese and cutting the olives.
3. Each child piles cheese, olives, and salsa on one tortilla bear and puts the other tortilla bear on top.
4. Cook the quesadillas in the microwave for 30 seconds. Take out and enjoy!

4. Cook the quesadillas in the microwave for 30 seconds. Take out and enjoy!
5. Explain how funny it is to substitute the word *beary* for *very* in the name of this treat.
6. Children describe how their quesadillas taste. The teacher writes sentences on the board. For example, *Sam's quesadilla is beary spicy!*

5. Mr. Bear, Are You Sleeping?
Target Areas: gross motor, social

What you need:

- Large area to move around in
- Small amounts of food items: popcorn, tea, stew, honey-nuts, onion, garlic, and lemon juice

What you do:

1. One child is the bear and lies on the floor "sleeping" on one side of the room.
2. The other children stand together on the other side of the room, each holding one of the food items. As a group, they quietly ask, "Mr. Bear, are you sleeping?"
3. The bear continues to sleep while the children take turns approaching and putting their food items under the bear's nose.
4. When the bear smells yummy food, he jumps up and chases that child back to the other side of the room. If the bear smells yucky food, he continues sleeping.
5. After the bear smells yummy food and chases the food-bearing child across the room, another child is chosen to be the bear. The game continues until each child has had a turn to be the bear.

6. Teddy Bear's Picnic Day and Honey Bear Toast
Target Areas: communication, social

What you need:

- Picnic baskets
- Blankets
- Extra teddy bears (for children who don't bring their own)
- Bread (1 slice per child)
- Honey (in a bear-shaped dispenser, if possible)
- Bear-shaped cookie cutters
- Lyrics to the "Teddy Bear's Picnic" song
- Family members and their potluck dishes

What you do:

1. If you haven't done so already, choose a date for the picnic. This picnic could happen on the last day of the unit as a grand finale.

2. Send home a letter to families reminding them of the Teddy Bear's Picnic. Invite the family members to join in the picnic. Ask them to bring foods that bears like to eat (since there will be so many bears there). Each family can decide what they think the bears would like. Each child should bring his or her own teddy bear too, if possible.

3. Find the lyrics and tune to "Teddy Bear's Picnic" at the library or online.

4. During the picnic, make Honey Bear Toast: Each child has a slice of bread. The children take turns using the cookie cutters to cut their bread into the shape of a bear. Then toast the bread. Using a honey dispenser (bear-shaped if possible), squirt honey onto the bread. Or, toast the pieces of bread before cutting them into bear shapes, then add the honey.

5. Discuss how bears love to eat honey and all of the other tasty treats the families brought. The children can pretend to feed their teddy bears the yummy treats!

6. Don't forget to teach everyone the "Teddy Bear's Picnic" song and to sing it throughout the festivities.

Who Snores?

Send a small tape recorder home with one child each night. Attach a note to families, asking them to turn on the tape recorder when they put their child in bed. The next day, the child can bring the tape in and play it for the class. Did he or she snore last night?? Families that have their own tape recorders could tape their child themselves and send just the tape to school.

All About Sneezing

Have a box of facial tissue on hand. Discuss how the bear sneezes. Why did he sneeze? What other things can make someone sneeze? Looking at a light? A feather tickling the end of your nose? Explain how germs come out of your nose when you sneeze, and that they need to be removed quickly. Demonstrate the steps to properly blowing your nose. Throw away the facial tissue when finished and wash your hands. The children can pretend to sneeze and then practice wiping their noses.

Note: Be sure no children are allergic to peanuts before serving them in any of these snack items. As appropriate, substitute other food items.

1. Eat what the animals eat by enjoying some black tea (look for decaffeinated) and some honey-nuts.

2. If you have an air popper, place it in the middle of a sheet, take the lid off, and let the popcorn fly! Look, it's a snowstorm!

3. **Trail Mix**
   Combine any or all of the following items together in a big bowl: small pretzels, cereal pieces, raisins, nuts, fruit snacks, dried fruit, granola. Each child can use a scooper to fill his or her own ziplock baggie. Talk about how this would be a healthy snack to take on a hike.

4. **Bear-in-the-Middle Muffins**

What you need:
- Box of pre-made, low sugar muffin mix
- Large mixing bowl
- Several mixing spoons
- Box of teddy bear shaped graham crackers

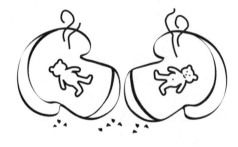

What you do:
   Using pre-made muffin mix, make a batch of muffins. Before you put them in the oven, sneak a teddy graham in the middle of each one. The children will be delighted when they find their little bear surprise!

Pretest and Posttest
Bear Snores On

Concepts	Pretest	Posttest
Bears		
Caves		
Popcorn		
Stew (what is in it?)		
Hibernation		
Ice/snow melting		
Snow		
Snoring		
Sneezing		
Animals in the wild (raven, wren, mouse, badger, hare)		
Tea		

Notes

The Little Mouse, the Red Ripe Strawberry, and the Big Hungry Bear

By Don and Audrey Wood
Illustrated by Don Wood

In this cute story, a nervous little mouse tries every trick he can think of
to protect a perfectly ripe, delicious strawberry from a hungry bear whose
footsteps grow ever closer and louder. After managing to pick the strawberry
from the vine, the mouse tries hiding it in a hole, wrapping it in chains
and locking it up, dressing it up in a disguise, and covering it up with a
tablecloth. As it turns out, the only way to truly protect the coveted fruit is
to eat it! The mouse shares the strawberry with the clever narrator
and the big bear goes without.

Dear Families,

We're anticipating lots of fun as we read our next story, *The Little Mouse, The Red Ripe Strawberry, and The Big Hungry Bear* by Don and Audrey Wood. We'll meet a little mouse who tries desperately to hide a delicious strawberry from a looming, hungry bear. In the end, the mouse eats the yummy treat (sharing half with the narrator), leaving the poor bear with none. The book is creatively written and illustrated so that we never actually see the bear, even though its footsteps grow ever closer and louder to the little mouse.

At school we will be discussing the concept of *a half*, various emotions, prepositions, and how different foods taste. We'll stomp our feet like hungry bears, hide like scared mice, and share delicious strawberries with each other.

There are so many fun activities you can do at home related to this story: Use red play dough to form strawberries of all shapes and sizes. Make a list of all the things your family eats that contain strawberries, and then eat an item off the list each day. (Use another fruit as a substitute if any family member is allergic to strawberries.) Pretend to go strawberry picking but watch over your shoulder for the big hungry bear. Go to the zoo and see the different kinds of bears. Do some research to find out if bears even like strawberries! Look in the grocery store for fruit that is ripe, too ripe, or not ripe enough. Cut fruits in halves or quarters to make a beautiful salad—and if you feel comfortable having your child use a plastic knife, this is a good time to talk about holding it by the handle and passing it to others with the handle first.

In addition to *The Little Mouse . . .*, you might want to check out these favorites at the library: *Mouse Paint* and *Mouse Count,* both by Ellen Stoll Walsh, *Eating Fractions* by Bruce McMillan, *Seven Blind Mice* by Ed Young, and *If You Give a Mouse a Cookie* by Laura Joffe Numeroff.

Enjoy your strawberries and
don't forget to watch out for that bear!

Room Setup

Dramatic Play Area

- Provide any of the following: mouse ears, a big stuffed bear, a large stuffed paper strawberry (see Week 1, Activity 1), a fake nose with glasses and mustache, and a hammock (if space allows).

- Build a bear cave using blankets or boxes.

- Hang a hammock in the room so that the children can pretend to be the mouse resting with a full tummy.

- Add a table with a tablecloth, candles, a toy knife, and plastic foods that children can pretend to cut in half.

Sensory Area

- Fill the sensory table with dirt and plastic strawberries for the children to bury.

- Put out red play dough for children to make strawberries. They can use a pencil to create little dimples like real strawberries.

Science Area

- Set out a variety of padlocks with all of the keys on a table. The children can explore the keys and locks, trying to find the matching sets.

- Provide red water (made with food coloring), eyedroppers, and cotton balls for children to make cotton "strawberries."

Art Area

- Set out smooth rocks, wiggly eyes, small pieces of string, tacky craft glue, and paint for children to make pet rock mice.

- Using paint and sponges shaped like a bear, a bear paw print, a mouse, and a strawberry, children paint on large sheets of white paper.

- Provide bear shapes cut out of sandpaper. Children tape white paper over the top of the sandpaper and rub with a crayon. When the bear rubbings are completed, put them on the bulletin board.

Book Area

- *Eating Fractions* by Bruce McMillan

- *Eating the Alphabet* by Lois Ehlert

- *If You Give a Mouse a Cookie* by Laura Joffe Numeroff, illustrated by Felicia Bond

- *Mouse Count* and *Mouse Paint* by Ellen Stoll Walsh

- *The Mouse Who Ate Bananas* by Keith Faulkner, illustrated by Rory Tyger

- *Seven Blind Mice* by Ed Young

- *A Story for Bear* by Dennis Haseley and Jim LaMarche

- *Totally Strawberries Cookbook* by Helene Siegel and Karen Gillingham

- Other books related to bears, mice, and strawberries

Bulletin Board

- Make a background resembling the mouse's tree trunk. Children interact with this scene on the bulletin board by moving mouse puppets, strawberries, and other props alongside the board to act out the story.

- Cut out and attach the sandpaper bear rubbings made in the Art Area. Write the words *stomp, stomp, stomp* under the bears' feet.

Other

- Laminate brown paper paw prints and tape them to the floor. Children attempt to jump from one to the next, or they follow the footprints along a path around the room.

Week 1

Focus of the Week: Strawberries, emotions, and the concept of *a half*

Songs, Poems, and Fingerplays

A Bear in Tennis Shoes

The teacher sings the lines and the children repeat them:

The other day (the other day)
I met a bear (I met a bear)
In tennis shoes, (in tennis shoes,)
A dandy pair. (a dandy pair.)

The teacher and the children sing together:

The other day I met a bear
In tennis shoes, a dandy pair.

Continue this repeating-then-together pattern for all the verses:

He looked at me. I looked at him.
He sized up me. I sized up him.

He said to me, "Don't just stand there.
Can you not see, I'm a great big bear?"

And so I ran . . . away from there,
But right behind . . . me was that bear.

Ahead of me . . . there was a tree,
A great big tree, O golly gee!

The lowest branch . . . was ten feet up.
I'd have to jump . . . and trust my luck.

And so I jumped . . . into the air,
And I missed that branch, oh way up there.

Now don't you fret. . . and don't you frown,
'Cause I caught that branch . . . on the way back down.

That's all there is, there is no more,
Until I meet . . . that bear once more.

<u>*I'm Bringing Home a Yummy Strawberry*</u>
(to the tune of "I'm Bringing Home a Baby Bumblebee")

I'm bringing home a yummy strawberry,
Half for you and half for me.
I'm bringing home a yummy strawberry,
SMACK, SMACK, SMACK, SMACK, SMACK!

Reading the Story

Introduce the book by discussing the title and author. Discuss the book's cover and ask the children to guess what the book will be about.

Read the story every day and, as the children become familiar with it, gradually add in any of the following activities:

- The teacher uses a mouse puppet and acts out the story while reading. Or, each child holds a mouse puppet and acts out the story as it is read.

- Place large stuffed bears sitting in chairs, hidden around the room, and/or holding various props. Point them out at appropriate points during the story.

- Every time a page is turned, the children take turns beating a drum to imitate the footsteps of the bear. They walk to the drumbeat slowly or run quickly—the drummer decides!

Group Activities

1. Stuffed Strawberry

Target Areas: cognition, fine motor, social

What you need:

- Spatulas, flyswatters, rollers, paint daubers, thread spools, rubber bands, and so on
- Red paint
- 2 large strawberries, exactly alike, cut out of large pieces of white paper
- Stapler
- Newspapers

What you do:

1. Place the paper strawberries on a table. Place one "right side up" and the other "right side down."
2. Children use the different utensils and work together to paint the sides of the strawberries that are now up.
3. When the paint is dry, staple the strawberries together with painted sides out (to make one strawberry), leaving an opening at the top.
4. Children stuff the strawberry with crumpled newspapers and staple the opening closed to create a large three-dimensional red ripe strawberry.

Optional: Use the strawberry as a story reading prop or have it out during free play time.

2. Half and Half

Target Areas: cognition, fine motor, social

What you need:

- Construction paper in different colors (red, orange, purple, yellow, blue, green)
- Velcro
- Index cards (a handful)
- Glue
- Pen
- Scissors (1 pair per child)
- Large basket
- Flannel board

161

What you do:

1. Cut the construction paper into 2"
   squares. Make one square for each
   pair of children.
2. Divide children into pairs and give
   each pair one of the paper squares.
3. Each pair decides what fruit to cut
   out of their piece of paper. The
   teacher draws an outline of that
   fruit on their paper.
4. They cut out fruit shapes and give them to the teacher.
5. When complete, the teacher holds up each fruit shape, writes the name of the
   fruit on an index card, then cuts the shape in half. Attach little pieces of Velcro to
   the backs of the fruit halves.
6. Put all the halves into a basket and shake them up.
7. Each child reaches into the basket and takes out one half piece of fruit.
8. When all of the children have a fruit half, the teacher selects an index card and
   reads the name of the fruit. The two children with the named fruit stand up and
   run to the flannel board to put their two halves together to create a whole.
9. Each pair of children can say, "Two halves of (<u>name of fruit</u>) make a whole (<u>name
   of fruit</u>)."

3. Plant a Strawberry

Target Areas: cognition, communication

What you need:

- Small indoor flowerpots, terra cotta or
  plastic (1 per child)
- Strawberry seedlings
- Potting soil
- Shovels, gloves, watering can

What you do:

1. Demonstrate how to transplant a young plant.
2. Each child fills his or her pot with potting soil and a strawberry seedling.
3. Place the strawberry plants near the window that gets the most sunlight or
   outside in a protected area.
4. Children water and track the growth of their plants.

4. Mr. Strawberry Head

Target Areas: fine motor, social

What you need:
- Washed potatoes (1 per child)
- Body parts from a Mr. Potato Head
- Red paint
- Very small doll clothes

What you do:
1. Each child paints his or her whole potato red to look like a strawberry, then allows it to dry.
2. Use the body parts and doll clothes to disguise the strawberries.
3. Alternatively, use an old Mr. Potato Head toy and paint it red.

5. Strawberry Relay

Target Areas: gross motor, social

What you need:
- Plastic, paper, or foil strawberries (three-dimensional, to roll on the floor) (1 per team)
- Masking tape
- Optional: Spoons (1 per team)

What you do:
1. Divide the class into teams with the same number of children on each team.
2. The teams line up on one side of the room.
3. Put down a piece of masking tape to indicate how far they need to go before they can turn around.
4. Give each team a strawberry.
5. The first person on each team rolls the strawberry on the floor to the line and back to the team—with his or her nose!
6. The next person in line does the same thing, until all children have had a chance to roll the strawberry with their noses.

Alternatives: This game can be modified by having the children use spoons, or carry the strawberries under their chins, or hold the strawberries between their knees.

6. Emotional Strawberries
Target Areas: cognition, fine motor, social

What you need:
- Laminated paper strawberries, about the size of an adult hand (1 per child)
- Dry erase markers (1 per child)
- Facial tissue

What you do:
1. Give each child a laminated strawberry and a dry erase marker.
2. Show children how they can show emotions on their strawberries by drawing facial expressions, giving them a wide range of emotions they can choose from.
3. Encourage the children to think of and depict as many emotions as they can.
4. Give the children different scenarios that might happen in their lives and ask them to draw the faces that show the emotions they might feel.
5. Use facial tissue to wipe off the drawings.

Week 2

Focus of the Week: Prepositions and problem solving

Songs, Poems, and Fingerplays

There's a Bear in the Middle
(to the tune of "The Wheels on the Bus")

There's a bear in the middle and (he/she) can't get out, can't get out, can't get out.
There's a bear in the middle and (he/she) can't get out.
Let's give (him/her) a hand to help (him/her) out!

The children stand in a circle with one child being "the bear" in the middle. The bear acts as if he or she is stuck in the middle. Everyone lends a hand to pull the bear out.

Did You Ever See a Brown Bear?
(to the tune of "Did You Ever See a Lassie?")

Did you ever see a brown bear, a brown bear, a brown bear,
Did you ever see a brown bear go this way and that?

Sing additional verses changing the action to: *doing jumping jacks, dancing on all fours, wiggling its nose, shaking its hands, stomping its feet,* and *touching the floor.* Children decide what the brown bear will do next!

Hickory Dickory Dock
Hickory dickory dock, the mouse ran up the clock.
The clock struck one, the mouse ran down.
Hickory dickory dock.

Reading the Story

Read the story every day and gradually add in any of the following activities:

- Children put line-drawn pictures of book pages in order of occurrence as the story is read.

- One child is selected to retell the story from beginning to end. The teacher sits outside the circle and videotapes the performance, if possible. Children take turns being the storyteller (on successive days).

- Children act out the motions of the story—climb the ladder, pick the strawberry, dig a hole and bury the strawberry, wrap it up with a chain, put it under a table, cut it in half, eat it up!

- Each child brings his or her own teddy bear to class for a "Teddy Bear Day!" The bears can sit in the children's chairs for story time. Be sure to have some extra teddy bears on hand for those who forgot theirs.

Group Activities

1. Sly Kids

Target Areas: cognition, social

What you need:
- Bear mask
- Blocks, beanbags, blankets, boxes, or pillows
- Large stuffed strawberry (see Week 1, Activity 1)

What you do:
1. Select one child to be the bear, and let him or her wear the bear mask.
2. The bear leaves the room.
3. The other children devise a plan to hide the strawberry from the bear. They work together to try to completely cover the strawberry, using whatever supplies they can find.
4. When the strawberry is hidden, call in the bear and see if he or she can find the strawberry.
5. Children can give the bear hints, if necessary.

2. Mini-Mousey Maze

Target Areas: cognition, fine motor

What you need:
- Large sheet of white butcher paper, enough to cover a long table
- Small toy cars
- Black paint

- Red ink pen
- Paint trays
- Optional: Small plastic mice

What you do:
1. Attach the butcher paper to the table at each end.
2. Explain to the children that they are going to be making a maze.
3. Draw a strawberry at one end of the butcher paper.
4. Distribute the cars to three or four children at a time.
5. Children dip their cars in the black paint until the tires are covered.
6. They make tracks along the paper leading to the strawberry. Encourage them to make loops, twists, and turns, avoiding making a straight line.
7. After the paint is dry, children use their fingers or small plastic mice (if available) to go through the maze and get the strawberry.

3. Preposition Obstacle Course
Target Areas: cognition, communication, gross motor

What you need:
- The storybook
- Stopwatch
- Dry erase board and marker
- Big red rubber ball (to represent the strawberry)
- Classroom furniture including tables, small stairs, a child-sized ladder, chairs, and large beanbags

What you do:
1. Point out prepositions that appear in the book and talk about these words. Show the strawberry ON the mouse's back, UNDER the dirt, and IN the mouse's mouth.
2. Set up the room as an obstacle course. For example, set up the following: a table for the children to crawl UNDER, stairs or a child-sized ladder for them to climb UP, beanbags for them to jump OVER.
3. The children carry the ball (strawberry) through the obstacle course. Instruct them, as part of the obstacle course, to do actions such as: sit down ON top of the strawberry, carry the strawberry ON their backs, roll the strawberry UNDER a chair, carry the strawberry OVER their heads. Point out and emphasize the prepositions when giving the instructions.

4. The teacher uses the stopwatch to time each child. Children take turns being the "note taker" and writing the competitors' names and times on the white board.

5. The other children cheer their classmates on and remind them that "The bear is coming!"

4. Clues, Clues, Clues

Target Areas: cognition, communication

What you need:

- Dry erase board
- Markers

What you do:

1. The teacher says: "I am small and have some fur" (teacher draws an oval). "I have small black eyes, a pink nose, and a few whiskers" (draws these items). "I squeak, but I don't purr" (draws a mouth). "I have a long, thin tail" (draws a tail). "I might live in your house!" (draws a house around the mouse). "I have two little ears" (draws ears). "What am I?"

2. Children raise their hands and take a guess at any time.

3. Next, the children take turns drawing their favorite animals, one part at a time, while giving clues.

4. To make this game more challenging, say the clues but don't draw them.

5. Lock It Up!

Target Areas: cognition, communication, social

What you need:

- Padlocks with keys (enough for half of the class)
- Paints

What you do:

1. Before playing the game, the teacher paints each key a different color.

2. Half of the children sit on the floor in a circle. The other half stand behind them outside the circle.

3. Each child sitting down gets a padlock.

4. The teacher puts all of the keys in the middle of the circle, spreading them out so they don't touch each other.

5. One at a time, each child with a lock picks a key he or she thinks will fit that lock. The children standing outside the circle help out their classmates by cheering them on and predicting which key would be right.

6. Children with locks continue taking turns trying keys. If they do not choose the right key, they set the key back down in the spot it had been in before, among the keys in the middle of the circle. With the help of their classmates outside the circle, they are to remember which keys they have already tried.

7. When all of the children have found their keys, the teams switch, and the other half of the class gets to sit in the circle.

Variation: Give half of the class the locks and the other half the keys. Children move around the room trying out lock-and-key combinations until all matches have been made.

6. It's Getting Bigger!!
Target Areas: fine motor, social

What you need:
- Several flashlights or an overhead projector
- Large, stuffed paper strawberry (See Week 1, Activity 1)

What you do:
1. Using flashlights or an overhead projector, make bear-, strawberry-, and mouse-shaped shadows on the wall with your hands. Ask the children how they could make the images bigger and smaller.

2. Slowly move the light source further away to create full body shadows of the characters.

3. Bring in the large stuffed strawberry for a huge image of the strawberry on the wall!

4. Of course, feel free to jump in the middle of the light at any point and tell them that you are a big hungry bear!

Note: Be sure no children are allergic to strawberries or peanuts before serving snacks with these items. As appropriate, substitute other fruits, almond butter, or another sandwich spread.

1. Nibble on teddy graham crackers and real or gummy strawberries.

2. Paint with frozen strawberries on crepes, and then eat!

3. Make fancy drinks in a blender: Combine strawberries, ice, and soda water. Yummy!

4. **Half a Snack**: When pouring juice or water, only fill children's cups halfway. Tell the children they can ask for a full cup or half a cup. Continue the activity with food items, giving the children half crackers, half a fruit bar, or half a strawberry.

5. Set the table with a tablecloth and real silverware. Then set battery-operated candles on the table. Turn the lights off and eat strawberries topped with vanilla frozen yogurt by candlelight.

6. Strawberry Taste Test

What you need:
- Variety of foods containing strawberries (fruit salad, jam or jelly, fruit bars, fruit chews, juice, Jell-O, pie, muffins, peanut butter and jelly mini-sandwiches)
- Pieces of paper for food labels
- 1 piece of chart paper
- Pens

What you do:
1. Make as many columns on the chart paper as there are separate food items. Write the name of one food at the bottom of each of the columns. Make paper labels for each food item. Place each food in a separate small dish. Place the labels in front of the dishes.

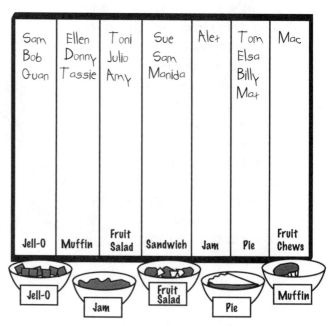

Sam Bob Quan	Ellen Donny Tassie	Toni Julio Amy	Sue Sam Manida	Alex	Tom Elsa Billy Mat	Mac
Jell-O	Muffin	Fruit Salad	Sandwich	Jam	Pie	Fruit Chews

2. Tell the children what all the food items are. Children ask for, and taste, the different foods. When they are finished, tell them it is time to vote. Children come up one at a time and write their names on the chart paper in the columns above the names of their favorite foods. When all of the children have voted, discuss the results. Which food was most popular and which was the least favorite?

7. Bury the Strawberry

What you need:
- Small paper cups and plastic spoons
- Box of graham crackers
- Gummy or real strawberries

What you do:

Each child has a cup, a spoon, and a graham cracker. The children use their spoons and crunch up their crackers in their cups. Add a real or gummy strawberry into the cup. Pretending that the broken cracker is dirt, the children use their spoons to dig a hole and attempt to bury their strawberry. Remind them of the lurking bear!

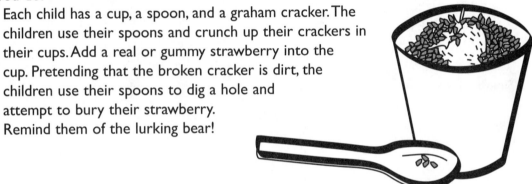

Pretest and Posttest

The Little Mouse, the Red Ripe Strawberry, and the Big Hungry Bear

Concepts	Pretest	Posttest
Concept of *a half*		
A disguise		
Strawberries		
Mice		
Bears		
Different emotions (name 5)		
Prepositions *(on, over, under, in, up)*		

The Kissing Hand

By Audrey Penn
Illustrated by Ruth E. Harper and Nancy M. Leak

This is a wonderful story to read at the beginning of the school year or around Valentine's Day. Chester Raccoon is scared to start school and wants to stay home in the arms of his mother. Her gentle words of encouragement and secret gift of the Kissing Hand reassure him that school will be fun and that he will carry his mother's love with him wherever he goes. Chester loves his Kissing Hand so much that he gives one to his mother in return.

Dear Families,

It is natural for children, and all of us, to feel anxious before entering a new situation. In the forward to our next storybook, *The Kissing Hand* by Audrey Penn, we learn that this story will help us with such feelings. Jean Kennedy Smith writes that this story is for all children—and indeed all adults—who need comfort and encouragement in facing a challenging circumstance.

Through gentle words and vibrant illustrations, we meet Chester Raccoon, who is nervous to start school and wishes to stay home with his mother. His mother gives him the secret gift of the Kissing Hand (a kiss right in the middle of his palm) and explains that, whenever he feels scared, he need only press his palm to his cheek and feel the warmth of her kiss to know he is safe and loved.

Our activities over the next two weeks will teach about love, hearts, the many uses for our hands, and forest animals. This would be a nice time to make cards covered in hearts and hand tracings to send to loved ones. Make heart collages from different papers and fabrics, or experiment with lipstick kisses to make wrapping paper. Talk about love and other emotions. Go on a walk after dark with flashlights and watch for animals you may see. Check out books on forest animals to learn which ones prowl around at night.

Try to make a trip to the library to find *The Kissing Hand* as well as some of our other favorites: *Guess How Much I Love You* by Sam McBratney; *Koala Lou* by Mem Fox; *Morning, Noon, and Night* by Jean Craighead George; and *I Love You As Much . . .* by Laura Krauss Melmed.

We hope you enjoy this sweet story and the connection it reinforces between you and your child.

With love,

Room Setup

Dramatic Play Area

- Set out lots of forest animal puppets or toys for the children to pretend with.

- Attach a large paper tree to a wall. Place a step stool in front of it and encourage the children to pretend to climb the tree.

Sensory Area

- Cut heart shapes out of various textured materials (sandpaper, corrugated cardboard, foam, fabric, bubble wrap, and so on) and place them in the sensory table.

Science Area

- Supply a variety of pieces of tree bark, leaves, and nuts for the children to examine. They can draw, trace, or glue these objects to cardboard that is cut out in the shapes of tree trunks.

Art Area

- Cover a large table with white paper. Provide red and pink drawing tools (pencils, crayons, markers) for the children to trace their hands on the paper. Provide heart rubber stamps and additional coloring materials so the children can draw and stamp hearts in the centers of their hand tracings.

Book Area

- *All the Ways I Love You* by Teresa Imperato, illustrated by Julie Downing

- *Guess How Much I Love You* by Sam McBratney, illustrated by Anita Jeram

- *I Love You As Much . . .* by Laura Krauss Melmed, illustrated by Henri Sorensen

- *Koala Lou* by Mem Fox, illustrated by Pamela Lofts

- *Love You Forever* by Robert N. Munsch, illustrated by Sheila McGraw

- *Morning, Noon, and Night* by Jean Craighead George, illustrated by Wendell Minor

- Other books related to love, hearts, new experiences, hands, feeling scared, and forest animals

Bulletin Board

- Add the words *Our Kissing Hands* to a white background. Decorate according to Activity 1 of Week 1.

- Put up Our Own Class Tree (see Week 2, Activity 1)

Week 1

Focus of the Week: Love, hearts, and kisses

Songs, Poems, and Fingerplays

Skidamarink
Skidamarink a dink a dink,
Skidamarink a doo,
I love you.
Skidamarink a dink a dink,
Skidamarink a doo,
I love you.

I love you in the morning
And in the afternoon,
I love you in the evening
And underneath the moon;
Oh, Skidamarink a dink a dink,
Skidamarink a doo,
I love you!

The More We Get Together
The more we get together, together, together,
The more we get together, the happier we'll be.
'Cause your friends are my friends, and my friends are your friends.
The more we get together, the happier we'll be.

Reading the Story

Introduce the book by discussing the title, author, and dedication. Discuss the book's cover and ask the children to guess what the book will be about.

Read the story every day and, as the children become familiar with it, gradually add in any of the following activities:

- When the mother raccoon gives Chester the Kissing Hand, stamp each child's hand with a rubber-stamp heart.

- Teach all the children how to say "I love you" in sign language (shown on the last page of the storybook and illustrated here). They all sign it together at the end of the story.

- Pass out a heart sticker to each child at the end of one story reading.

- While looking in hand mirrors, children practice making kissing motions with their lips before the teacher begins to read the story. Make loud kisses and quiet kisses, long kisses and short kisses. Children wait for the last word in the story, then demonstrate their favorite kissing sounds all together.

"I love you"

1. Our Kissing Hands
Target Area: fine motor

What you need:
- Bulletin board covered with white paper
- Colored pens
- Tubes of lipstick (1 per child)
- Mirrors

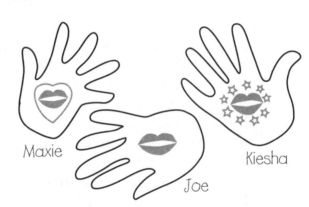

Maxie

Joe

Kiesha

What you do:
1. Help the children trace outlines of their hands on the white paper on the bulletin board.
2. Each child applies lipstick and admires himself or herself in a mirror before placing a giant kiss right in the middle of his or her traced hand.
3. The children either draw or trace a heart around their lipstick print and add their names under their hands.
4. Invite family members to add their lipstick kiss prints to their child's handprint. Or, they can make their own handprint and make a lipstick kiss print in it.

2. Find Those Hearts!
Target Areas: cognition, gross motor

What you need:
- Paper geometric shapes and heart shapes of all sizes and colors
- Paper sacks or bags
- Glue

What you do:

1. Look at all of the shapes and label them with the children.
2. Children leave the room or turn away while the teacher hides the shapes around the room.
3. Explain to the children that they are to go on a scavenger hunt, looking only for the hearts to put in their bags. They are to leave the other shapes where they find them.
4. Once the children have found all the hearts, they empty their bags and look over the different sizes and colors they have collected.
5. Play again or go to the table to decorate the bags with the collected hearts.

3. Matching Hearts

Target Area: cognition

What you need:

- All of the suit of hearts cards from a deck of playing cards, cut in half

What you do:

1. This game is played like Memory, in which the children try to remember where cards are placed in order to match the pairs.
2. Begin with only half the card halves (both halves of aces through fives or sixes). Place these card halves face down on a smooth surface.
3. Explain the rules: Children take turns turning over two cards to see if they match. If so, they remove the matching cards from the playing surface and go again. A child's turn continues as long as matches are uncovered. When no match is uncovered, the two cards are replaced exactly where they had been, face down, and the next child takes a turn.
4. Play until all of the cards have been matched and removed from play.

Optional: Make the game more difficult by adding in more cards from the deck.

4. Love Lists

Target Areas: communication, fine motor

What you need:

- Writing paper (1 piece per child)
- Transparent tape
- Colored markers
- Heart and love stickers and stamps

What you do:

1. Each child writes <u>(Child's name)</u> loves . . . at the top of the paper and hands it back to the teacher.

2. Tape the papers up on the wall or chalkboard.
3. Go around the circle asking the children what they love. Write their answers on their papers to create a list for each child.
4. Once the papers are full, the children decorate their Love Lists with the stickers and stamps.

5. Mailing Kisses

Target Areas: cognition, fine motor

What you need:

- 11" x 14" sheets of white paper, with a large heart drawn on each (1 per child)
- Several sponges cut out in the shape of lips
- Large envelopes and stamps for mailing
- Scissors
- Red paint
- Shallow paint dishes

What you do:

1. The children cut out the hearts on their papers.
2. The teacher writes *I send you a kiss for all that you do—made with love from me to you!* in the center of each heart.
3. The children then decorate their hearts with the sponges and paint. Allow time for the hearts to dry.
4. The children watch as the teacher addresses the envelopes to their special family member (parent or someone else special for whom the teacher has an address).
5. Children place the hearts in the envelopes and seal them. They attach the stamps.
6. Walk out to the mailbox together to mail off the kisses!

6. Sticky Hearts

Target Areas: cognition, fine motor

What you need:

- Large heart cut from white paper (1 per child)
- Food coloring in a variety of colors
- Small foam paint rollers or paintbrushes
- Corn syrup

What you do:

1. Children slowly pour about 2 tbsp. of corn syrup all over their paper hearts.
2. Each child chooses and drips 3 or 4 colors of food coloring onto the corn syrup.
3. Using paintbrushes or paint rollers, the children move the corn syrup and food coloring around to cover the paper.
4. Allow the hearts to dry overnight before sending them home. When dry, the hearts will have a beautiful shimmer.

Week 2

Focus of the Week: Hands and forest animals

Songs, Poems, and Fingerplays

Here We Go Loopty-Loo
Here we go loopty-loo, here we go loopty-lie,
Here we go loopty-loo, all on a Saturday night.
You put your right hand in.
You put your right hand out.
You give your hand a shake, shake, shake,
And you turn yourself about. Oh . . . .

Start over, singing *left hand* instead of *right hand*, then end with *both hands*.

Chester the Raccoon
(to the tune of "Mary Had a Little Lamb")

Chester's climbing up the tree
With his friends 1, 2, 3.
He's ready now for school to start,
With a kiss in hand and love in his heart.

Reading the Story

Read the story every day and gradually add in any of the following activities:

- Use Chester and Mom Raccoon hand, finger, or Popsicle stick puppets to help tell the story.
- Create a paper tree with tape loops placed all over the trunk and branches. Attach the tree to a board or wall in the story area. Before reading, give the children small pictures of the animals in the story. As the animals in the story appear, the children with the corresponding pictures come to the front to place their animals on the tree.

- Either before or after reading the story, practice blowing kisses to each other and catching them.

Group Activities

1. Our Own Class Tree

Target Areas: cognition, communication, fine motor, social

What you need:
- Pictures of the forest animals in the story
- White circles the sizes of the animals' heads
- Large paper cutout of a tree with branches
- Colored pencils or markers
- Glue

What you do:
1. Attach the paper tree to the wall. Explain that the children will create their own forest animal classroom.
2. Children choose an animal to be either by naming it and taking the animal's picture or by picking out an animal picture at random from a bag.
3. Children draw pictures of their own faces on the white paper circles. Ask them to think about how their animals feel about going to school. Have them draw their faces to represent those emotions.
4. Glue the self-portraits on top of the animals' heads and let the children select where on the wall tree to place their animals. Glue the animals onto the tree.
5. Children sit in a circle. The teacher asks each child how his or her animal feels and then writes a sentence to reflect that feeling (*Jared the Fox feels happy; Emily the Bunny feels scared*).

2. Mystery Box

Target Areas: cognition, communication

What you need:

- Shoebox with a lid and 2 holes cut out—one on each end—large enough to fit adult hands through. (Optional: Secure a piece of fabric on the top of each hole to prevent peeking.)
- Various items from the story small enough to fit in the shoebox (puppets, a toy tree, various animals, anything heart-shaped)

What you do:

1. Explain to the children that for this game they can use only their hands to help them determine what is in the box.
2. Secretly place an item in the box. Children each take a turn putting their hands through the holes to feel the item.
3. The children whisper their guesses to the teacher.
4. The teacher reveals the item once all have had a turn. Talk about how the item felt, using vocabulary related to size, texture, and shape.
5. Pass the item around so that the children can look at it while they feel it.
6. Play again and again.

3. Can You Hide It in Your Hand?

Target Areas: cognition, communication

What you need:

- Variety of objects, all shapes and sizes, from the story

What you do:

1. Set out all of the items in front of the children.
2. The children take turns naming an object and predicting whether they will be able to hide it in their hand.
3. Ask them to predict whether the item will fit in a classmate's hand or if it is too big.
4. Try variations: Will an item fit in *both* hands, or *under* one or both hands?
5. Be sure the children test out all their predictions.

4. Clapping Cards

Target Area: fine motor

What you need:

- 11" x 17" sheets of paper, any color (1 per child)
- Colored markers
- Glitter, jewels, sequins, other fun decorations
- Thin dowels, at least 10" long (2 per child)
- Packing or duct tape

What you do:

1. Children place their papers in front of themselves lengthwise and fold them in half to create cards.
2. On the insides of the cards, the children draw pictures of themselves right in the center creases. Tell them to draw long, outstretched arms but no hands.
3. On the ends of the long arms, help the children trace their hands. Near each traced hand, either the teacher or the children write the word *CLAP!*
4. Children decorate their huge hands with the glittery supplies.
5. Use strong tape to attach a dowel on the backside in the center of each side of the card. Let 6" of the dowels come down below the card. Children hold onto the dowel ends and use them to open and close their cards—the hands clap!

5. Owl Eyes

Target Area: fine motor

What you need:

- Empty toilet paper rolls, cut in half (2 halves per child)
- Feathers in a variety of colors
- Glitter
- Liquid glue
- Several shallow dishes
- Stapler or tape

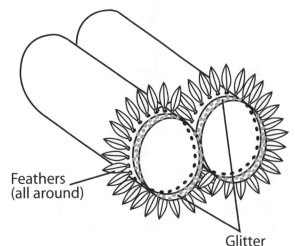

Feathers (all around)

Glitter

What you do:

1. Ahead of time, staple or tape two rolls together, side by side. They will look like binoculars. Each child needs one set.
2. Also ahead of time, use a sharp pencil or a nail to poke several small holes around the edges of one end of the tubes, about 1/2" in.
3. Children poke the feather tips through the holes just far enough so that they will stay in. The feathers frame the owl eyes.

4. Pour about 1/2" of glue into a shallow dish, and about 1/2" of glitter into a separate shallow dish.
5. Children dip the feathered ends of their rolls into the glue, then into the glitter. Glitter now also frames the owl eyes.
6. Children hold their owl eyes up to their eyes and practice their best hooting.

6. Animals in the Night

Target Areas: communication, gross motor

What you need:
- Flashlight

What you do:
1. Talk about the animals in the story and how they are most active at night when the moon is out.
2. Turn off the lights and shine the flashlight up high like the moon.
3. Ask the children to choose an animal in the story to pretend to be. Shine the light on each child as he or she flies or crawls around the room.
4. Now ask the children to freeze when they sense that the light is on them and to quietly keep moving when they are "in the dark" again.
5. Move the light around the room quickly to see how fast the children can freeze when they sense the light is on them.

Note: Be sure no children are allergic to strawberries or peanuts before serving snacks with these items. As appropriate, substitute other fruits, almond butter, or another sandwich spread.

1. See how easy or hard it is to eat without using hands. Or, eat as animals do, without using thumbs.

2. Play a guessing game: Which hand is the cracker (or other food item) in?

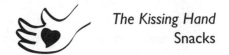

3. Honey Heart Sundae

What you need:
- Small heart-shaped cookie cutter or paring knife
- Large strawberries
- Frozen yogurt
- Bowls
- Spoons

What you do:
1. Slice strawberries.
2. Use the cookie cutter or the paring knife to make strawberry slices look like hearts. They may already look like hearts when they are sliced.
3. Help the children dish one scoop of frozen yogurt into their bowls.
4. Children scoop the heart-shaped strawberries onto their yogurt and taste the love on their tongues!

4. Make together and enjoy a heart-shaped fruit salad (kiwis, pears, apples, and strawberries). Create the fruit hearts with a heart-shaped cookie cutter or a paring knife.

5. Make peanut butter and jelly sandwiches cut in the shapes of hearts. Yum!

Pretest and Posttest

The Kissing Hand

Concepts	Pretest	Posttest
Forest animals		
Heart (what the symbol represents)		
Heart (how it differs from other shapes)		
Concept of *love*		
I love you in sign language		
Things we do with our hands		
Emotions related to starting something new		
Descriptive words *(strange, scary, warm, cozy)*		

Pete's a Pizza

By William Steig

Who says rainy days have to be boring? Young Pete's parents save the day
when they decide to make him into a pizza. Just roll him like dough, sprinkle
some toppings on his tummy, and pop him into the couch-oven. Luckily for
Pete, the sun comes out just before he's going to be sliced up and
gobbled down, and he's off to play football. This creative story will keep
the children laughing and wishing they, too, could be a pizza.

Dear Families,

For a child who longs to play outside, a rainy day can seem to last an eternity. Luckily for Pete, the little boy in our next story—*Pete's a Pizza* by William Steig—his creative parents come up with a way to liven up the day. Why not make Pete into a pizza? It's simple: knead, roll, and toss the dough (that'd be Pete), sprinkle on the cheese and pepperoni (colored paper and checkers), toss him in the oven (the couch), and slice him up. Wait just a minute! What was that last part? Is that the sun peaking out from behind the clouds? Hooray! See ya, Mom and Dad!

You'll definitely want to be eating lots of pizza over the next couple of weeks—both real and pretend. Why not send us your favorite homemade pizza recipe? We'll have the children illustrate the recipes and create a cookbook for each family. See how creative you and your child can be in making pretend pizzas. Invent crazy ingredients just by using items from around your house. Try a "theme" pizza (for example, green pizza, square pizza, or soft pizza). Let us know what you come up with. Of course, we'd like for you to head to the library and get your own copy of this story to reinforce the activities we do at school as well as those you do at home. We also suggest *Hold the Anchovies!* by Shelley Rotner and Julia Pemberton Hellums, *"Hi, Pizza Man!"* by Virginia Walter, and *Curious George and the Pizza* by Margret and H.A. Rey.

We'll be busy here at school playing pizza games, learning about ingredients, and, naturally, making and eating a few different pizzas. Who knew pizza could be so educational?

We'll try to save you a slice,

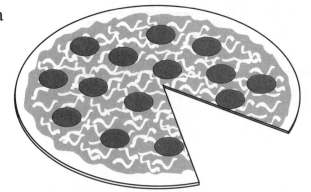

Room Setup

Dramatic Play Area

- Provide aprons, pretend pizza cutters, cardboard pizza boxes, cutout pieces for toppings, pizza pans, notepads to write orders on, play money, and chef hats.

- Draw and color a variety of slices of pizza, cut them out, and laminate them. The children make special-order pizzas for each other by putting individual slices together into whole pizza pies.

- Use masking tape to make large triangular "slices of pizza" on the floor. Use plastic or paper foods to decorate the pizza slices.

Sensory Area

- Mix water and flour in the sensory table to make "dough." Mix cornstarch, water, and red food coloring to make "sauce." Add plastic vegetables for the toppings. Children make pretend pizzas.

- Smell test: Set out several baby food jars with tiny holes in the lids. Put a variety of pizza spices (oregano, garlic, anchovies, chilies, marjoram, thyme, basil, fennel seeds, pepper) inside the jars, one spice per jar. On each jar, put a ring of glue around the perimeter of the lid, then put the lid on the jar. Label the jars with permanent markers. Children smell the jars and try to identify the spices. Then they can check the labels to see if their guesses are correct. *Optional:* Cover the outsides of the jars with construction paper so the contents and labels are hidden from view.

Science Area

- Put small magnets on the backs of some plastic or paper pizza toppings. Children attach the magnets to a metal pizza pan, thus creating their own pizzas.

Art Area

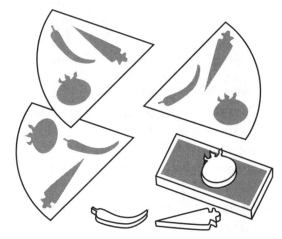

- Provide laminated circles on which children draw pizza toppings and slices. Provide dry erase markers and facial tissue so the same circle can be used to make multiple pizzas, one after the other.

- Set out paper cut into triangles (pizza slices) and sponges cut in the shapes of different vegetables. Children apply paint to the sponges and print the vegetable shapes on the pizza slices.

- For each child, provide a circular piece of cardboard and a paper lunch bag containing a variety of art materials (paper clips, cotton balls, scrap paper and fabrics, markers, buttons, pennies, yarn, rice, beans, foam cutouts, Popsicle sticks, foam peanuts, pictures from magazines, rubber bands, self-stick notes, stickers, ribbons). Set out glue, scissors, a stapler, tape, and a hole punch for all to share. Children open their bags and make creative pizzas using their materials. It is fine for them to swap items with each other!

Book Area

- *Curious George and the Pizza* by Margret and H.A. Rey
- *"Hi, Pizza Man!"* by Virginia Walter, illustrated by Ponder Goembel
- *Hold the Anchovies!* by Shelley Rotner and Julia Pemberton Hellums
- *The Little Red Hen (Makes a Pizza)* by Philemon Sturges, illustrated by Amy Walrod
- Pizza cookbooks with color pictures
- Other stories related to pizza, cooking, and rainy days

Bulletin Board

- Create a scene of an Italian restaurant containing an umbrella, grapes cascading down the walls, and red-and-white checkerboard tablecloths on the tables.

- Attach the Giant Doodle Pizza (see Week 1, Activity 2) to the board.

- Display the Classy Pizza (see Week 1, Activity 4).

Other

- Play Italian music in the background during free play.

Week 1

Focus of the Week: Making a pizza

Circle Time

Songs, Poems, and Fingerplays

P *is for* Pizza
(to tune of "Peanut, Peanut Butter")

P *is for pizza (pizza).*
P *is for pizza (pizza).*
First you get the dough
And you knead it and you knead it
And you knead it, knead it, knead it.
Then you toss it and you toss it
And you toss it, toss it, toss it.

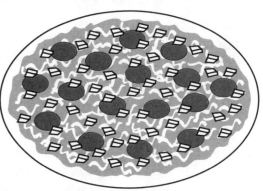

P *is for pizza (pizza).*
P *is for pizza (pizza).*
Next you get the veggies
And you chop 'em and you chop 'em
And you chop 'em, chop 'em, chop 'em.
Then you place 'em and you place 'em
And you place 'em, place 'em, place 'em.

P *is for pizza (pizza).*
P *is for pizza (pizza).*
Next you get the cheese
And you shred it and you shred it
And you shred it, shred it, shred it.
Then you sprinkle and you sprinkle
And you sprinkle, sprinkle, sprinkle.

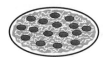

P *is for* pizza (pizza).
P *is for* pizza (pizza).
Next you take the pizza
And you bake it, and you bake it
And you bake it, bake it, bake it.
Then you cut it and you cut it,
And you cut it, cut it, cut it.

Time for the pizza (pizza)!

P-I-Z-Z-A
(to the tune of *"B-I-N-G-O"*)

There was a man who had a restaurant
And pizza's what he made-oh!
P-I-Z-Z-A, P-I-Z-Z-A, P-I-Z-Z-A
And pizza's what he made-oh!

Repeat the song and, with each successive verse, replace another letter
in *P-I-Z-Z-A* with an "mmmm" sound.

Pete Was a Pizza
(to the tune of "You Are My Sunshine")

Pete was a pizza, Pete was a pizza,
Pete was a pizza when skies were gray.
His mom and daddy were gonna eat him,
Then the sun came out, hooray!

Reading the Story

Introduce the book by discussing the title, author, and dedication (the dedication is at the
back of the book). Discuss the book's cover and ask the children to guess what the book
will be about.

Read the story every day and, as the children become familiar with it, gradually add in any
of the following activities:

- Each child has a laminated set of the following items cut from paper: light brown
  circle (dough), slightly smaller red circle (sauce), white paper strips (cheese), small red
  circles (tomatoes). Each child also has a saltshaker with a small amount of powder
  (flour) and a spray bottle with a small amount of water (oil). Children make their
  own pizzas as the story is read to them.

- Before story time, cut out pictures from magazines showing ingredients that might be in a pizza. Put the pictures in a bag. Give each child a blank paper pizza. As the ingredients are added in the story, each child picks out a pizza ingredient and says whether it is the same or different from the one just mentioned in the book. Children use glue sticks to affix the ingredients to their pizzas.

- As the story is read, the children stand up every time they hear the word *pizza*.

1. Sticker Pizza

Target Areas: cognition, communication, fine motor, social

What you need:

- Cardboard circle cutouts the size of the bottom of a pizza box (1 per child)
- Red construction paper
- Clean milk jug caps (at least 6 per child)
- Black markers (1 per child)
- Multiple sets of matching stickers
- Plastic sandwich baggies

What you do:

1. Children cut the red construction paper out to resemble tomato sauce and then glue it onto their pieces of cardboard.
2. With the marker, they trace circles (using milk jug caps) onto the pizza.
3. With matching sets of stickers, children place one sticker inside each circle on the pizza and matching stickers on the insides of the milk jug caps.
4. Children keep their game pieces (caps) together in their plastic baggies.
5. Children play their very own matching games. They pull out caps and find matches for them on their own pizzas. They can switch their pizzas and pieces with classmates to see what kinds of crazy pizzas their classmates have.

Optional: Children make up names for their specialty pizzas based on the stickers they used ("Half American flag, half flowers," "Large dog with extra cats," and so forth).

2. Giant Doodle Pizza

Target Areas: fine motor, social

What you need:

- A circle about 6 ft. across cut from white butcher paper (tape 2–3 sheets together)
- Black markers (1 per child)
- Colored pencils or crayons

What you do:

1. The teacher stands in the middle of the huge paper circle and draws as many pizza slices on the circle as there are children in the class.
2. Each child has his or her own slice to decorate.
3. Using black markers, children begin making designs in the middle of their slices. When they get near the edges, they try to have their lines meet their neighbors' lines. If their neighbors have already drawn something up to the edge, the children attach their drawing lines to their neighbors' lines. If their neighbors have not yet reached the edge, the children stop at the edge and their neighbors then draw to meet their lines. The children try to fill up their slices with their own designs.
4. Ultimately, all of the lines will connect piece to piece around the entire circle.
5. Encourage the children to color in their designs.
6. Display this huge piece of art on the ceiling or bulletin board.

3. Order Up!

Target Areas: cognition, communication

What you need:

- White board
- Dry erase markers
- Telephone with speakerphone capability
- Phone book
- Money

What you do:

1. Explain that the class will be ordering a pizza to be delivered to the classroom and that first the children need to vote on what they want on their pizza.

2. Make a graph on the board. Draw pictures of all the ingredients that could be on a pizza along the bottom of the graph. On the side, write numbers *1* though however many children are in the class.

3. Name each ingredient. Children vote on what they would like by raising their hands. They can vote for more than one ingredient.

4. Color in the graph up to the appropriate number. When the voting is complete, look at the graph together and see which are the most popular ingredients.

9							
8							
7							
6							
5							
4							
3							
2							
1							
	Pepperoni	Peppers	Tomato	Olives	Cheese	Sausage	Anchovies

5. Get out a phone book and explain the whole process of finding a phone number. Point out specific categories in the phone book and mention that the book is in alphabetical order. Write the name and number of the pizza place on the white board.

6. Call in the order with the phone on speakerphone so that the children can hear what the pizza person is saying.

Optional: If no delivery service is available during class time, have a friend pose as a delivery person, answering the phone and delivering the pizza (could be a cooked frozen or take-and-bake one).

4. Classy Pizza

Target Areas: cognition, communication, fine motor, social

What you need:
- Small black-and-white photocopied picture of each child, cut into a circle
- Large white paper circle (approx. 1 1/2 ft. across)
- Pencils (1 per team)
- Clipboards (1 per team)
- Checklists of tasks (1 per team)
- Glue
- Crayons

What you do:
1. Ahead of time, the teacher decides on a list of tasks for the children to complete in teams and makes a checklist of these tasks. Include a check box next to each task for the children to mark as they finish each one. Some ideas for tasks include:
   - Think of a compliment for each member of your team.
   - Write down (or copy) your first and last name.

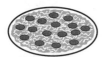

- Count the children in the class and have one team member write that number on the board.
    - Using your favorite color, draw a picture of your family.
    - Tell the teacher your favorite part of school.
2. Divide the children into teams.
3. The teacher explains each task on the checklist and how to use the checklist.
4. As each team finishes all of the tasks, all members of the team get to put their pictures onto the big class pizza (the big paper circle). Those that finish first can start decorating the pizza with crayons while the other children finish.
5. The end result will be a big, beautiful, *classy* pizza—perfect for the hallway or bulletin board!

5. Pizza Match

Target Areas: cognition, communication, social

What you need:
- Poster board
- Markers
- Scissors

What you do:
1. Before class, draw and color several pizzas on poster board. Make enough for half the children in the class and make each one unique (sausage and mushroom, tomato and olive, olive and pepperoni, and so on). Cut them all in half and laminate the two parts.
2. Pass out the halves to the children.
3. Select one child to come up and describe his or her pizza. The child hides the half pizza while describing it so that the other children cannot see it.
4. The other children listen to the description to see if it matches their halves.
5. When a match has been found, those two children sit together and pretend to eat their pizza.
6. Continue until all the pizzas have been put back together.

6. Pizza-on-Your-Head Relay

Target Areas: gross motor, social

What you need:
- 3–4 empty pizza boxes
- Variety of plastic vegetables
- 3–4 spatulas

What you do:

1. Divide the class into three or four teams.
2. Line the teams up at one end of the classroom.
3. Use masking tape to make a line 20 feet away from the starting line.
4. Explain the relay: The first child in each team is to run to the line, bend down and touch it, and run back to the team. The child runs while carrying a spatula and balancing a pizza box filled with fake vegetables on his or her head!
5. When the child returns to the team, he or she puts the pizza box on the next child's head and hands over the spatula.
6 Anyone who drops his or her pizza box uses the spatula to pick up all of the pieces and put them back in the box, and then continues on with the race.

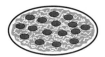

Week 2

Focus of the Week: More pizza

Songs, Poems, and Fingerplays

Aiken Drum
There was a man who lived in the moon, in the moon, in the moon.
There was a man who lived in the moon, and his name was Aiken Drum.
And he played upon a ladle, a ladle, a ladle.
He played upon a ladle, and his name was Aiken Drum.
And his <u>eyes</u> were made of <u>cheese, cheese, cheese</u>.
His <u>eyes</u> were made of <u>cheese</u>, and his name was Aiken Drum.

Continue through the parts of the face, changing the underlined words.
Children name the food item—preferably a pizza ingredient:

ears were made of _____
hair was made of _____
nose was made of _____
mouth was made of _____

Draw pictures of Aiken's face including the named food items. Sing the song
once or twice a day and keep the pictures to make a classroom book.

Name Game
Pete Pete po peet
banana fanna fo feet
me my mo meet,
Pete!

Choose a couple of children to sing about each day. Soon they will be able
to sing the "Name Game" on their own.

Pizza Starts with P
(to the tune of "*C is for Cookie*")

P *is for* pizza, *that's good enough for me.*
P *is for* pizza, *that's good enough for me.*
P *is for* pizza, *that's good enough for me.*
Oh, pizza, pizza, pizza *starts with P!*

Reading the Story

Read the story every day and gradually add in any of the following activities:

- As the story is read, three children act out the roles of Pete, Mom, and Dad. They use paper for the toppings and a large pillow or beanbag for the oven. Others watch and alternate roles each day.

- Create hand movements for working with each of the ingredients (sprinkle, shake, spread, roll). Model the movements for the children to copy. They join in when the actions occur in the story.

- With each new page, ask the children if it is raining or sunny outside in the book. If it's raining, the children stand up and wave their arms like rain. Finally, on the last page, they stand and raise their arms in a circle overhead to be the sun.

- Use a boy doll "Pete" as a prop for the children to enact the story. They take turns being the parents and turning the doll into a pizza, following the steps as the story evolves.

Group Activities

1. Reading, Writing, and Hula-Hoops?
Target Areas: cognition, fine motor

What you need:
- Ball of yarn

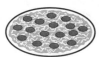

- 1 Hula-Hoop
- Pennies (1 per child)
- Plain paper (8 1/2" x 11")
- Pizza Worksheets (4 per child)
- Pencils (1 per child)

What you do:

1. Make the Pizza Worksheets—a drawing of a large circle with lines dividing it into 4 equal "slices."

2. Wrap yarn around the Hula-Hoop to make it too look like a pizza cut into 4 equal slices.

3. Decide on 4 topics for which children will learn and write the names of examples. One of these topics will be used each day (examples of topics: animals, numbers, colors, and foods).

4. For each topic, make 4 pieces of paper with a target word and a corresponding picture or symbol (some examples: for the colors topic—a paper with the word *red* and a big red circle; for the foods topic—a paper with the word *cheese* and a picture of cheese; for the numbers topic—a paper with the word *three* and the numeral *3*).

5. Choose the topic for the day. Place the appropriate papers in the Hula-Hoop slices, one paper in each slice. Write the topic of the day at the top of a Pizza Worksheet for each child.

6. Give each child a Pizza Worksheet, a pencil, and a penny.

7. Children line up and take turns throwing a penny into the Hula-Hoop. They look at the slice it landed in and copy the *name* of the example from the paper onto one of the slices on their Pizza Worksheet. When they finish their turn, they go to the back of the line.

8. The game continues until all children have all 4 slices filled in on their Pizza Worksheets. If a child's penny lands on the same slice twice, he or she picks it up and aims for a different slice.

9. After their pennies land, children move aside and copy their words down. Each child works at his or her own pace. Remind the children that this is not a race.

10. Repeat steps 5 through 9 for each of the next three days, using a different topic each day. When all four days are done, staple each child's 4 papers together for a nice collection of pizzas with words.

2. Making the Real Thing!
Target Areas: cognition, communication, fine motor, social

What you need:

- Refrigerated biscuit dough (1 biscuit per child)
- Tomato slices in plastic baggies (1–2 slices per child)
- Toppings (olives, pepperoni, mushrooms, and so on)
- Grated cheese
- Toaster oven
- Spatula
- Oven mitts
- Sequence cards with pictures of ingredients (first the dough, second the sauce, . . .)

What you do:
1. Discuss the sequence cards, showing the process of putting a pizza together.
2. Children smash the tomatoes in their plastic baggies.
3. They pour the tomato mixture onto their own biscuit.
4. Add whatever toppings they want, plus cheese.
5. Bake in the toaster oven following directions on the biscuit package.
6. Using oven mitts, remove and enjoy!

Note: Remember to use sequential words throughout the process. Ask the children what they did first, second, and so on.

3. Potato Print Pizza
Target Areas: cognition, fine motor

What you need:
- Bag of clean potatoes
- Small paint trays
- Paint in a variety of colors
- Sharp knife
- Construction paper (1 piece per child)
- Permanent markers

What you do:
1. The teacher cuts all of the potatoes in half and passes the halves out to the children.
2. Each child uses a permanent marker to draw a picture of a favorite pizza topping on the cut edge of the potato.
3. When their pictures are complete, the teacher uses a sharp knife to cut around the edges of the design. Use the knife to cut away the background and discard it. This will leave a raised image in the middle that can be used as a stamp.

4. On the construction paper, each child paints a large circle. Using the potatoes as stamps, they put paint on the images and then stamp them onto their pizzas. The children can switch with classmates, using whatever potato picture they want, to create their yummy potato print pizzas!

4. A Very Particular Pizza

Target Areas: cognition, communication, fine motor

What you need:
- Paper (1 piece per child)
- Marking pens in different colors (3–4 per child)

What you do:
1. Following the teacher's directions, each child draws a large circle for a pizza.
2. The teacher gives *very specific* directions about what ingredients he or she wants on this pizza and where to draw the ingredients in the circle.
3. The children draw the items on their pizzas.
4. As the list goes on, the teacher continues adding more complex language into the activity—using words such as *a few, in the middle, around the edges, a pinch, piled high, a dash.*
5. The children draw whatever the teacher requests, following each set of directions.
6. When the activity is finished, the children can compare their drawings. Discuss some of the terms used in the activity and whether different children understood the terms in different ways.

5. Velcro Pizza Stick-Ons

Target Areas: cognition, gross motor, social

What you need:
- Large piece of cardboard (approx. 3 ft. square)
- Lots of Velcro
- 10 small, soft balls in various colors, or Ping-Pong balls
- 2 sheets of poster paper

What you do:
1. Draw a pizza on the large piece of cardboard, dividing it into 8 slices. Write the numbers *1* through *8*, one number on each slice. On each slice, put one side of 8 squares of Velcro. Draw around the Velcro pieces to make them look like pizza ingredients.
2. Wrap the other side of the Velcro around the balls.
3. Divide the class into two teams and give each team 5 balls.

4. The first member from each team throws a ball at the pizza. A scorekeeper keeps track of which numbers the balls land on. The whole class can help add up the points as the game goes along.

5. Choose what will be the "winning score." The game continues until a team reaches that score.

6. Pizza Tag

Target Areas: gross motor, social

What you need:
- Masking tape
- Large open space

What you do:
1. Create a large pizza made of masking tape on the floor. Use tape to divide the pizza into 8 slices.
2. Start with one child in the middle of the pizza. He or she is "Pete." The other children stand in a line outside the pizza.
3. The first 8 children in line move to stand on the tape on the perimeter of the pizza pie (1 child per pizza slice).
4. When the teacher says "Go," Pete tries to tag the other children, but the catch is that Pete and the children must stay on the tape lines. If they fall off of the line, they become "Pete" and the original Pete goes out of the pizza to the back of the line.
5. If the original Pete tags someone, the tagged child becomes the new Pete. At that point, the next child in line joins in the game and the original Pete goes to the back of the line. There should always be 9 players in the game.

Additional Activities

Crazy Name Books

Talk about the title of the storybook and why it is funny. Discuss other children's names in the class to see what the titles of their books could be (for example, *Sandy's a Candy, Lou's a Shoe, Sam's a Clam*). After the class has come up with a title for each child, help children create their own books. Take 5 minutes every day to let children dictate a page for their book—and to add illustrations, of course!

Our Families' Favorite Pizzas Cookbook

Send home an index card with each child. Ask each family to write down a favorite recipe for pizza and send it back to school (see letter to families introducing this idea at the beginning of this unit). Photocopy all entries and assemble them into a class cookbook. Every child gets a cookbook to bring home.

Name That Ingredient

Make a mystery box (see the Kissing Hand unit, Week 2, Activity 2) and secretly place inside it, one at a time, typical pizza toppings: pepperoni stick, cube of cheese, tomato, garlic clove, olives, and so on. Children feel inside the box and guess what the item might be by asking questions about it. Encourage the children to ask about the size, color, texture, taste, shape, and scent of the item. Children can also take turns secretly placing the item in the box for their classmates to guess.

Oh No! My Pizza Melted!

Set out waxed paper, an old iron, and small paper cups, each filled with a different color of crayon shavings—black, red, green, orange, yellow, and brown. For each child, make 2 circular paper frames out of card stock (about 1 ft. across on the outside). Following the directions for "Crayon Melt Butterflies" (See the Very Hungry Caterpillar unit, Week 2, Activity 6), the children create pizzas on pieces of waxed paper using the crayon shavings: black for olives, red for sauce, green or yellow for peppers, orange for cheese, and brown for mushrooms or pepperoni. After ironing, see what happened to the pizza! Attach the frames and trim to make circular pizzas.

Snacks

1. Have a cheese taste test: Who likes mozzarella, cheddar, American, jalapeño jack?

2. Spread any of the following on crackers to make fruity pizzas: yogurt, cream cheese, applesauce, or pure fruit jam. Then, add slices of apple, grape, orange, or any other fruits the children like.

3. Bagel Pizzas

What you need:
- Bagels (one half per child)
- Tomato sauce
- Pizza toppings (cheese, and pepperoni, olives, pineapple, tomatoes, peppers, and/or mushrooms)
- Toaster oven
- Oven mitts
- Spatula
- Plastic tongs

What you do:
Each child puts together his or her own bagel pizza. Use plastic tongs to pick up the toppings. Depending on the size of the toaster oven, bake as many as possible (until the cheese is melted), let cool, and munch. The children can eat their pizzas next to the bulletin board that looks like a pizza parlor. Play Italian music while cooking and eating!

4. Eat olives off fingers, counting 1 to 10.

5. Sip on tomato or pineapple juice.

6. Peel mozzarella string cheese into big, medium, and tiny strings.

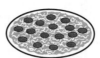

Pretest and Posttest

Pete's a Pizza

Concepts	Pretest	Posttest
Process of making a pizza		
Pizza ingredients		
Ordering a pizza on the phone		
Vocabulary related to amount: *pinch, a little, dash, a few*		
Identifying numerals 1–8		
Smells of spices and foods		
Italian music		
Letter sounds (e.g., *P* for *Pete* and *pizza*)		
Reading and writing simple words (colors, animals, numerals)		

The Napping House

By Audrey Wood
Illustrated by Don Wood

In this charming tale about a house full of sleeping people and animals, all is quiet and peaceful. That is, until the wakeful flea shows up! Beautifully illustrated, this story begins when everyone in the house decides to take a nap on a dark, rainy afternoon. One by one, the characters climb into the cozy bed and fall into a restful sleep. All is well until a not-so-sleepy flea shows up and bites the mouse who wakes the cat who wakes the dog and so on, until the house is no longer sleepy but alive and active. The wonderful illustrations add to the moods throughout the story.

The rhyming text is cumulative and therefore predictable, making it easy for children to read along and help tell the story.

207

Dear Families,

"This is a house, a napping house, where everyone is sleeping." Sounds pretty peaceful, right? Our next story, *The Napping House* by Audrey Wood, starts out calm, but it quickly escalates into a less-than-restful nap none of the characters were expecting. The story ends with a startling wake-up call, a broken bed, and animals and people everywhere!

The story begins with perfect napping weather—clouds and rain. But by the end, the sun appears and we see a bright, cheery rainbow. Who can sleep through that? We'll be learning about sleep routines and, naturally, about pretty, colorful rainbows. Any home activities you can do to tie in with these themes will help your child build a strong connection between home and school as well as reinforce new vocabulary and concepts. Help your child create a step-by-step chart for his or her nap or bedtime routine. Go outside or to the window and talk about the weather. Be on the lookout for rainbows or any other interesting weather. Draw or take pictures of what you see and send them to school with your child. Or, compile the images to create a *Weather Out Our Window* book to keep at home.

When you are at the library, look for *The Napping House* and for these other favorite books as well: *Maisy Goes to Bed* by Lucy Cousins, *Time for Bed* by Mem Fox, *Ten Out of Bed* by Penny Dale, *Good Night* by Claire Masurel, *Tell Me Something Happy Before I Go to Sleep* by Joyce Dunbar, *A Rainbow of My Own* by Don Freeman, and *Planting a Rainbow* by Lois Ehlert.

Wishing you restful naps,

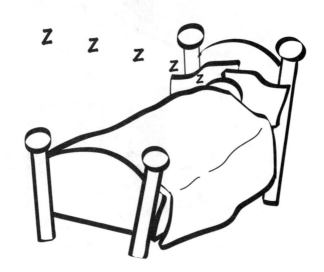

Dramatic Play Area

- Add some pajamas, robes, and slippers to the dress-up area.

- Create a bedroom or house using a large box.

- Wind some yarn or string all around the room. Place a bowl of chocolate coins at the end of the yarn. Children work together to follow the rainbow (yarn) to the pot of gold.

Sensory Area

- In a baggie, combine 2 cups of rice with 1/3 cup rubbing alcohol and several drops of food coloring. Shake the baggie vigorously until all the rice is colored. Spread the rice out on a cookie sheet covered in waxed paper and let it dry overnight. Repeat this process several times with different colors (rainbow colors would be best), then mix the different colors of rice together in the sensory table.

Science Area

- Rainbow Cubes: Put out 5 cups of water, each colored with food coloring in one of the rainbow colors (red, orange, yellow, green, blue, purple). Give children eyedroppers to drip the colored water onto ice cubes or shapes made by freezing water in margarine tubs or molds made for the sandbox or play dough.

- Hang prisms up in the windows of the classroom. Set some out on a table, too, for manipulation and experimentation. Point out the rainbows that are created by the prisms.

Art Area

- Supply white play dough and colored pipe cleaners. Children make two white clouds out of the white play dough and create a rainbow by bending the colored pipe cleaners and placing their ends into each cloud of dough.

- Provide waxed paper, paint in rainbow colors, eyedroppers, and white paper. Allow children to experiment with the materials. What if they dropped paint onto the white paper and then placed the waxed paper on top?

- Place spoonfuls of blue and white finger paint on a clean table. Children mix the blue and white finger paint with their fingers on the table, creating images of clouds. Make a print by pressing paper onto the paint and then lifting it carefully.

Book Area

- *Good Night* by Claire Masurel, illustrated by Marie H. Henry
- *Goodnight Moon* by Margaret Wise Brown, illustrated by Clement Hurd
- *Maisy Goes to Bed* by Lucy Cousins
- *Planting a Rainbow* by Lois Ehlert
- *The Rainbow Goblins* by Ul De Rico
- *A Rainbow of My Own* by Don Freeman
- *Swinging on a Rainbow* by Charles Perkins
- *Tell Me Something Happy Before I Go to Sleep* by Joyce Dunbar, illustrated by Debi Gliori
- *Ten, Nine, Eight* by Molly Bang
- *Ten Out of Bed* by Penny Dale
- *Time for Bed* by Mem Fox
- Other stories related to napping, rainbows, and rain

Bulletin Board

- Take photos of the children when they are awake and when they are pretending to be asleep. Divide the bulletin board with the headings *Napping* and *Awake*. The children tape their photos on the appropriate sides.

- Make a simple house out of paper with several windows. Children pick a window and attach a photo of themselves napping inside. Add the heading *Our Napping House*.

- Create a handprint rainbow to display on the board (see Week 1, Activity 5).

- Display the Rainbow Napping Quilt (see Week 1, Activity 3) on the board.

Week 1

Focus of the Week: Rainbows

Songs, Poems, and Fingerplays

<u>*I Wish That I Could Find Myself a Rainbow*</u>
(to the tune of "I Wish I Were an Oscar Mayer Wiener")

Oh I wish that I could find myself a rainbow,
I look for all the colors in the sky.
Red, orange, yellow, green, blue, and purple,
This is what I search for with my eyes.

....

Look for a version of "The Rainbow Connection" song to play during free play time.

Reading the Story

Introduce the book by discussing the title, author, and dedication. Discuss the book's cover and ask the children to guess what the book will be about.

Read the story every day and, as the children become familiar with it, gradually add in any of the following activities:

- When the rainbow appears at the end of the story, talk about the colors of the rainbow. Point a flashlight at different things in the classroom that have rainbow colors, discussing each color separately. For example, "Find something yellow . . ."

- Pause before reading the last word in a line. See if the children can fill in the blank. Or, substitute a nonsense word and see if the children catch the substitution.

- Give each child a rainbow-colored streamer to hold during the story reading (they could use their Rainbow Wands from Week 1, Activity 2). When the last page of the story is reached, the children wave their streamers overhead, dance around, and have a rainbow-streamer parade.

Group Activities

1. Weather Mobile

Target Areas: cognition, fine motor

What you need:
- White construction paper (enough for 4 shapes per child)
- Tempera paint in a rainbow of colors
- Paintbrushes
- Hole punch
- Yarn
- Clothes hangers (1 per child)

What you do:
1. Children (or the teacher) cut out shapes of the sun, clouds, rainbows, and lightening rods from the white construction paper (4 shapes per child).
2. Children paint each of their 4 shapes with the paint.
3. When the paints dry, punch holes in the top of each shape and thread yarn of different lengths through the holes.
4. Tie the children's painted shapes with the yarn to their hangers and hang their beautiful mobiles around the room.

2. Rainbow Wands

Target Areas: cognition, fine motor, gross motor

What you need:
- Ribbons in 6 rainbow colors
- Paper towel tubes (1 per child)
- Hole punch
- Music
- Dancing area

What you do:
1. Punch 6 holes around one end of each paper towel tube using the hole punch.
2. Give one tube to each child. Children then request a colored ribbon.
3. Help each child guide the ribbon through one of the holes on the end of the tube (wand) and tie it on.
4. Repeat with all the ribbons in all the colors of the rainbow.
5. Turn on some dancing music and dance with the rainbow wands. (We recommend "The World Is a Rainbow" by Greg & Steve in *We All Live Together, Volume 2,* Youngheart Records.)

3. Rainbow Napping Quilt

Target Areas: cognition, fine motor

What you need:

- 4" x 4" squares of patterned paper (scrapbook paper or wallpaper in rainbow colors) (4 squares per child)
- 8" x 8" squares of colored construction paper in rainbow colors (1 per child)
- Glue
- Scissors

What you do:

1. Talk about different shapes with the children. Describe and demonstrate how squares can be folded in half diagonally to make triangles.
2. Let the children choose 4 squares each from the patterned paper and fold them diagonally to make triangles.
3. Cut the squares on the folds. Children should now each have 8 triangles.
4. Hand out the construction paper squares. Children arrange the triangles back into squares, mixing up the patterns. Then they glue their triangles in their new arrangements onto the construction paper.
5. When all the quilt squares are complete, hang them up together to make a large quilt.

4. Floor Rainbows

Target Areas: cognition, fine motor

What you need:

- Colored cubes, building blocks, bears, or coins in red, orange, yellow, green, blue, and purple
- 2 large cloud shapes cut out of paper or cardboard
- Tape

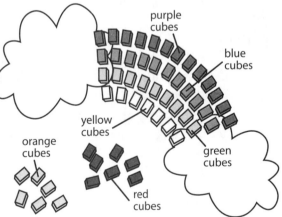

What you do:

1. Tape the clouds on the floor or table with enough space between to create a three-dimensional picture of the arc of a rainbow.
2. Create the rainbow arc out of the blocks, cubes, bears, or coins.

Optional: Children order the rainbow colors as they are in nature: from outside to inside, red, orange, yellow, green, blue, and purple.

5. Handprint Rainbow

Target Area: cognition

What you need:
- Paint—red, orange, yellow, green, blue, and purple
- Large piece of white paper

What you do:
1. Explain to the children that they will all be contributing their handprints to a big handprint rainbow.
2. Dip one child's hand into the purple paint and that child makes one purple handprint on the left side of the white paper.
3. Then the next child makes a purple handprint just to the right of the first child's, and so on, until all the children have made purple handprints to look like the arc of a rainbow.
4. Start over with the blue paint, making an arc above the purple arc, and continue until all the colors of the rainbow have been used (in order, from inside to outside: purple, blue, green, yellow, orange, red).
5. The end result is a colorful rainbow made from all the children's handprints.
6. Put the handprint rainbow up on the bulletin board.
7. At the end of the unit, donate the rainbow to a nursing home or hospital.

6. Squeegee Paint Pull

Target Areas: cognition, fine motor

What you need:
- Tempera paint in rainbow colors
- Window squeegee
- White or light blue paper

What you do:
1. Tape the paper to a table.
2. Drip several colors along the edge of the paper in the order of rainbow colors (see Week 1, Activity 5).
3. Pull the colors across the paper with the squeegee and see how they blend. (If a squeegee is not available, use the edge of a piece of cardboard).

Week 2

Focus of the Week: Napping

Songs, Poems, and Fingerplays

It's Raining, It's Pouring
It's raining, it's pouring,
The old man is snoring.
He went to bed and bumped his head
And couldn't get up in the morning.

Rain, Rain, Go Away
Rain, rain, go away.
Come again some other day.
All the children want to play!

Reading the Story

Read the story every day and gradually add in any of the following activities:

- Use the stuffed characters from Week 2, Activity 1 to act out the story.

- Make a simple bed shape out of paper and lay it on the floor. Give the children Popsicle stick puppets of the story characters to hold during the story reading. As their characters are mentioned, they lay their puppets on the bed or on top of the other characters.

Bed on the floor

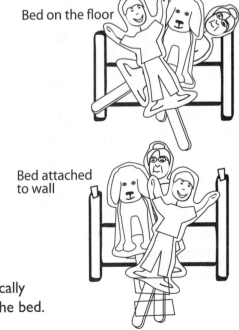

Bed attached to wall

- Make a simple bed out of construction paper glued onto a large piece of paper. Attach this whole scene to the wall or bulletin board before starting the story reading. As characters are mentioned during the story, children tape stick puppets of the characters—stacked vertically on top of each other—in the middle of the bed.

- Turn off as many lights as possible and tell the story by flashlight. Turn the lights on when the characters wake up and the sun comes out. Ask a child to be in charge of the lights.

- After reading the story, see if the children can tell the story in reverse order. Who is on the very top? Under that? And under that? . . . until they get to the empty bed. Use stick puppets to create the story backwards.

1. Puppet Stack
Target Areas: fine motor, social

What you need:
- Large paper or felt cutouts of the book's characters (2 cutouts of the same character per child)
- Fiberfill or cotton balls
- Stapler
- Glue
- Markers (plain or fabric)
- Decorations: yarn, buttons, foam cutouts, sequins, ribbon

What you do:
1. Each child decorates 2 cutouts (for a front and a back) of a character from the book with markers and decorations.
2. When the decorations dry, place the two sides of each character together and glue or staple them to make one character, leaving a small opening at the top.
3. Stuff the characters with fiberfill or cotton balls.
4. Close the openings and use the characters to act out the story.
5. Take turns stacking the characters and see how high they can go before the stack falls!

2. Sweet Dreams Pillowcases
Target Areas: cognition, communication, fine motor

What you need:
- White pillow cases (1 per child)
- Fabric paints in a variety of colors
- Sponge shapes for stamping
- Fabric markers

What you do:
1. Give each child a pillowcase.
2. Children use paints and sponges to decorate their pillowcases.
3. Write or assist children with writing their names on their pillowcases.
4. Let the pillowcases dry and then send them home with the children.

3. Mini Pillow Sachets
Target Areas: cognition, fine motor

What you need:
- Pairs of fabric or felt 4" x 4" squares cut out with regular or decorative scissors (1 pair per child)
- Fabric markers and/or fabric paint
- Stencils and/or sponge stamps
- Star-shaped or other decorative buttons
- Fiberfill
- Potpourri
- Needle and thread or sewing machine

What you do:
1. Give each child a pair of fabric squares. They decorate them with fabric paint, markers, stencils, or sponges.
2. When the paints dry, the children choose 1 or 2 buttons to sew on one piece of their fabric as decoration. Children help as much as possible.
3. With a sewing machine or by hand, sew around the edges of each pair of squares, leaving a small opening for stuffing.
4. The children fill their pillow sachets with fiberfill and a pinch of potpourri.
5. Sew the mini pillow sachets closed.
6. The children take their pillow sachets home to help them sleep.

4. Folding Blankets Relay
Target Areas: cognition, fine motor, social

What you need:
- Variety of blankets

What you do:
1. Demonstrate ways to fold blankets. Children then practice folding blankets.
2. Then divide the children into two teams and give each team one blanket.
3. In each team, one child folds the blanket and then hands it to the next child in the team. The next child unfolds the blanket, then folds it again and hands it to the next child. The sequence continues until all the children have had a chance to fold the blanket.
4. When all players on a team have folded the blanket once, the whole team gets under their blanket and pretends to be sleeping.

5. Napping Families

Target Areas: cognition, fine motor

What you need:

- Photocopied pictures or children's drawings of each child's family members (at least 5 per child—can include pets, dolls, and so on)
- Popsicle sticks
- Glue
- Sandwich baggies

What you do:

1. Give each child one Popsicle stick for every family member photo or drawing.
2. Children glue their photos and drawings onto the Popsicle sticks.
3. Act out *The Napping House* with each individual child's puppet family.
4. Send home the puppet families in sandwich baggies.

6. Slipper Match

Target Areas: cognition, gross motor

What you need:

- Variety of pairs of slippers
- Masking tape

What you do:

1. Divide the slippers into two piles—each pile having one slipper from each pair of slippers.
2. Make a line on the floor with masking tape. Line the children up along the line, and give each child one slipper from one of the piles of slippers.
3. Place the other pile of slippers (the matching slippers) in the center of the room.
4. Count to 3, and then the children put on their slipper and run to the pile in the center of the room and find their matching slippers.
5. Children put on their matching slippers (no matter how ill-fitting!) and run back to the line and sit down.

Note: Be sure that no children are allergic to strawberries before serving them in any of these snacks. As appropriate, substitute other fruits.

1. Serve a variety of rainbow-colored fruits and/or vegetables (strawberries, blueberries, kiwi fruit, carrots, tomatoes, corn, celery, and so forth).

2. Use an air popper to make rainbow-colored popcorn. Ask the children if they think the color will stay on the popcorn once it pops. When the popcorn is done, the children can cuddle up with a bowl of this yummy snack, a book, and a blanket and get ready for sleep.

3. Rainbow Fruit Salad

What you need:
- Purple grapes
- Blueberries
- Kiwi
- Oranges
- Mangoes
- Strawberries
- Large clear bowl to hold the salad

What you do:
Cut the fruit up and layer it in the bowl in the following rainbow order: strawberries, oranges, mangoes, kiwi, blueberries, and purple grapes.

Pretest and Posttest

The Napping House

Concepts	Pretest	Posttest
Rainbows		
Colors in a rainbow		
Rain		
Items used for napping		
The concept of *on*		
Family members		
Sleep-related words (*dozing, dreaming, snoring, waking, slumbering*)		

Five Little Monkeys Bake a Birthday Cake

(formerly *Don't Wake Up Mama!*)

By Eileen Christelow

The same five monkeys who jump on the bed and bump their heads are at it again, this time preparing a special birthday surprise for their sleeping mother. Chaos ensues as they bake (and burn) a cake, hammer together homemade gifts, and deal with the firefighters who come to help with the smoking oven. Somehow, Mama sleeps through it all, only to be awakened by the voices of her darling children singing "Happy Birthday." The fun never ends in this silly story.

Dear Families,

Remember the children's rhyme *Five Little Monkeys Jumping on the Bed*? You know, the monkeys that fall off the bed, bump their heads, and get into a bit of trouble with the mother? Well, those same five monkeys are getting into mischief again, this time while trying to secretly plan a birthday celebration for their sleeping mother. Anytime five little monkeys get together to make a birthday cake, you just know there's going to be trouble.

Our next storybook, *Five Little Monkeys Bake a Birthday Cake* by Nancy Christelow, is one in a series of Five Little Monkeys books that are all action packed and full of adventure. Along with *Five Little Monkeys Bake a Birthday Cake,* you'll want to check out as many other Five Little Monkeys books as you can from the library and laugh your way through them all.

From making a giant mess in the kitchen to creating homemade birthday cards and gifts and having the fire department come to help with the burning cake, the monkeys will keep the children endlessly entertained. Miraculously, Mama sleeps through it all (with the help of fuzzy earmuffs) and is only awakened by the sweet voices of her dear children singing "Happy Birthday." If she only knew . . .

Do you have any upcoming birthdays in your family? If so, do as the monkeys do (with a little less chaos) and make your own cake, card, and gift. Anything homemade is always appreciated. Practice singing "Happy Birthday" together. Better yet, make up your own version of the song to sing at family birthdays. Designate a short time during the day as "quiet time" when everyone whispers and walks around on tiptoes. Visit the fire station for a look at the big engines. This book provides endless opportunities for fun both at home and at school.

Gotta run—cake's burning!

Dramatic Play Area

- Set out slippers and robes of all sizes (ask families to send some); a bedroom with a small bed and a chest of drawers (the bed could be made out of a blow-up mattress, a sleeping bag, and some pillows); and earmuffs.

- Add a play kitchen area with a refrigerator, sink, and table. Put plastic food in the refrigerator and on the shelves. Include a bottle with the word *oil* written on it, some plastic eggs, and some flour for "cooking." Provide bowls, spoons, and pans.

Sensory Area

- Set out a variety of wrapped presents varying from light to heavy. The children can put them in order of weight.

- In the sensory table, start with flour for a couple of days. Throughout the unit add water and oil. Provide an eggbeater, mixing spoons, and a flour sifter.

Science Area

- Put out sealed bottles of oil and water mixed together with food coloring and floating objects. Children shake the bottles and watch what happens. (See Week 2, Activity 5).

- Provide several blank felt "cakes" along with felt candles, numbers, and decorations for putting on the cakes.

- Set out a Barrel of Monkeys game.

Art Area

- Provide a box filled with small boxes, scrap wrapping paper, gift bags, bows, tissue paper, scissors, and tape. Children practice wrapping presents.

- Put out white play dough for the children to make their own eggs. Provide empty egg cartons for safekeeping.

Five Little Monkeys Bake...

Book Area

- *Bedtime, Everybody!* by Mordicai Gerstein

- *Happy Birthday to You!* by Dr. Seuss

- *Shhhhh! Everybody's Sleeping* by Julie Markes, illustrated by David Parkins

- *Ten, Nine, Eight* by Molly Bang

- *Ten Out of Bed* by Penny Dale

- Any *Curious George* books by H.A. Rey

- Books by Eileen Christelow:

    Five Little Monkeys Jumping on the Bed

    Five Little Monkeys Play Hide-and-Seek

    Five Little Monkeys Sitting in a Tree

    Five Little Monkeys Wash the Car

    Five Little Monkeys with Nothing to Do

- Other books related to birthdays, baking, and monkeys

Bulletin Board

- Display children's drawings of their mamas and papas sleeping.

- Create a class birthday cakes exhibit: Display each child's name and birthday written on his or her own little cake.

- Attach Egg White Cakes (see Week 2, Activity 1) to the bulletin board.

Week 1

Focus of the Week: Sleeping, *noisy* and *quiet*

Circle Time

Songs, Poems, and Fingerplays

Five Little Monkeys Jumping on the Bed

Five little monkeys jumping on the bed,
One fell off and bumped (his/her) head.
Mama called the doctor and the doctor said:
"No more monkeys jumping on the bed!"

Continue to count down until there are no more monkeys on the bed.

Monkey See, Monkey Do
(to the tune of "Twinkle, Twinkle, Little Star")

Monkey see and monkey do.
What will (child's name) monkey do?

When the class sings a child's name, that child does a trick. The rest of the class imitates that child. Continue until each child has had a turn, encouraging the children to think of different tricks.

Are You Sleeping?
(to the tune of Frère Jacques)

Are you sleeping,
Are you sleeping,
Mama monkey, Mama monkey?
Little monkeys singing,
Little monkeys singing,
Happy Birthday, Happy Birthday!

<u>*Clap Your Hands*</u>
Clap, clap, clap your hands, as loudly as you can.
Clap, clap, clap your hands, as softly as you can.
Stomp, stomp, stomp your feet, as loudly as you can.
Stomp, stomp, stomp your feet, as softly as you can.

Continue with *pat your legs, snap your fingers,* or whatever the children suggest.

Reading the Story

Introduce the book by discussing the title, author, and dedication. Discuss the book's cover and ask the children to guess what the book will be about.

Read the story every day and, as the children become familiar with it, gradually add in any of the following activities:

- Give each child a prop for story time: earmuffs, oven mitts, bowls, mixing spoons, wood blocks, toy hammer, and plastic eggs. They use their props at the appropriate time during the story.

- Read the story in a whisper, incorporating fun sound effects as events occur in the story (cracking eggs, hammers banging, fire engine sirens, loud singing at the very end, and so forth).

- Children stand up and practice tiptoeing in place when the monkeys tiptoe in the story.

- Wear earmuffs while reading the story. The children take turns trying them on when the story is finished. Experiment: Can they hear whispering, normal talking, or loud singing through the earmuffs?

1. Let's Get Ready For Bed!
Target Areas: cognition, communication

What you need:
- A bed (see Dramatic Play Area)
- Toothbrushes (1 per child)
- Pajamas

- Books
- Slippers

What you do:

1. The teacher demonstrates all of the steps involved in going to bed. Add language to all of the steps so the children will know the vocabulary.
2. Explain why the order is what it is. Ask questions such as: Why do we put on our pajamas before we jump into the bed? (Try and put jammies on while under the covers!) Why do we brush our teeth in the bathroom? (Walk around the room dripping water and toothpaste on the floor.)
3. After the teacher has modeled all of the steps, the children go through the steps while explaining them using the vocabulary they just learned.

2. Lights Out, Little Monkeys
Target Areas: gross motor, social

What you need:

- Flashlights (1 per child)
- Mama monkey costume: earmuffs, a robe, Mama monkey ears (a paper headband with ears on it)

What you do:

1. One child is Mama monkey (wearing her costume). All of the other children have flashlights.
2. Turn out the lights.
3. Mama monkey walks quietly throughout the room dodging the flashlights.
4. Children all look for Mama monkey with their flashlights. When a child finds Mama monkey, he or she goes over to Mama and waits for all of the other children to arrive.
5. When everyone is together, sing "Happy Birthday" to Mama monkey.
6. Continue playing, with children taking turns being Mama monkey.

3. Turn Up the Music, Little Monkeys
Target Areas: fine motor, social

What you need:

- Mama monkey ears (See Week 1, Activity 2)
- Earmuffs
- **Wind chimes**—Punch holes out of

the rim of a pie tin, thread yarn through

the holes, and hang any of the following on the yarn: spoons, seashells, nails, pop tops, or bottle caps. Hang the chimes near an open window or fan.

- **Oatmeal box drums**—Decorate long strips of paper to wrap around the oatmeal box, using the lid as the top of the drum. Use spoons as drumsticks.
- **Maracas**—Fill 2 paper cups with beans and tape them together. Cover with aluminum foil and decorate with tissue paper.
- **Other noisemakers**: bubble wrap, horns, wooden sticks, and so forth (use your imagination!)

What you do:

1. Make and collect enough noisemakers/instruments for each child to have one.
2. Select someone to be the Mama monkey (he or she wears the ears and earmuffs). Mama tries to sleep throughout the chaos, trying to keep a "sleepy demeanor" as long as possible.
3. The rest of the children have their instruments ready. They stay at least 10 feet away from Mama monkey.
4. When someone says "Go," the children play their music. . . . Is it enough to wake up Mama?
5. Mama monkey waits for a short time, wakes up, and chases her little monkeys around the room!

4. Monkey Tunes

Target Areas: fine motor, gross motor, social

What you need:

- Large butcher paper taped to the walls
- Markers or crayons
- Tape or CD player
- Tape or CD of some lively music
- Mama monkey ears (see Week 1, Activity 2)
- Earmuffs

What you do:

1. Choose a child to be Mama monkey (wearing ears and earmuffs) and a child (or teacher) to be in charge of the music.
2. Mama pretends to be sleeping and the monkeys (children) try to be quiet.
3. Turn the music on, and the monkeys start coloring designs all over the paper.
4. After a while (the child playing Mama decides when), Mama slowly wakes up. Mama says, "Please turn off the music so I can take my nap!" The music is turned off, and the monkeys stop coloring.
5. Then Mama picks another child—someone who was being VERY quiet—to be the next Mama. Repeat steps 2 through 5 until all children have had a chance to be Mama.

5. Mama's in the Middle . . . Shhhhh!

Target Areas: communication, social

What you need:

- Large floor space
- Warm potato

What you do:

1. Children sit in a large circle.
2. Explain that they will be trying to move a warm potato around the circle without waking up Mama.
3. Choose a child to be Mama. Mama lies in the center of the circle pretending to be asleep. Children pass the potato around the circle quickly, but silently.
4. Mama decides when to wake up. When she does, the child holding the potato goes into the center and becomes the next Mama.

6. Sound Walk

Target Areas: cognition, fine motor

What you need:

- Old magazines
- Large piece of white paper
- Glue
- Scissors
- Clipboards (1 per child)
- Pencils
- White paper, 8 1/2" x 11" (1 piece per child)

What you do:

1. Discuss how some things make noise and other things do not.
2. Draw a line down the center of the large piece of paper. On one side write *Makes Noise* and on the other side write *Does Not Make Noise*.
3. Ask children to suggest ideas of things to draw on both sides of the paper. After a few examples, hand out the magazines.
4. Children look through the magazines and cut out various pictures.
5. The children glue their pictures on the appropriate sides of the paper.
6. After 5-10 minutes, bring the children back together for a discussion of the pictures.
7. Give each child a clipboard with a piece of paper. Explain that they are going to go on a Sound Walk. They need to be very quiet to hear the noises around them.
8. They each draw a line down the middle of the paper and copy the headings *Makes Noise* and *Does Not Make Noise*.
9. Walk around the school and listen. Remind them to draw pictures of things that do not make noise, not only to draw the noisy things!

Optional: Do this activity on two consecutive days (collage one day, sound walk the next day).

Week 2

Focus of the Week: Birthday parties

Songs, Poems, and Fingerplays

This Little Monkey
This little monkey ate bananas,
This little monkey ate peas,
This little monkey did a somersault,
This little monkey slapped her knees,
And this little monkey went "Ooh! Ooh! Ooh!"
Swinging through the trees.

......

Use a speakerphone to call a few popular family restaurants. Ask the staff person who answers to sing the special birthday song they sing to customers celebrating a birthday at their restaurant. Write down the words and sing these different birthday songs at circle time.

......

Sing the "Happy Birthday" tune in monkey language ("Oo-oo Oo-oo Ooo-oo")!

......

Teach the "Happy Birthday" song in sign language.

Happy   **birthday**   **to**   **you**   **dear**   **Mama**

Reading the Story

Read the story every day and gradually add in any of the following activities:

- Create a storytelling glove using a glove and five felt monkeys attached with Velcro to each finger and the thumb. Make these monkeys tiptoe, stir the cake batter, write on birthday cards, and dance while singing. The children can take a turn wearing the glove after the story reading.

- Bring out surprise birthday hats and party blowers at the end of the story. Celebrate with Mama, then move into the class snack time and a party of your own.

Monkey Glove Template

- Designate five children to be the monkeys. They can act out the scenes as they occur in the book. Switch to five new monkeys halfway through, or as many times as necessary to allow all the children to participate.

1. Egg White Cakes

Target Areas: cognition, fine motor

What you need:
- Several "birthday cakes" cut out of white poster board (or thick paper)
- 1 dozen eggs
- Food coloring
- Painting dishes (bowls)
- Paintbrushes
- Smocks

What you do:
1. Separate the yolks from the egg whites. Put egg whites into several painting dishes.
2. Explain to the children they are *not* to eat the egg whites.
3. Add several drops of food coloring to the egg whites in each dish—one color per dish. Mix with a paintbrush.

4. Children use paintbrushes to decorate the paper cakes with the egg-white paints.
5. The paint will be slimy, but when it is dry, it will be shiny and beautiful!
6. Put the cakes up on the bulletin board.

2. That's a Wrap!

Target Areas: cognition, fine motor

What you need:

- Several rolls of birthday wrapping paper
- Variety of bows and ribbons
- Children's scissors (1 pair per child)
- Lots of scotch tape
- Pieces of children's artwork or objects made in class to give as gifts (1 per child)
- Boxes suitable for the gifts (1 per child)

What you do:

1. Demonstrate (while explaining, step by step) how to wrap a present. Emphasize going slowly and using only a small amount of tape. Show how to rip the tape off of the dispenser.
2. Children decide which boxes would best fit their presents.
3. Children select the wrapping papers they would like to use.
4. While the children are wrapping their presents, the teacher walks around and reminds them of the steps of present wrapping.
5. When their presents are wrapped, children choose and attach bows and ribbons to their gifts.

3. Better than Hallmark

Target Areas: cognition, fine motor

What you need:

- Card stock in a variety of colors
- Marbles
- Salad tongs
- Drinking straws
- Sponges in different shapes
- Box lid or baking pan
- Magazines
- Tempera and watercolor paint in a variety of colors

- Paintbrushes
- Scissors
- Glue

What you do:

1. Demonstrate five different ways to decorate a card:

   Watercolor painting—Paint a lovely, flowing picture on the card stock paper.

   Marble painting—Put card stock paper in the lid of a box or in a baking pan, use tongs to dip marbles into the paint, then drop the marbles onto the paper and jiggle the lid/pan around. Watch the marbles make a beautiful design.

   Blow painting—Drop small piles of paint onto the card stock paper. Use a straw to blow the paint around in different directions.

   Sponge painting—Dip sponges into the paint and press them onto the card stock paper.

   Collage—Cut out a variety of pictures from magazines and glue them all together on the card stock paper in any chosen design.

2. Establish five areas, each with the necessary materials for one of the ways of decorating cards.

3. Children pick which type of card they would like to make and go to the appropriate areas.

4. When the cards are dry, the children dictate what they want written as a greeting, and sign their names. Or, alternatively, they can copy the words *Happy Birthday* onto their cards themselves.

5. Attach their cards to the presents they wrapped (Week 2, Activity 2). They can give their gifts to anyone they choose (and it doesn't even need to be the recipient's birthday!).

4. Birthday Cake Hats

Target Areas: cognition, communication, fine motor

What you need:

- 3"-wide paper strips that will fit around a child's head (1 per child)
- Marking pens
- Candles cut out of paper (enough for all children to have as many as the number of years old they are)
- Glitter
- Glue
- Stapler
- Transparent tape
- Index cards with children's birthdays written on them (1 per child)

What you do:

1. Pass out the strips and the index cards to the children.
2. Children write their names and copy their birthdays onto the strips.
3. Ask the children how old they are. Give them the appropriate number of paper candles. They decorate their candles with glitter and tape them onto their strips.
4. Staple the strips together into "hats." The children put on their hats and march around showing off their Birthday Cake Hats.

5. Oil and Water Just Don't Mix!

Target Areas: cognition, communication

What you need:

- Large, clear pitcher
- Water
- Vegetable oil
- Super glue
- Several clear 2-liter plastic bottles
- Small items such as plastic toys, ribbons, beads, glitter, and plastic animals (monkeys, if possible)

What you do:

1. Fill the pitcher half full with water.
2. Open the oil and let the children touch it and smell it. Show them the page in the story where the monkeys spill the oil.
3. Ask the children what they think will happen when the oil is poured into the water. Write down any suggestions on the board.

4. Pour the oil into the water so that the mixture is half water, half oil. Children describe what happened.

5. Pour the concoction into clear 2-liter bottles. Add glitter, small plastic toys, ribbons, and beads. Super glue the tops on the bottles.

6. Children shake the bottles and watch what happens. They describe what they see. It's a birthday party inside of the bottle!

7. Leave the bottles in the Science Area for further exploration.

Alternative: This activity could be done with smaller plastic bottles so each child could make his or her own to take home.

6. Goop

Target Areas: cognition, communication

What you need:
- Cornstarch
- Water
- Cake decorations made of sugar
- Small tubes of frosting
- Small cake or cupcake tins
- Small plastic items (monkeys, candles, food, small firefighters)

What you do:
1. Explain to the children that they will be making something goopy like the monkeys' goopy cake batter.

2. Pour some cornstarch in a bowl or on the tabletop. Let the children touch it and describe how it feels.

3. Start adding drops of water. Let the children continue to manipulate it until the texture has changed completely. The goal is for the goop to feel wet to the touch, but when picked up it becomes more solid.

4. Children transfer the goop to the small tins (as well as they can).

6. Encourage the children to let the goop run through their fingers. They can use tools to cut through it and poke it. (Make sure they don't eat it.)

7. Experimenting and mixing to see what happens, children add small plastic toys to the goop. They use tubes of frosting to add color and add sugar decorations to their wonderful cakes!

8. The teacher compliments them and they compliment each other on what great chefs they are!

Additional Activities

What's That Sound?
Behind a screen, have a variety of objects that can be used to make noise. The children take turns going behind the screen and making noise with an object while the other children guess what the object is. Some ideas for noisemakers are: a boingy rubber band, a stapling stapler, a fluttering pad of paper, some crinkling cellophane, a book opening and closing, a zipper going up and down.

When Is My Birthday?
The teacher has a reference list of all the children's birthdays. The teacher and the children go through a wall calendar together and, as the appropriate months appear, the children (with prompting from the teacher) come up and write their names on their birthday squares. Discuss the different months of the year. What might be happening outside on the different birthdays (snow, flowers blooming, sunshine, rain)?

Birthday Candles
Put some old birthday cards that have large numbers showing the ages (for example, *You're 5 today!*) in a paper bag. The children take turns picking out a card, secretly reading it, and counting out the number of candles that correspond to the number on the card. They put the candles into holes in a 3/4"- to 1"-thick piece of wood cut and painted to look like a birthday cake (with 10 holes for candles drilled partway into the wood with a 3/8" drill bit). The "birthday child" says, "Guess how old I am today!" The other children say how old their classmate is by exclaiming, for example, "Happy Birthday! You are three!"

Snacks

1. Throw a Birthday Party!! Either make cupcakes at school, or buy them from the store. Have hats, balloons, the whole shebang! Don't forget to blow out the candles (fake) and sing the song!

2. Noisy vs. Quiet Foods

What you need:
- Crunchy items: carrots, potato chips, celery sticks, apple wedges, crackers
- Quiet items: bananas, yogurt, applesauce, Jell-O

What you do:

Pass out the crunchy items first. Children taste them. Note how noisy they are. Pass out the quiet foods. Now children taste them. Note how quiet they are. Ask the children which would be better to eat when you are trying to be quiet?

crunchy

quiet

3. Party Gift Bags

Children each add ingredients for a Party Mix to a large bowl: raisins, pretzels, crackers, dried fruits, and cereal. Using a scoop, fill up a party gift bag to send home with each child.

4. Using an ice cream maker, follow the directions to make frozen yogurt—a perfect treat for a birthday party!

Pretest and Posttest

Five Little Monkeys Bake a Birthday Cake

Concepts	Pretest	Posttest
When is your birthday? (month, day, year)		
Steps in making a cake		
Steps in wrapping a gift		
Things that are "noisy"		
Things that are "quiet"		
Getting ready for bed		

The Very Hungry Caterpillar

By Eric Carle

This artfully illustrated storybook is about a caterpillar's metamorphosis into a magnificent butterfly. The children follow along as the tiny, insatiable caterpillar spends a week eating his way through a huge quantity of food, culminating in an uncomfortable stomachache. A healthy green leaf helps calm the queasy stomach, and the now big caterpillar spins a cozy cocoon to rest in. Children never tire of the last-page surprise—a gorgeous butterfly. Many concepts are covered in this very popular children's book including counting, days of the week, excessive eating, and of course metamorphosis.

Dear Families,

The metamorphosis from caterpillar to butterfly is truly amazing to watch, both in real life and in our next story, *The Very Hungry Caterpillar* by Eric Carle. This story is a long-standing favorite for many reasons: The pictures are beautiful, the little caterpillar is quite funny as it eats through pages and pages of food, the related activities are endless, and the reader learns so much from it!

Eric Carle is a very accomplished children's book author, and we're sure you'll find several of his stories, including this one, at the library or even at used bookstores. See if you can find *The Very Quiet Cricket; The Grouchy Ladybug; The Very Busy Spider;* and *Brown Bear, Brown Bear, What Do You See?* Keep your eyes out for other caterpillar and butterfly stories as well. We especially enjoy *Caterpillar's Wish* by Mary Murphy, *I'm a Caterpillar* by Jean Marzollo, and *The Color of My Wings: A Lace & Learn Book* by Linda Williams Aber.

We'll use this story to teach about counting, food, and the sequence of the stages of this insect's life. Consider creating a caterpillar garden of your own. Library books or a quick Internet search will give you an outline of how to do it to ensure a fun experience. Your caterpillar may not become a butterfly right before your eyes, but it will still be fun to watch for a few days. Pretend with your child that you are caterpillars searching for food and growing bigger and bigger until you finally fall asleep and then wake up as beautiful butterflies. Find a simple calendar to put on your wall at your child's eye level and talk about the days of the week and special upcoming events. Expand the conversation to include vocabulary related to months and seasons. The concepts may be too hard for your child to fully understand right now, but it's still important to introduce new vocabulary and concepts all the time.

Time to flutter off,

Room Setup

Dramatic Play Area

- Set out a blanket or sleeping bag (cocoon), butterfly wings, and caterpillar antennae for role-playing. Also provide plastic items (fruit, other foods, leaves) for the caterpillars to pretend to eat.

- Using a large collapsible tunnel set on end, the children pretend to wrap and unwrap themselves in a cocoon.

Sensory Area

- Place a piece of artificial grass cut to size or a few green grass doormats in the bottom of the sensory table. Add a few toy caterpillars, butterflies, and food items that are mentioned in the story. Provide tweezers and magnifying glasses for examining the small creatures.

Science Area

- Grow a Chia Pet as a large group activity. Monitor the growth with the class on a daily or weekly basis.

- Create a butterfly garden and watch the pupae turn into butterflies. Butterfly kits can be found at science stores and online. They come with directions.

- Set up an insect farm that includes live ladybugs, caterpillars, ants, and any other insects found in your area. Provide magnifying glasses for extra-close observations. Teach the children about the food and care requirements of insects, and about careful handling. Help them return the insects to their outdoor homes after a short time in the farm.

- Create a "living" fuzzy caterpillar: Fill a knee-high stocking with potting soil mixed with grass seed. Close the end of the stocking with a rubber band. Wrap different-colored hair ties around the stocking to create the caterpillar's body segments. Place the stocking-caterpillar on a plate and set it in a sunny spot. Water it regularly using a spray bottle. Grass should begin to grow, creating a fuzzy little caterpillar. Toy facial features from a Mr. Potato Head can be added to create a face.

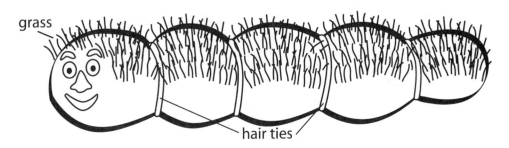

grass

hair ties

Art Area

- Children make coffee filter butterflies: Provide small containers of food coloring mixed with water or liquid watercolors in various colors, or watercolor markers; square or rectangular coffee filters; eyedroppers; spray bottles filled with water; twist ties; paper clips; and colored pipe clearers. Children create butterfly wings one of three ways:
  1. Squeeze drops of the food coloring mix or liquid watercolor onto the coffee filters and create a design with the various colors.
  2. Fold the coffee filters and dip them into the liquid colors. Unfold some great designs.
  3. Color the filters with watercolor markers and then spray them with water.
  Hang the filters to dry. When they are dry, use twist ties, tied or cinched around the middle, for the butterfly bodies.

- Put out 10 large white circles cut from heavy paper, yellow and green tempera paint, containers to hold the paint, newspapers, and a wide variety of objects to use as painting tools (fun-looking kitchen gadgets, cleaning tools, toothbrushes, flyswatters, toilet plungers, or tools you make yourself). Children use the tools to cover the circles with painted designs. When dry, staple the circles together in pairs, leaving an opening, and let the children help stuff them with crumpled newspaper. Close the opening with staples. Tape on black paper feet and antennae, and use yarn to hang the circles in a row from the ceiling to make a big, long class caterpillar.

- Set out small plastic snack bags that close on the top, various colors of cut up tissue paper, and twist ties, paper clips, and pipe cleaners. Children choose the colors they want in their butterfly wings and put tissue paper of those colors into the plastic bags. They close the bags, cinch them in the middle (from top to bottom) with twist ties, paper clips, or pipe cleaners, and a beautiful butterfly appears! Add a small magnet to the back for a nice gift to send home.

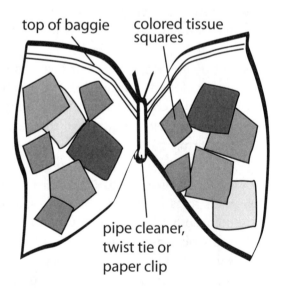

top of baggie   colored tissue squares

pipe cleaner, twist tie or paper clip

Book Area

- *Caterpillar's Wish* by Mary Murphy
- *The Color of My Wings: A Lace & Learn Book* by Linda Williams Aber, illustrated by Peggy Tagel
- *Gregory the Terrible Eater* by Mitchell Sharmat, illustrated by Jose Aruego
- *I'm a Caterpillar* by Jean Marzollo, illustrated by Judith Moffatt
- *The Picnic* by Kana Riley
- *Potluck* by Anne Shelby, illustrated by Irene Trivas
- Other books by Eric Carle
- Other stories related to caterpillars, butterflies, days of the week, and eating

Bulletin Board

- Glue a picture of each child's face onto a separate green-paper circle frame. Put them all together in a row to create a classroom caterpillar.

- Make an outline of a tree with large branches as the focus. Add caterpillars, cocoons, and butterflies as they are completed during the two weeks' activities.

Other

- Bring in plants from home to display around the room.

Week 1

Focus of the Week: Caterpillars and fruits

Songs, Poems, and Fingerplays

<u>Caterpillar, Caterpillar</u>
(to the tune of "Teddy Bear, Teddy Bear, Turn Around")

Caterpillar, caterpillar, turn around. (turn around)
Caterpillar, caterpillar, touch the ground. (touch the ground)
Caterpillar, caterpillar, make your cocoon. (roll into a ball)
Caterpillar, caterpillar, you'll be a butterfly soon! (flap wings)

<u>The Itsy Bitsy Caterpillar</u>
(to the tune of "Itsy Bitsy Spider")

The itsy bitsy caterpillar
Ate and ate, but soon . . .
It got so very tired
So spun a nice cocoon.
It spun and it spun
And when its nap was done,
A happy butterfly was floating in the sun!

Reading the Story

Introduce the book by discussing the title, author, and dedication. Discuss the book's cover and ask the children to guess what the book will be about.

Read the story every day and, as the children become familiar with it, gradually add in any of the following activities:

- Draw and cut out small pictures of caterpillars and of the different foods used in the story. Laminate them for use in a variety of the activities in this unit. Lay the pictures on the floor as they are named in the story.

- Put the small laminated fruit pictures (see previous activity) in paper lunch bags with the corresponding numbers written on the bags (one apple in a bag with a *1*, two

pears in a bag with a 2, and so on). Hand out the bags to the children as they sit in the circle. Depending on the class size, children may share bags or the teacher can create more than one bag per fruit. As the story is read, each child holds up his or her bag when the corresponding fruit is named. Then all the children help count the fruits as they are removed from the bag.

- Make a caterpillar using a tube (potato chip can). Cover the can with a piece of green construction paper. Add some black construction paper eyes on the plastic lid and construction paper antennae above the eyes. Cut a hole in the plastic lid for a mouth big enough for the small laminated food pictures (see previous activity) to fit through. At story time, pass out the food pictures to the children. As the story is read, the children can feed the caterpillar.

- Put three tennis balls into a green sock. Use colored rubber bands to separate the body parts. Draw on eyes, nose, and mouth with a felt tip marker and glue on cotton swabs for antennae. This caterpillar can sit in a chair at story time.

1. Caterpillar Headbands
Target Area: fine motor

What you need:
- 8" x 10" colored paper, each sheet with 4 circles drawn on (1 sheet per child)
- Long strips of paper, large enough to be a child's headband (1 strip per child)
- Cotton swabs cut in half (2 halves per child)
- Markers
- Glue
- Glitter
- Scissors

What you do:
1. Children cut out the circles from the colored paper, decorate them, and attach them to the long strips (their headbands).
2. Dip the cotton ends of the swabs in glue, then dip them in some glitter.
3. Glue the cotton swabs to the first circle (head of the caterpillar) for antennae.

2. Shaving Cream Fruit

Target Areas: cognition, fine motor

What you need:

- Large pieces of durable white paper
- Shaving cream
- Powdered tempera paint—red, yellow or green, blue or purple, and orange
- Aprons

What you do:

1. Make large fruit shapes out of the white paper. Make multiple copies of each of the five fruits in the story. It's a good idea to make enough shapes to have a classroom set (1 apple, 2 pears, 3 plums . . .) for display.
2. Each child chooses a shape to paint. Talk about the colors of the fruits in the book, and then the children choose a color from the paint colors.
3. Lay the chosen shape on the table and sprinkle some powdered tempera on top.
4. Children help spray the shaving cream on the shape.
5. Using their hands, the children mix the tempera with the shaving cream and spread it all around the shape. Be sure to comment on the colors of the tempera and the shaving cream before and after they mix them together. Hang to dry.
6. Cut a small circle out of each fruit shape to create the hole the caterpillar made.

3. Caterpillar Tag

Target Areas: gross motor, social

What you need:

- Large area to move around in

What you do:

1. Children stand in a line. Each child puts his or her hands on the waist of the child in front.
2. The first child is the head of the caterpillar and the last child is the end.
3. The head tries to touch the end without the other children in the middle letting go of each other.
4. When the head touches the end, then the game stops, the head goes to the end, and everyone moves up in the line. The new head takes his or her turn at trying to touch the end.
5. The game continues until each child has had a turn being the head.
6. If necessary, put a 1-minute time limit on each child's turn.

4. Apple Prints

Target Areas: cognition, fine motor

What you need:

- Sponge pieces or paintbrushes
- Paper
- Red and green tempera paint
- Paper towels
- Apples sliced in half through the middle to show the "star" (pattern in the core)

What you do:

1. Pat the sliced apples dry with a paper towel.
2. Use the sponge pieces or paintbrushes to apply paint to the flat, cut surface of the apples and then press them on the paper.
3. If it is easier, dip the apple in the paint, blot on a damp towel, and print.

5. Egg Yolk Fruits

Target Area: fine motor

What you need:

- Large paper shapes of the various fruits in the story
- 3–4 egg yolks
- Food coloring or liquid watercolor in 3–4 different colors
- 3–4 small containers
- Paintbrushes

What you do:

1. Children mix the egg yolks with each of the colors in separate small containers.
2. Divide children into groups and give each group a fruit shape and a paint mixture.
3. Children paint the fruit, and then allow it time to dry with a glossy finish.
4. Hang the fruits around the room to add to the caterpillar décor.

6. Rocky the Caterpillar

Target Area: fine motor

What you need:

- Large quantity of small smooth rocks
- Tempera paint in a variety of colors
- Googly eyes (1 pair per child)
- Glue
- Paintbrushes

What you do:

1. Each child chooses 3 to 5 rocks and paints the rocks each a different color.
2. When dry, glue googly eyes on one rock.
3. Set out the painted rocks in a line to create a caterpillar.

Week 2

Focus of the Week: Butterflies and metamorphosis

Songs, Poems, and Fingerplays

Big Butterfly
(to the tune of "Happy Birthday")

Look up in the sky,
A big butterfly!
It floats way up high,
That big butterfly!

Little Caterpillar
(to the tune of "Little Bunny Foo-Foo")

Little caterpillar crawling up a tree,
Eating all the nice green leaves that she can see.
Then comes a big cocoon,
And, finally . . .
Big butterfly floating on the breeze,
Showing off her lovely wings for everyone to see.

Reading the Story

Read the story every day and gradually add in any of the following activities:

- Give each child a laminated picture of a caterpillar and begin telling the story. The children curl into balls on the floor and "hatch" as the caterpillar does at the beginning of the story. Using their caterpillar pictures, they eat their way through each of the foods (use the classroom set of laminated food pictures—see Week 1, Reading the Story). Have a piece of lettuce available for them to nibble on before weaving their cocoon. They then climb into large boxes or under sheets and fall asleep inside their cocoons. Include colored scarves inside the cocoons for the children to use as wings when they climb out as butterflies.

- Use the Snack Bag Butterflies from the Art Area activity and attach them with rubber bands to unsharpened pencils or sticks. The children hold these behind their backs to bring out at the end of the story.

- Give each child a card with Velcro on the back and a picture of the caterpillar in one of its four life stages on the front. As the story is read and the caterpillar reaches (or is in) each life stage, the children with the appropriate card come up and put their cards on the flannel board.

1. Metamorphosis Relay
Target Areas: gross motor, social

What you need:
- 4 or more rolls of toilet paper
- 4 colored scarves
- Lively music on a CD or tape
- Large area to move around in

What you do:
1. Divide the class into two teams.
2. Send half of each team across the room, creating four lines, each with the same number of children.
3. The first child in each line on one side of the room holds two colorful scarves. The second child in those same lines holds a roll of toilet paper.
4. When the teacher says "Metamorphosis begin!" the two children with the toilet paper wrap up the children in front of them (with the scarves) in the toilet paper, as if they were in cocoons. (Four children are "in motion" at once.)
5. Once a child is wrapped up, his or her team counts to 5, and then the beautiful butterfly breaks out of the cocoon, fluttering its wings (the scarves).
6. When both butterflies are out, they run across the room to the other halves of their teams and hand the butterfly scarves to the first children in those lines. The second child in those lines is given a roll of toilet paper.
7. This continues until everyone has metamorphosed.

Note: For added excitement, play lively music while the relay is happening.

2. Shoe Flies

Target Area: fine motor

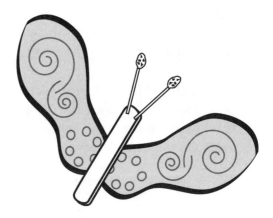

What you need:

- Paper
- Pencils or black markers
- Cotton swabs cut so just the cotton tip and 1/2" of the stick remain
- Glue
- Glitter
- Tongue depressors or Popsicle sticks
- Colored markers or watercolors

What you do:

1. Children stand on a piece of paper with the toes of their shoes pointing outwards and the heels touching each other.
2. Children trace around their shoes.
3. They glue a Popsicle stick (or tongue depressor) on the paper between the shoes to create the body of the butterfly.
4. Children decorate the butterfly with the watercolors or markers.
5. Dip the cotton swabs in glue, rub them in glitter, and attach them to the butterfly as antennae.

Optional: Children can also make Hand Flies, using their traced hands instead of shoes.

3. Bug Hunt

Target Areas: cognition, communication, gross motor

What you need:

- Plastic or rubber insects (at least 2 per child)
- Objects to make an obstacle course: tables to crawl under and over, slides to go down, tunnels to crawl through, boxes to climb in and out of, and so on

What you do:

1. Set up an obstacle course in the room for children to follow.
2. Hide the bugs where the children can find them easily in many places along the obstacle course as well as in other parts of the room.
3. Children try to find the bugs. Guide them through the obstacle course (through tunnels, over the chairs, and so on) and encourage them to hunt throughout the room.
4. Children bring back 2 bugs each and report on where they found them ("I found this caterpillar under the chair").

4. Butterfly Dancing

Target Area: gross motor

What you need:

- Multicolored scarves, handkerchiefs, or fabric pieces
- Music
- Large area to dance and move around in

What you do:

1. Each child chooses a scarf and holds it with both hands behind his or her back like a cape.
2. Turn on the music and encourage the children to dance and flutter around the room like butterflies.
3. Provide different options for dancing: stop and go dancing while turning the music off and on, fast/slow dancing, spinning, or leaping.

5. Symmetrical Butterfly Wings

Target Areas: cognition, fine motor

What you need:

- Large poster-size precut symmetrical butterfly-shaped paper (1 per child)
- Multiple colors of tempera paints
- Paintbrushes

What you do:

1. Give each child a butterfly shape and a paintbrush.
2. Children fold their butterflies down the middle, make a crease, then open them up again.
3. Children then paint on one half of the wings, stopping at the crease.
4. While the paint is still wet, children fold the other wing over and on top of the painted wing and press down.
5. Open the paper to see a beautiful symmetrical butterfly!

6. Crayon Melt Butterflies
Target Area: fine motor

What you need:
- Variety of broken crayons
- Iron
- Oven mitts
- Multicolored paper butterfly frames (cut out a large shape of a butterfly, then cut out the inside to create a frame) (1 per child)
- Waxed paper in pieces larger than the butterfly frames (2 pieces per child)
- Scissors
- Stapler

What you do:

1. Turn the iron on a low setting and set it away from the children's reach.
2. Children sprinkle broken crayon bits on one piece of waxed paper and cover it with their other piece of waxed paper.
3. One at a time, assist the children with placing the iron on their waxed paper and ironing. Children can wear oven mitts for protection.
4. Discuss what the crayons looked like before and after ironing. Comment on the colors and shapes of the crayons.
5. When all the crayon projects have been ironed, cover each with a butterfly frame and staple together the frame and crayon project.
6. Trim edges if needed, and hang the butterflies around the room.

Note: Be sure no children are allergic to strawberries or peanuts before serving snacks with these items. As appropriate, substitute other fruits, almond butter, or another sandwich spread.

1. Serve the fruits from the story.

2. Make butterfly-shaped peanut butter sandwiches using a butterfly cookie cutter.

3. Fresh Squeezed Orange Juice

What you need:
- Electric juicer (shop thrift stores!)
- Oranges sliced in half
- Bowl for juice
- Cups (1 per child)

What you do:

Give each child an opportunity to hold an orange on the juicer. This requires some concentration and the ability to hold the orange while the base moves. Adult supervision is necessary. Direct the children to observe the juice as it flows into the bowl. When finished, compare the oranges that were juiced to those that weren't. Pour the juice into a cup and let the children enjoy.

Note: If an electric juicer is not available, use a hand juicer instead.

4. Strawberry Ice

What you need:
- Ice cubes
- Strawberries (fresh or frozen)
- 1/2 c. frozen lemonade concentrate
- 1/2 c. water
- Blender

What you do:

Children put all the ingredients into the blender. Blend and enjoy!

5. Strawberry Milkshakes

What you need:
- Strawberries, whole (4 per child)
- Vanilla frozen yogurt
- Milk
- Ziplock baggies (1 per child)
- Large bowl
- Paper or plastic cups (1 per child)

What you do:
1. Put all the strawberries in a bowl. Give each child a ziplock baggie.
2. Ask the children how many strawberries the caterpillar ate through in the book. Let them take out the same amount from the bowl and put them in their baggie, counting as they do so.

3. Pour a small amount of milk into a cup and help each child pour it into his or her baggie.
4. Add a scoop of frozen yogurt to each baggie and help the children seal them.
5. Children squish and squeeze the baggies to mix the contents.
6. They open the baggies, pour the contents into their cups, and enjoy!

6. Fruit Salad

What you need:
- Each of the fruits in the same amount as in the book (1 apple, 2 pears, 3 plums, and so on)
- Plastic knives (1 per child)
- Mixing bowl and large spoon
- Cutting boards

What you do:
1. The children choose fruits and chop them up. (Peel fruit to make cutting easier.)
2. Place the cut fruit in the large bowl and mix.
3. Serve to everyone and enjoy, just like the caterpillar!

7. Grape Skewer Caterpillars

What you need:
- Wooden shish-kabob skewers (1 per child)
- Large bunch of green grapes
- Jelly or peanut butter
- Box of toothpicks

What you do:
1. Give each child a skewer.
2. Children stick the grapes onto their skewers until the skewers are full.
3. Add toothpicks as the antennae for the caterpillar, and add small dots of jelly or peanut butter for the eyes.

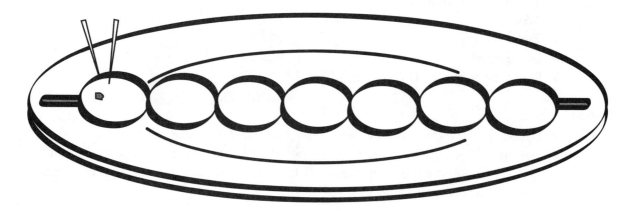

Pretest and Posttest

The Very Hungry Caterpillar

Concepts	Pretest	Posttest
Four stages of metamorphosis		
Caterpillars		
Butterflies		
Fruits (apple, orange, strawberry, plum, pear)		
Healthy eating		
Days of the week		
Counting 1–5		
Colors (of butterflies and caterpillars)		

Notes

Grow Flower, Grow!

(formerly *Fran's Flower*)

By Lisa Bruce
Illustrated by Rosalind Beardshaw

This is a fun springtime story about a little girl's initial excitement and eventual frustration as she tries to grow a flower. After numerous attempts to feed the tiny stem all of her favorite foods in hopes that it will grow, Fran finally gives up and tosses the pot out the window. With a little help from nature, her flower eventually grows into the most beautiful flower ever.

Dear Families,

Is it happening at your house yet? Are those tiny little signs appearing that let us know spring is just around the corner? Birds chirping? Trees sprouting tiny buds and leaves? At school, we are anxiously waiting for the spring flowers to poke their heads out of the ground and start blooming, which is why our next book is sure to be a favorite. *Grow Flower, Grow!* by Lisa Bruce is the funny story of little Fran and her dog Fred, who try desperately to get a flower to grow by feeding it Fran's favorite foods. Not until Fran becomes frustrated and throws the plant outside does she see what plants really need to grow tall and healthy.

We'll be spending our time digging, watering, planting, and (we hope) watching things grow over the next few weeks. We'll experiment together and, most likely, make some mistakes we can learn from.

You can extend school activities at home by having your child help water and re-pot your house and garden plants. Take special notice of springtime plants that are starting to appear and check their growth each day. Or pick a specific flower to photograph as it grows. Compile the photos into a sequence book with captions. Make a growth chart at home to periodically check your child's height through the years and explain the things that children need to grow tall and healthy. And feel free to think of your own activities to try out and to share with us!

Be sure to visit the library, which has loads of stories related to growing plants. In addition to *Grow Flower, Grow!* see if you can find *The Carrot Seed* by Ruth Krauss, *The Tiny Seed* by Eric Carle, and *Mrs. McNosh and the Great Big Squash* by Sarah Weeks.

Enjoy the flowers,

Room Setup

Dramatic Play Area

- Supply gardening aprons, gloves, sun hats, and other gardening items or supplies for the children to play dress-up with.

- Set up a play kitchen stocked with plastic foods related to the story or other children's favorites.

Sensory Area

- Fill the sensory table with potting soil, small plastic pots, and scoops. After a few days, add some small plants, some seeds, and spray bottles. Children plant the seeds and spray them and the plants regularly.

Science Area

- Provide a magnifying glass, whole and split seeds, soil, clipboards, paper, and pens so the children can examine and draw what they see.

Art Area

- Provide supplies (watercolors, other paints, markers, crayons) and various pictures related to plants and flowers for the children to paint and color. Supply cardboard flowers in a variety of shapes for the children to practice tracing.

- Lay out flower-shaped sponges and paints along with various sizes of blank paper.

Book Area

- *The Carrot Seed* by Ruth Krauss, illustrated by Crockett Johnson
- *Dinofours, My Seeds Won't Grow* by Steve Metzger, illustrated by Hans Wilhelm
- *The Enormous Carrot* by Vladimir Vasilevich Vagin
- *Flora's Surprise* by Debi Gliori
- *Mrs. McNosh and the Great Big Squash* by Sarah Weeks, illustrated by Nadine Bernard
- *The Stubborn Pumpkin* by Laura Geringer, illustrated by Holly Berry
- *The Tiny Seed* by Eric Carle
- Other books related to plants, flowers, and gardening; and seed catalogs

Bulletin Board

- On a white background add the heading *How Does Our Garden Grow?* Attach pictures of the sun, rain, and empty flowerpots. Add plant pictures as children complete them. Add words as children describe their art (*Samuel's pink rose, Kelly's tall sunflower*).

- Display the children's Watch It Grow! sequence cards (see Week 1, Activity 3).

Week 1

Focus of the Week: Growing and seeds

Circle Time

Songs, Poems, and Fingerplays

In Our Pretty Garden Green
(to the tune of "Here We Go 'Round the Mulberry Bush")

This is how we plant a bean,
In our garden, in our garden.
This is how we plant a bean,
In our pretty garden green.
(dig a hole in the ground)

Now we plant it with our foot,
In our garden, in our garden.
Now we plant it with our foot,
In our pretty garden green.
(while standing, "plant" bean with foot)

Now we plant it with our elbow,
In our garden, in our garden.
Now we plant it with our elbow,
In our pretty garden green.
(crouch down and "plant" bean with elbow)

Now we plant it with our knee,
In our garden, in our garden.
Now we plant it with our knee,
In our pretty garden green.
(while kneeling, "plant" bean with knee)

Now we plant it with our chin,
In our garden, in our garden.
Now we plant it with our chin,
In our pretty garden green.
(on all fours, "plant" bean with chin)

......

Roses Are Red
Roses are red,
Violets are blue,
Do something silly
And I'll copy you!

Children take turns standing up
front and doing a silly action for
the others to copy.

......

Sing "The Farmer Plants a Seed" from Week 1, Activity 6.

Reading the Story

Introduce the book by discussing the title and author. Discuss the book's cover and ask the children to guess what the book will be about.

Read the story every day and, as the children become famil-iar with it, gradually add in any of the following activities:

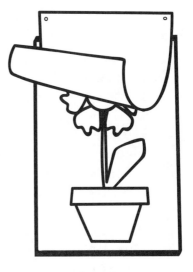

- Use props during the story reading—a watering can or small spray bottle to represent the rain, a fan for the wind, a large paper sun, and so forth.

- Attach a large piece of butcher paper to a wall or board in front of the children. Draw on it or cut out of colored paper and attach a flowerpot with a flower in it. Cover the flower and most of the stem with another piece of paper. Roll up the paper bit by bit as the flower in the story grows. At the end, remove the entire paper to reveal a beautiful full-grown flower.

- Invite the children to sit on the floor for the beginning of the story. As the flower grows, the children move into a kneeling position, then standing, and finally standing with their arms waving overhead as the flower blooms on the last page.

Group Activities

1. Window Gardens

Target Areas: cognition, communication

What you need:

- Clear plastic cups with a few small holes cut in the bottoms (1 per child)
- Potting soil
- Seeds (bean seeds work well, or try peas or a variety of flower seeds; try to find seeds with quick germination times)
- Small scoops or shovels
- Tray or dishes for holding cups
- Water

What you do:

1. Pass out a few seeds to each child to examine.
2. Using scoops or shovels, children fill their cups three-fourths full with potting soil.
3. Place the seeds on top of the soil.
4. Fill the cups the rest of the way with soil.
5. Water the soil until water begins to drip through the holes in the bottoms of the cups.
6. Put the cups in a tray or in dishes and place in a sunny window.
7. Water the cups each day and watch for the roots to begin reaching down while the stems and leaves climb up out of the soil.

2. Fish Bowl Garden

Target Areas: cognition, communication

What you need:

- 1 large or a few small fish bowls
- Garden pea seeds
- Cotton balls
- Clear plastic wrap
- Eyedroppers
- Water

What you do:

1. The children use the eyedroppers to saturate cotton balls with water and put them in the bottom of the fish bowl.

2. Once a thick, wet layer is in the fish bowl, each child sprinkles several seeds onto the wet cotton balls.

3. Cover the bowl with clear plastic wrap and set it near a window.

4. Check each day to see if the seeds have sprouted. Eventually, the plants will climb and cover the sides of the bowl.

3. Watch It Grow!

Target Areas: cognition, communication, fine motor

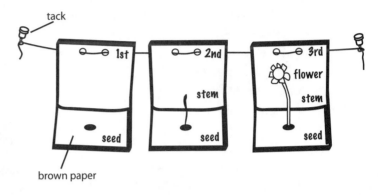

What you need:

- 8" x 8" squares of white construction paper with a 1" piece of brown paper attached to the bottom (3 per child)
- Sunflower seeds (3 per child)
- 4" pieces of green yarn (2 per child)
- 30" pieces of yarn (1 per child)
- Yellow and orange markers to share
- Black marker
- Hole punch
- Liquid glue
- Thumbtacks

What you do:

1. Explain to the children that they will be making cards to show the 3-step sequence of a blooming flower. As they watch, write *1st, 2nd,* and *3rd* respectively at the tops of each of their paper squares.

2. On the bottom of the *1st* square, children glue a seed in the "dirt" (brown paper at the bottom). The teacher writes the word *seed* next to each seed.

3. On the *2nd* square, children repeat step 2, then glue on the piece of green yarn to represent the stem growing from the seed. The teacher writes the words *seed* and *stem* next to those items.

4. On the *3rd* square, children repeat steps 2 and 3, then use the markers to draw a sunflower on the top of the stem. The teacher writes the words *seed, stem,* and *flower* next to those items.

5. Use the hole punch to punch 2 holes an inch apart in the middle of the top of each square. Either the teacher or each child then laces the long piece of yarn through the holes to connect the cards in a line. Tie knots in the ends and use thumbtacks through the yarn to hang the children's sequence cards on the bulletin board.

4. Seed Collage

Target Areas: communication, fine motor

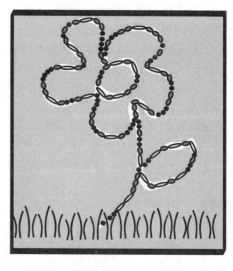

What you need:

- Variety of seeds of different sizes and shapes
- Glue with a paintbrush or in small glue bottles
- Blue 8 1/2" x 11" construction paper (1 piece per child)
- Green paint
- Paintbrushes

What you do:

1. While the children watch, open the seed packets and examine each kind of seed.
2. Ask the children which kinds of seeds they would like to use in their projects and pass them out.
3. Using the glue, children outline the shape of a flower or a plant on their piece of blue paper.
4. They attach the seeds to the glue to create their flower or plant.
5. Use the green paint and paintbrushes to add grass to the bottom of the paper.

Optional: Children may want to add a sun or rain to their art as well.

5. Grow Flower, Grow!

Target Areas: communication, gross motor, social

What you need:

- Paper bag filled with items from the story that will and will not help a flower grow (a small bag of soil, a paper sun, a picture of rain or small bottle of water, a picture representing wind, various food items, a dog bone . . .)
- Doll representing Fran

What you do:

1. The children sit in a circle with one child crouched in the middle pretending to be a flower.
2. Pass the doll around the circle chanting "Grow flower, grow!" five times (hold up a finger each time to help the children remember when to stop). Whoever is holding the doll when the chanting stops reaches into the paper bag to retrieve an item to feed the "flower" in the middle.

3. The flower must decide whether to grow (jump up tall and straight) or not to grow (shake his or her head "no" and fall to the floor).

4. Whoever fed the flower now sits in themiddle and play continues until all the children have had a chance to be the flower.

6. The Farmer Plants a Seed

Target Areas: communication, gross motor, social

What you need:
- Small spray bottle
- Yellow streamers

What you do:
1. To the tune of "The Farmer in the Dell," sing and act out the following song (the teacher is the farmer the first time through):

The farmer digs a hole, (pretend to dig a hole in front of each child)
The farmer digs a hole, heigh-ho the derry-o, the farmer digs a hole.

The farmer plants the seed, (gently push the children's heads down so they are now sitting)
The farmer plants the seed, heigh-ho the derry-o, the farmer plants a seed.

(Continue the pattern with the rest of the verses:)
The farmer waters the seed . . . (lightly spray each child with water)

The sun begins to shine . . . (wave yellow streamers over their heads)

The seed begins to sprout . . . (children rise up onto their knees)

The flower raises its head . . . (children stand up tall with their arms raised)

The farmer says "Hooray!" . . . (everyone shouts "Hooray!")

2. Continue singing, with the children taking turns being the farmer, or sing the song daily with a different child playing the farmer each day.

Week 2

Focus of the Week: Flowers

Songs, Poems, and Fingerplays

Counting Flowers
One, two, three, four, five, (raise fingers one at a time)
Pretty flowers all alive. (wiggle fingers)
Five flowers in a row,
The sun and the rain will help them grow. (raise arms up high and wiggle fingers)

......

Listen to "The Four Seasons" by Vivaldi. Ask the children to listen for parts of the music that remind them of rain, wind, and sun. Find the pages in the storybook that depict the corresponding weather when the children think the music sounds like a particular season. Also point out aspects of the music that relate to weather (example: babbling brook in spring).

Reading the Story

Read the story every day and gradually add in any of the following activities:

- Cut the bottom out of a plastic flowerpot. Add a few decorations to the pot. Create a flower puppet using either a long sock or glove (color a green stem on the leg or arm part, then create colorful petals up on the toes or fingers part). Put the sock puppet on and pull the colorful petals down into your fist, so that only the green stem is visible to the children. Then put the plastic pot over the puppet so that only a little of the stem is showing and start reading the story. As the story progresses, push the puppet up bit by bit, revealing more of the stem. When the last page is read, open the fist of the puppet to reveal the beautiful flower.

The teacher reads and uses the puppet the first time through, and then the children get to be the puppeteers.

- Make a simple flower hat. Children take turns wearing it and being the flower in the story all curled up in a ball at the beginning, then finally popping open into a flower at the end. The child-flower shakes his or her head "yes" or "no" as different things are offered to help it grow.

- Bring an assortment of real flowers for the children to smell and look at before the story begins. They can pick their favorites to hold gently during the story reading. After the story, put all the flowers in a vase with water and keep in a visible place in the classroom.

1. Giant Flower Petals

Target Areas: communication, fine motor, social

What you need:
- Large pieces of white butcher paper (3–4 children can share one paper)
- Tempera paints in a variety of vibrant colors
- Large paintbrushes of all kinds

What you do:
1. Out of the middle of each piece of butcher paper, cut a circle large enough for one child to stick his or her head through, like wearing a collar. Draw petals around the outside of the circle.
2. Hold up one of the large pieces of paper for all the children to see. Explain that the flower needs some color to make it more beautiful, but it will be up to them to decide what it will look like.
3. Divide the children into groups of three or four.
4. Give each group one piece of paper, a variety of paint colors, and several paintbrushes.
5. Encourage the children to cover each petal thoroughly with paint and to talk with each other about what colors to use.
6. Once the flowers are dry, cut them out and model how the children can wear them over their heads as if their bodies were the stems for their beautiful flowers. Set out the flowers for the children to play with during free choice time or as story props.

2. Painted Pots

Target Areas: communication, fine motor

What you need:

- Small terra cotta pots (1 per child)
- Paints, in a variety of paint colors, that won't wash off the pot when it gets wet
- Paintbrushes
- Soil
- Variety of flower seed packets

What you do:

1. Spend a few minutes looking through the seed packets with the children. Explain that they will be picking their favorite flower and planting it in a special pot.
2. Once the children have selected their favorite flower, they say what colors they see (in the petals, stem, center, and so forth). Give them the corresponding paint colors.
3. The children can now paint their pots to represent their favorite flower.
4. Once the paint is dry, the children fill their pots partially with dirt, plant the seed they selected, cover the seed with more dirt, and sprinkle with water.

3. Fingerprint Flowers

Target Areas: cognition, fine motor

What you need:

- White construction paper (1 piece per child)
- Several ink pads in various colors
- Colored and black markers and pencils

What you do:

1. Model for the children how they can use their own unique fingerprints to create gardens of beautiful flowers on paper. Here are some ideas:
   - Use fingerprints to create petals around a drawn center.
   - Use fingerprints to create a flower center to draw petals around.
   - Use the entire length of one finger to make a long, thin stem. Add thumbprint leaves.
   - Create a flower bush with several fingerprints coming off several stems.
2. Encourage the children to come up with their own ideas for creating fingerprint flower gardens.

4. Painting with Flowers
Target Area: fine motor

What you need:
- Variety of fresh flowers and leaves (daisies, sunflowers, ferns, anything that will make a nice print)
- Paints in several bright colors
- Small paintbrushes
- White construction paper

What you do:
1. Pass the flowers and leaves around the circle so the children can feel the bumps in the flower centers, the spores on the ferns, the ridges on the petals, and so forth.
2. Model for the children how to paint delicately on the flower petals and leaves.
3. Turn the flower or leaf over and press it onto the paper to create a print.
4. The children will probably try to make a few prints and then want to use the flowers and leaves to create messier pictures. Go for it!

5. A Pocket of Posies
Target Area: fine motor

What you need:
- Gardening catalogs
- Scissors
- Paper plates (1 1/2 plates per child)
- Crayons
- Glue
- Yarn
- Stapler

What you do:
1. Punch a hole in the top of each child's whole paper plate.
2. Encourage the children to color their whole paper plates in shades of blue to represent the sky and to color their half paper plates dark browns and grays to represent the dirt.
3. Help the children staple their whole and half plates together so the edges line up and they create a pocket.
4. The children now look through catalogs to decide what to "plant" in their pocket garden. Encourage them to look for flowers with a variety of sizes and colors. They can cut out as many flower pictures as will fit in their gardens.
5. Children glue the flower pictures onto their blue paper plates.
6. Attach yarn through the hole in the top and hang the pocket gardens as a display in the classroom.

6. Nature Artists
Target Areas: cognition, communication, fine motor

What you need:
- Clipboards (1 per child)
- Pencils (1 per child)
- White paper (1 piece per child)
- Crayons and colored pencils
- An outdoor area with a variety of vegetation

What you do:
1. Go outside with the children and search for a place with lots of different flowers and plants.
2. Talk about what you see: the colors, shapes, heights, textures, and so forth.
3. Give each child a pencil and a clipboard with a piece of paper attached to it.
4. The children now draw the different flowers and plants around them.
5. Come back in the classroom to add color to the sketches with crayons and colored pencils.
6. Write the children's words on their papers as they describe what they saw outside.

Plant Nursery Field Trip
Take a field trip to a local garden or nursery. Buy flowers to plant on the school grounds. Decorate small paper bags with handles to take to the nursery for bringing the plants back to the school.

Our Field Trip Experience Book
Take pictures on the field trip (see above) to make into a flower-shaped experience book. Use this book one day during circle time, and then keep it in the book corner. Invite the children to check out the book to take home for a night to share with their families.

Snacks

1. Use a flower-shaped cookie cutter to cut out bright pieces of watermelon or cantaloupe.

2. Use breadstick dough to create flower shapes. Bake and eat while warm!

3. Gobble up sunflower seeds.

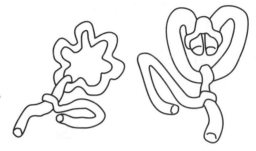

4. Nibble on foods with seeds inside (kiwi fruit, tomatoes, cucumbers, peppers). Match the seeds with the foods they came from.

5. Edible Flowers

What you need:
- Graham crackers
- Cream cheese
- Plastic knives
- Thin slices of carrots and celery
- Green and red pepper rings

What you do:

Model for the children how to spread cream cheese over their graham crackers. Then decorate the crackers using the vegetables to create flower shapes. Celery can be used to create stems and leaves. Munch and enjoy!

6. Dirt and Worms? YUM!

What you need:
- Ziplock bags (1 per child)
- Graham crackers (2 per child)
- Chow mein noodles (for worms) (a few per child)
- Small rolling pins, toy hammers, other pounding toys
- Paper plates
- Forks and spoons

What you do:
1. Children put the crackers into their bags and seal them.
2. Using their hands, the rolling pins, or pounding toys, children crush their crackers into crumbles resembling dirt.
3. Add the chow mein to the bag and shake it all together.
4. Dump the mixture out onto paper plates and eat the "dirt and worms" with hands, forks, or spoons.

Pretest and Posttest

Grow Flower, Grow!

Concepts	Pretest	Posttest
Different kinds of seeds		
Steps in the growing process		
Parts of a flower		
Parts of a plant		
What flowers need to grow		
Colors of various flowers		

Fidgety Fish

By Ruth Galloway

It's hard to be a fidgety, curious fish living in the great big, beautiful ocean. Our friend Tiddler finds out the hard way just how safe and cozy his little home is when he heads out into the unknown to expend some of his unending energy. Meeting some new sea friends is fun for Tiddler, but after accidentally spending a little time in the belly of a Big Fish, his wiggles are cured for good, and he realizes that there's no place better than home.

Dear Families,

Aren't we all a little curious about life under the sea? Our friend Tiddler the fish is no different. Even though he has a nice, cozy home safe from danger, he is endlessly fidgety and seizes the opportunity to go exploring when his mother sends him out to expend some of his energy. In *Fidgety Fish,* by Ruth Galloway, we'll read about all kinds of sea life—some friendly, and some, well, to be avoided if you're a little fish. We'll learn new vocabulary, make beautiful art projects, do a little fishing right here in our room, and, of course, play lots of fidgety games.

If you can, take a trip to the library this week and pick up *Fidgety Fish* and a few other stories about sea life. We recommend *Sea, Sand, Me!* by Patricia Hubbell, *Smiley Shark* by Ruth Galloway, *The Rainbow Fish* by Marcus Pfister, *Commotion in the Ocean* by Giles Andreae, and *Fish Eyes: A Book You Can Count On* by Lois Ehlert.

Visit an aquarium or the pet store to look at and learn about all the varieties of fish. If you feel your child is ready for a pet, buy a couple of goldfish and set up a small fish tank at home. Play fidgety, action-filled games, such as Freeze Tag, Simon Says, and Red Light, Green Light. This is also a nice time to talk with your child about safety and staying close to you when out in unfamiliar places. Don't forget to eat plenty of goldfish crackers and tuna fish sandwiches!

Off for a swim,

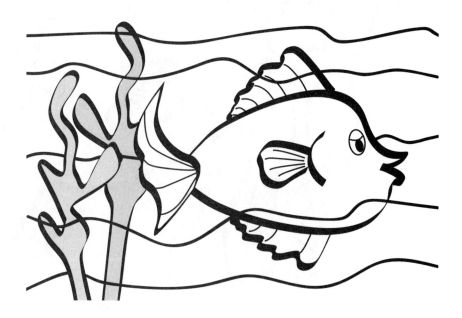

Dramatic Play Area

- Cover a corner of the room with a sea life-theme shower curtain to create an "underwater" area. Fill the area with play fish and shells.

- Add flippers, goggles, and masks to the "underwater" area (see above) so the children can pretend to explore the sea.

Sensory Area

- Fill a plastic swimming pool with water and a variety of toy sea animals, shells, and coral. Optional: Add sand to the water in the pool.

- Play music with the sounds of ocean waves, seagulls, and wind. Provide earphones for individual listening. Use a fan to create a gentle sea breeze.

- Show the children how they can "hear the ocean" in a large conch shell.

Science Area

- Set up a simple fish tank with a goldfish or two (be sure they are compatible). If the tank is large enough, consider adding some other type of compatible fish as well. Put out magnifying glasses for the children to get a close-up look. Teach the children how to feed the fish: one pinch of food daily. Designate a child to do the feeding each day. Be sure to clean the tank with warm soapy water once a week.

Art Area

- Provide white paper with outlines of fish and coral made with thick black pen. Children use sponges and bright, neon-colored paint to bring the scenes to life. Cut out the fish and coral when they are dry. Add them to the bulletin board.

- Provide transparent contact paper cut in rectangles and a variety of sequins and other flat, sparkly art decorations. The children attach decorations to the sticky side of half of a contact paper rectangle, then fold the other half on top to stick the sides together, enclosing the decorations. Using a permanent marker, the teacher draws the

outline of a fish on each child's contact paper. The children cut out their fish. Punch holes in the tops of the fish and hang them from the ceiling, on the bulletin board, or in a window.

Book Area

- *Commotion in the Ocean* by Giles Andreae, illustrated by David Wojtowycz
- *Fish Eyes: A Book You Can Count On* by Lois Ehlert
- *One Fish, Two Fish, Red Fish, Blue Fish* by Dr. Seuss
- *The Rainbow Fish* by Marcus Pfister
- *Sea, Sand, Me!* by Patricia Hubbell, illustrated by Lisa Campbell Ernst
- *Shake My Sillies Out* by Raffi, illustrated by David Allender
- *Smiley Shark* by Ruth Galloway
- Other books related to sea life and movement

Bulletin Board

- Add the words *Under the Sea* to an aqua blue background. Place the creations from the Art Area and from the weeks' activities on the board.

- Attach green crepe paper to the top of the blue background on the board and allow it to hang down. The children can pull back the "seaweed" to uncover their creations.

Week 1

Focus of the Week: Sea life

Circle Time

Songs, Poems, and Fingerplays

I'm a Little Fishy in my Cave
(to the tune of "I'm a Little Teapot")

I'm a little fishy in my cave. (arms in a circle overhead)
I'm going out, feeling very brave. (swimming motion with arms)
I meet many friends in the ocean deep, (shake hands with classmates)
Then swim on home and go to sleep. (lay head in hands and close eyes)

If I Were an Jellyfish
If I were an jellyfish (wave arms gently up and down)
Swimming in the sea,
If I were a crab, (create pinchers with thumb and index finger)
Then I wouldn't be me!

Encourage the children to come up with other animals to use in this poem.

Reading the Story

Introduce the book by discussing the title, author, and dedication. Discuss the book's cover and ask the children to guess what the book will be about.

Read the story every day and, as the children become familiar with it, gradually add in any of the following activities:

- Use plastic sea creatures (mom fish, child fish, crab, jellyfish, starfish) to help tell the story.

- Attach a large piece of aqua blue paper to a wall in the story reading area. Before reading, go around the circle and ask the children to describe the animals and objects

277

in the story. Draw what they say, encouraging them to use descriptive language. As an animal or object appears in the story, the child who suggested the corresponding drawing comes to the front to draw a circle around it.

- Children select animals in the story that they would like to be. Give them a moment to practice the movements that their animals make (a jellyfish waving arms, a crab pinching, a Big Fish with puffed cheeks, and so forth). When their animals appear in the story, take a second to allow the children to imitate their animals' movements.

Group Activities

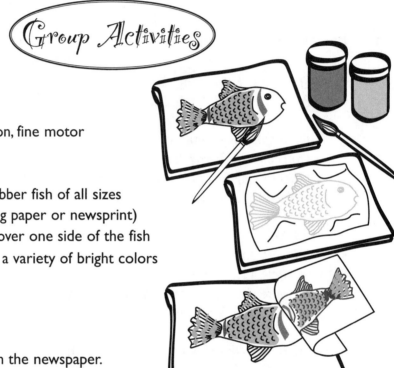

1. Fish Prints

Target Areas: cognition, fine motor

What you need:

- Real, plastic, or rubber fish of all sizes
- Thin paper (tracing paper or newsprint) large enough to cover one side of the fish
- Tempera paints in a variety of bright colors
- Paintbrushes
- Newspaper

What you do:

1. Lay a fish down on the newspaper.
2. Children decorate the top of the fish with the brightly colored paints.
3. Press the thin paper over the fish, applying firm pressure over the entire length.
4. Lift the paper to see the beautiful fish print!

2. Tissue Paper Fish

Target Areas: cognition, fine motor

What you need:

- 8 1/2" x 11" or larger pieces of white paper (1 per child)
- Black permanent-ink markers (1 per child)
- Small spray bottles filled with water
- Colorful tissue paper cut into small squares

What you do:

1. Each child traces, copies, or independently draws a large fish with the black marker on the white paper.

2. Children cover their fish with dry squares of tissue paper.
3. Now it's time to go in the ocean: The children use the spray bottles to completely soak the tissue paper on their fish until the colors start to bleed.
4. Allow the squares some time to dry. Then the children peel the squares off the paper to reveal their gorgeous animals.
5. When completely dry, cut out the fish along the black lines.

3. Sea Life Headbands

Target Areas: cognition, communication, fine motor

What you need:

- Sponges cut into simple sea life shapes (starfish, fish, whale, coral, shark)
- Paint in a variety of colors, each color in a shallow container
- Strips of paper long enough to fit around a child's head (1 per child)
- Stapler
- Optional: Paintbrushes
- Optional: Camera and film

What you do:

1. Introduce the different sea life shapes and model for the children how to dip the sponges into the paint and apply the paint to the strip of paper. (It may work better to apply the paint to the sponges using paintbrushes so the prints don't come out too gloppy.)
2. Children move around the table, select the different shapes and colors, and cover their headbands with prints.
3. When everyone is finished, even if the paint is still wet, encourage the children to come to the front of the group to "read" their headbands from left to right ("red starfish, yellow whale, blue coral," and so on). Set the strips aside to dry.
4. Once dry, staple the ends together to create the headbands.
5. Consider a class picture of the children with their headbands on, pretending to swim!

Note: This activity can be modified to introduce the concept of patterns. Children create a sea life pattern on their headbands. They point out and emphasize the pattern when reading the headband aloud.

4. Handprint Sea Creatures

Target Areas: cognition, fine motor

What you need:

- Paint in a variety of colors
- White construction paper
- Paintbrushes
- Wiggly eyes
- Glue
- Scissors

What you do:

1. To make a fish shape, children keep the fingers of one hand straight and held closely together (for the body of the fish) and their thumbs pointing up (for a fin).
2. Help the children paint their palm, thumb, and fingers and press them firmly down on the paper.
3. To make a jellyfish print, paint the fingers and palms of both hands (no thumbs). One at a time, press the hands down on the paper, overlapping the palms so that the fingers create the jellyfish's tentacles and the palms create the body.
4. See what other animals the children can create.
5. When dry, glue on wiggly eyes and cut out the shapes.
6. Add the prints to the bulletin board.

5. To Salt or Not to Salt

Target Areas: cognition, communication, social

Note: Be sure that no children are allergic to peanuts before doing this activity. As appropriate, substitute another salted and unsalted food item.

What you need:

- Salt in a saltshaker
- Pretzels with and without salt
- Canned peas with and without salt
- Salted and unsalted peanuts
- Cups (1 per child)
- Spoons
- Napkins or plates
- White board or large piece of paper
- Marker

	Salt	No Salt
water	III	HHH
pretzels	HHH II	I
peas	III	HHH
peanuts	HHH I	II

What you do:

1. Explain that the ocean consists of saltwater, and that certain animals can only survive in saltwater. (Check the library and the Internet for more details to include in the discussion.)
2. Pour some water into the children's cups and let them taste it.
3. Next, the children shake some salt into their cups and swish their cups around to mix in the salt. Then they taste the saltwater.
4. Divide the board into two parts with a vertical line. Label the parts *Salt* and *No Salt* respectively.
5. Ask the children to vote on which water they like the best.
6. On the left side of the board, write *water, pretzels, peas,* and *peanuts*.
7. Continue on with the voting process to see what the majority of the class likes. Don't forget to tally the results of the taste tests out loud!

Optional: This would be a good opportunity to discuss "a pinch" versus "too much salt" and the dangers of eating too much salt. Ask, "Who wants to live in the ocean and drink saltwater all day??"

6. Let's Go Fishin'

Target Areas: cognition, communication, social

What you need:

- Barrier that the children cannot see over (couch, painting easel, room divider)
- Magnetic fishing poles (tie a magnet to one end of a long string and attach the other end to the top of a dowel)
- Variety of paper sea creatures and objects with their names written on them and paper clips attached to their tops
- Containers labeled with the same sea creatures' and objects' names

What you do:

1. Place the sea creatures and objects on one side of the barrier, the children on the other side.
2. Children take turns tossing their line and magnet over the barrier and waiting to get "a bite." They guess what they think they will catch.
3. As the child waits for something to tug on his or her line, everyone chants: "Ocean, Ocean, Water so cold. What will tug on my fishing pole?"
4. Behind the barrier, the teacher attaches the "catch" to the fishing line by attaching the paper clip on a paper creature or object to the magnet.
5. After "reeling in" the catch, the child looks at the printed word on the creature or object and tries to match it with one of the words on the containers. The child puts the item in the correct container.

Week 2

Focus of the Week: Movement

Circle Time

Songs, Poems, and Fingerplays

I Can Jump
I can jump, jump, jump.
I can hop, hop, hop.
I can clap, clap, clap.
I can stop, stop, stop.
I can nod my head for "yes."
I can shake my head for "no."
I can bend my knees a little bit and sit down slow.

Don't Get Wet!
(to the tune of "Jingle Bells")

Clap your hands, stomp your feet,
Fidget all around.
Throw your hands up in the air,
Now touch them on the ground.
Shake your hips, nod your head,
Now let's take a rest.
Lay yourself down on the floor . . .
Be careful — DON'T GET WET! (spray the children lightly with water)

Reading the Story

Read the story every day and gradually add in any of the following activities:

- Make a Big Fish mouth out of a black plastic garbage bag and, following the story as it is read, have the Big Fish swallow a stuffed animal representing Tiddler. Once Tiddler is inside, shake and toss the bag around as if Tiddler were trying to escape. Then open the bag to allow him to escape.

282

- When Tiddler goes into the Big Fish's mouth during the story, cover the children with a large, dark blanket. They can squirm around underneath until you uncover them.

- Give each child a flashlight. Give them the opportunity to play with their flashlights, turning them on and off, shining them on the ceiling, the floor, each other (not in the eyes, please), and on different objects in the room. Try this both with the lights on and off. While reading the story, a helper turns the lights off when Tiddler is swallowed up. The children pretend they are in the Big Fish. They use their flashlights to search around the room for a way out of the Big Fish. Read some of the action words in the story individually—and the children act out the words: *fidget, giggle, swim, dive, flip, leap, dip, speed fast, glide gently, click, tremble, shiver, rumble, grumble, turn, tumble, flutter, groan.* When the lights come on, the flashlights go off.

Group Activities

1. Jellyfish Says

Target Areas: communication, gross motor, social

What you need:
- Open space to play in
- Jellyfish hat or headband

What you do:
1. Check to see which, if any, children have played Simon Says before, and explain the rules of the game as needed. Children can either sit out when they goof or just to continue to play.
2. The teacher begins by being the leader (the Jellyfish) and wearing the hat or headband. Give the children simple actions to perform either with the Jellyfish's permission or without.
3. Once the game seems clear to all, select children to come to the front to wear the hat or headband and be the Jellyfish leader.

2. Fidgety or Tired?

Target Areas: gross motor, social

What you need:
- Fun, lively music (like the Beach Boys)
- Open space to play in

What you do:

1. When the music comes on, the children quickly begin to fidget and dance like Tiddler.
2. When the music is turned off, the children drop to the floor and pretend to be asleep.
3. Celebrate who is the quickest to get up and down.
4. Stagger the time between turning the music on and off to try and fool the children.

3. Off to the Races!

Target Areas: gross motor, social

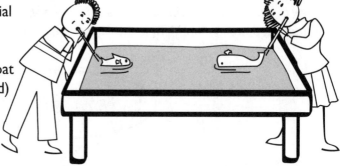

What you need:

- 2 animal water toys that float
- Drinking straws (1 per child)
- Water in the sensory table
- Some lively music

What you do:

1. Divide the children into two teams lined up at opposite ends of the sensory table.
2. Each team picks an animal water toy to represent their team. They put their animals in the water, one at each end of the table.
3. When the teacher says "SWIM!" the first child in each team blows through the straw to move the animal to the other end of the table and back.
4. When the first child returns to the starting place, the second child then blows the animal to the end and back.
5. The play continues until all players have had a chance to race.
6. Play some lively music to help with the excitement.

4. Pass the Big Fish

Target Areas: communication, social

What you need:

- Dark paper bag decorated with 2 white eyes and a mouth with teeth (to resemble the Big Fish)
- Variety of toy sea animals, each small enough to fit in the bag

What you do:

1. Children stand in a circle.
2. Show the children the different animals. Then hide the animals from view.
3. With the children not watching, place one sea animal in the bag.
4. Show the children how to stomp their feet to the beat as they chant "Fish, Fish, What's inside? It's dark in here, now open wide!" Once they can do this, start passing the bag around the circle as they chant.

5. Whoever is holding the bag on the last word looks inside, but doesn't show what the animal is. The child gives clues about which animal it is to help the other children make logical guesses.

6. Continue play until all the children have had a turn to give clues.

5. No Wet Toes!
Target Areas: gross motor, social

What you need:
- Graduated widths of blue paper (representing water)
- Optional: Squirt bottle filled with water

What you do:
1. Place the children in a line, one behind the other.
2. Place the narrowest width of paper on the floor.
3. Go through the line instructing the children to *jump over* the water. Demonstrate a jump. Children jump over the water one at a time.
4. The children line up and jump over the water again and again, with the paper width gradually increasing, until they have jumped over the widest paper.
5. Now play again, this time *leaping* over the water.
6. Try again with *hopping* or *jumping backwards*.

Optional: Have a small spray bottle nearby to squirt those who accidentally land in the water!

6. Fidgety Raisins
Target Areas: cognition, communication

What you need:
- Clear plastic cups (1 per child)
- Raisins (5 per child)
- Club soda or flavored seltzer (1/2 c. per child)

What you do:
1. Demonstrate by filling a cup halfway with seltzer.
2. Quickly add 5 raisins, one at a time.
3. Observe how the raisins dance and jump around in the cup because of the bubbly liquid.
4. Now assist the children as they create their own fidgety raisins.
5. Eat and drink the concoctions!

1. Make popcorn using an air popper. Experiment with leaving the lid off for a few seconds now and then to allow the popcorn to pop into the air. Watch the kernels go from sleepy to fidgety to sleepy again, just like Tiddler!

2. Make toast and try to predict when it will pop from the toaster. Children crouch down on the floor and pop up when the toast pops up!

3. Show the children how goldfish crackers can swim into their mouths.

4. Make tuna fish sandwiches and cut them out in the shape of a starfish or other sea life. Munch away!

5. Tropical Delight

What you need:
- Pineapple juice
- Club soda
- Straws
- Cups
- Little paper umbrellas

What you do:
Fill each child's glass halfway with pineapple juice. Fill the glass the rest of the way with club soda. Stir with a straw. Pretend to be at the beach watching and listening to the ocean. Visors, sunglasses, and beach towels may be necessary. Drink the Tropical Delights and enjoy!

6. An Ocean of Fish

What you need:
- Small fish bowl
- Small tongs or spoons
- Blue Jell-O (1 or 2 packages)
- Gummy fish or Swedish fish (1 per child)

What you do:
1. Using the fish bowl as your container, make the Jell-O according to the directions on the box. Include the children in each step—everyone smells the Jell-O, tastes a

little bit, pours a little into the bowl, and takes turns stirring in the hot and cold water.

2. Hand out the gummy fish. It's time to go swimming! The children drop their candies into the colored Jell-O (they can use tongs or spoons to put them in the Jell-O to avoid spreading germs). Make predictions: Will the fish sink or float? Put the creation in the refrigerator and enjoy when ready!

Pretest and Posttest

Fidgety Fish

Concepts	Pretest	Posttest
The ocean (What lives in it?)		
Sea animals (fish, crab, jellyfish, starfish, shark, etc.)		
How different sea animals move		
Concept of patterns		
Salt		
Concept of *fidgety*		
Action words (*fidget, giggle, swim, leap,* etc.)		

Appendixes

Lesson Plan

Week of: _____

Book/Author: _____

	Monday	Tuesday	Wednesday	Thursday	Friday
Free Play Dramatic Play Sensory Science Art					
Circle Time Song, Poem... Story Activity					
Group Activity	TA: _____	TA: _____	TA: _____	TA: _____	
Snack					

TA: = Target Area (cognition, communication, fine motor, gross motor, social)

Target Areas and the Activities

	Cognition	Communication	Fine Motor	Gross Motor	Social
There was a Bold Lady Who Wanted a Star					
Week 1: Transportation					
1. Running Shoes	X		X		
2. Rollin' Roller Skates	X		X		
3. Trike Relays				X	X
4. Bike Paintings	X			X	X
5. Box Cars	X	X		X	X
6. Highway to the Stars		X	X		
Week 2: Space and stars					
1. Space Hop	X			X	
2. Star in a Jar	X		X		X
3. Star Finder	X		X		X
4. Rocket Ships	X		X		X
5. Constellation Makers	X	X	X		
6. Balloon Rockets	X		X		X
Silly Sally					
Week 1: Silly movement					
1. Silly Sally Says	X	X			
2. Block Maze	X		X	X	X
3. Leap Frog	X			X	X
4. Dancing Sticks		X		X	X
5. Walk This Way	X	X		X	
6. Silly Cubes	X	X		X	
Week 2: Silly art					
1. These are the Silly Things I Can Do	X	X			
2. Silly Bag Art		X	X		
3. Silly Sally Magnet Maze	X	X	X		
4. Silly Wigs	X		X		X
5. Silly Class		X	X		
6. Silly Faces	X	X	X		

My Little Sister Ate One Hare	Cognition	Communication	Fine Motor	Gross Motor	Social
Week 1: Counting					
1. Number Hopping	X			X	
2. People Graph	X	X			
3. Bugs in a Bucket	X			X	
4. One Potato, Two Potato				X	X
5. Number Scavenger Hunt	X				
6. Line 'Em Up!	X				X
Week 2: Insects and other critters					
1. Frog Tongues	X	X	X		
2. Slinky Snakes	X		X		
3. Flyswatter Painting	X		X	X	
4. Fishing for Worms	X				X
5. Bat Tag				X	X
6. Ants at the Picnic	X		X		
Go Away, Big Green Monster!					
Week 1: Monsters and emotions					
1. Monster Masks	X		X		X
2. Monster Toes	X	X			X
3. Monster Partners	X	X	X		X
4. Silly Spaghetti Monsters	X		X		
5. Our Many Emotions Book	X	X	X		
6. Monster Spray	X	X			X
Week 2: Shapes					
1. Felt Monsters	X	X	X		
2. Shape Treasure Hunt	X	X			X
3. Lost My Shape	X	X		X	X
4. Shape Twister	X			X	X
5. Rip Face!	X	X	X		
6. Make a Shape with Your Body	X			X	

	Cognition	Communication	Fine Motor	Gross Motor	Social
Barn Dance!					
Week 1: Farm animals					
1. Marble Paint Hay	X		X		
2. Paper Bag Puppets			X		X
3. The Guessing Game	X	X			
4. Swingin' Characters			X		
5. Bat Feet	X		X		
6. Boingy Nose Pig Hat	X		X		
Week 2: Dancing, movement, verbs					
1. Dance Time!	X			X	X
2. Walk Like the Animals		X		X	
3. Drawing to the Music			X	X	X
4. Corny Relay					X
5. Corn on the Cob Painting	X		X		
6. Make Your Own Band	X	X	X		X
I Know an Old Lady Who Swallowed a Pie					
Week 1: Thanksgiving food and turkeys					
1. Thanksgiving Pie	X		X		
2. Thankful Turkeys		X	X		X
3. Colors of the Season	X	X	X		
4. Feathered Friends		X	X		X
5. Pumpkin Patch	X		X		
6. Corn on the Run				X	X
Week 2: Harvest and fall season					
1. Veggie Head Fred		X	X		X
2. Maple Leaf Turkeys	X	X	X		
3. Leaf Rubbing Book	X	X	X		
4. Cranberry-Red Napkins	X	X	X		
5. Growing Popcorn	X	X	X		
6. Handy Turkey	X	X	X		

	Cognition	Communication	Fine Motor	Gross Motor	Social
Gingerbread Baby					
Week 1: Gingerbread					
1. Applesauce Ornaments	X		X		
2. Life-Size Gingerbread Friends			X		X
3. Class of Gingerbread Babies			X		X
4. Gingerbread Lace-Up			X		
5. Gingerbread Play Dough	X		X		
6. Gingerbread Sandpaper Ornaments	X		X		
Week 2: Cold weather					
1. Indoor Ice Skating	X			X	X
2. Ice Cube Relay	X		X	X	
3. Gingerbread Baby Snow Globe	X		X	X	
4. Freeze Tag				X	X
5. Ice Sculptures	X	X			X
6. Winter Trees	X		X		X
Geraldine's Big Snow					
Week 1: Winter weather and winter clothing					
1. Winter Clothes Relay			X	X	X
2. What's Missing?	X	X			
3. Describe It!	X	X			
4. Winter Class Collage		X	X		
5. What Will the Weather Be?		X			
6. Summer in Winter				X	X
Week 2: Waiting, being patient, getting ready for snow					
1. Snowball Bowling	X			X	
2. Biscuit Bird Feeders	X		X		
3. Book Search	X	X			X
4. Hungry Birds			X	X	
5. Be Patient!	X	X			
6. Here Comes the Snowplow	X			X	X

	Cognition	Communication	Fine Motor	Gross Motor	Social
Bear Snores On					
Week 1: Habitats and snow					
1. Create a Cave!					X
2. Snowstorm		X	X		
3. Shaving Creme Snow	X		X		
4. Wilderness of Arms		X	X		X
5. Sparkling Snow Dough	X				
6. Footprints in the Snow	X	X			
Week 2: Cold weather cooking					
1. Pepper Letters	X	X	X		X
2. Stew		X			X
3. Parachute Popcorn				X	
4. Beary Good Quesadillas		X	X		
5. Mr. Bear, Are You Sleeping?				X	X
6. Teddy Bear's Picnic Day and Honey Bear Toast		X			X
The Little Mouse, The Red Ripe Strawberry, and The Big Hungry Bear					
Week 1: Strawberries, emotions, concept of a half					
1. Stuffed Strawberry	X		X		X
2. Half and Half	X		X		X
3. Plant a Strawberry	X	X			
4. Mr. Strawberry Head			X		X
5. Strawberry Relay				X	X
6. Emotional Strawberries	X		X		X
Week 2: Prepositions and problem solving					
1. Sly Kids	X				X
2. Mini-Mousey Maze	X		X		
3. Preposition Obstacle Course		X		X	
4. Clues, Clues, Clues	X	X			
5. Lock It Up!	X	X			X
6. It's Getting Bigger!!	X		X		X

	Cognition	Communication	Fine Motor	Gross Motor	Social
The Kissing Hand					
Week 1: Love, hearts, and kisses					
1. Our Kissing Hands			X		
2. Find Those Hearts!	X			X	
3. Matching Hearts	X				
4. Love Lists		X	X		
5. Mailing Kisses	X		X		
6. Sticky Hearts	X		X		
Week 2: Hands and forest animals					
1. Our Own Class Tree	X	X	X		X
2. Mystery Box	X	X			
3. Can You Hide It in Your Hand?	X	X			
4. Clapping Cards			X		
5. Owl Eyes			X		
6. Animals in the Night		X		X	
Pete's a Pizza					
Week 1: Making a pizza					
1. Sticker Pizza	X	X	X		X
2. Giant Doodle Pizza			X		X
3. Order Up!	X	X			
4. Classy Pizza	X	X	X		X
5. Pizza Match	X	X			X
6. Pizza-on-Your-Head Relay				X	X
Week 2: More pizza					
1. Reading, Writing, and Hula-Hoops?	X		X		X
2. Making the Real Thing!	X	X	X		X
3. Potato Print Pizza	X		X		
4. A Very Particular Pizza	X	X	X		
5. Velcro Pizza Stick-Ons	X			X	X
6. Pizza Tag	X			X	X

	Cognition	Communication	Fine Motor	Gross Motor	Social
The Napping House					
Week 1: Rainbows					
1. Weather Mobile	X		X		
2. Rainbow Wands	X		X	X	
3. Rainbow Napping Quilt	X		X		
4. Floor Rainbows	X		X		
5. Handprint Rainbow	X				
6. Squeegee Paint Pull	X		X		
Week 2: Napping					
1. Puppet Stack	X		X		X
2. Sweet Dreams Pillowcases	X	X	X		
3. Mini Pillow Sachets	X		X		
4. Folding Blankets Relay	X		X		X
5. Napping Families	X		X		
6. Slipper Match	X			X	
Five Little Monkeys Bake a Birthday Cake					
Week 1: Sleeping, noisy and quiet					
1. Let's Get Ready For Bed!	X	X			
2. Lights Out, Little Monkeys				X	X
3. Turn Up the Music, Little Monkeys			X		X
4. Monkey Tunes			X	X	X
5. Mama's in the Middle...Shhhhh!		X			X
6. Sound Walk	X		X		
Week 2: Birthday parties					
1. Egg White Cakes	X		X		
2. That's a Wrap!	X		X		
3. Better than Hallmark	X		X		
4. Birthday Cake Hats	X	X	X		
5. Oil and Water Just Don't Mix!	X	X			
6. Goop	X	X			

	Cognition	Communication	Fine Motor	Gross Motor	Social
The Very Hungry Caterpillar					
Week 1: Caterpillars and fruits					
1. Caterpillar Headbands	X		X		
2. Shaving Cream Fruit			X		
3. Caterpillar Tag	X			X	X
4. Apple Prints			X		
5. Egg Yolk Fruits			X		
6. Rocky the Caterpillar			X		
Week 2: Butterflies and metamorphosis					
1. Metamorphosis Relay	X		X	X	X
2. Shoe Flies			X		
3. Bug Hunt	X	X		X	
4. Butterfly Dancing				X	
5. Symmetrical Butterfly Wings	X		X		
6. Crayon Melt Butterflies			X		
Grow Flower, Grow!					
Week 1: Growing and seeds					
1. Window Gardens	X	X			
2. Fish Bowl Garden	X	X			
3. Watch it Grow!	X	X	X		
4. Seed Collage		X	X		
5. Grow Flower, Grow!		X		X	X
6. The Farmer Plants a Seed		X		X	X
Week 2: Flowers					
1. Giant Flower Petals		X	X		X
2. Painted Pots		X	X		
3. Fingerprint Flowers	X		X		
4. Painting with Flowers			X		
5. A Pocket of Posies			X		
6. Nature Artists	X	X	X		

	Cognition	Communication	Fine Motor	Gross Motor	Social
Fidgety Fish					
Week 1: Sea life					
1. Fish Prints	X		X		
2. Tissue Paper Fish	X		X		
3. Sea Life Headbands	X	X	X		
4. Handprint Sea Creatures	X		X		
5. To Salt or Not to Salt	X	X			X
6. Let's Go Fishin'!	X	X			X
Week 2: Movement					
1. Jellyfish Says		X		X	X
2. Fidgety or Tired?				X	X
3. Off to the Races!				X	X
4. Pass the Big Fish		X			X
5. No Wet Toes!				X	X
6. Fidgety Raisins	X	X			X

Notes

Notes

Notes

Notes